THE PRICE OF THIRST

THE PRICE OF THIRST

GLOBAL WATER INEQUALITY AND THE COMING CHAOS

Karen Piper

University of Minnesota Press

Minneapolis • London

The publication of this book was assisted by a bequest from Josiah H. Chase to honor his parents, Ellen Rankin Chase and Josiah Hook Chase, Minnesota territorial pioneers.

Portions of chapter 5 were previously published as "Revolution of the Thirsty," *Places* (July 2012), http://places.designobserver.com.

Published by the University of Minnesota Press
111 Third Avenue South, Suite 290
Minneapolis, MN 55401–2520
http://www.upress.umn.edu

Library of Congress Cataloging-in-Publication Data
Piper, Karen Lynnea, 1965-
The price of thirst : global water inequality and the coming chaos / Karen Piper.
Includes bibliographical references and index.
ISBN 978-0-8166-9542-3 (hc : alk. paper)
1. Water supply—Economic aspects. 2. Water consumption—Economic aspects.
3. Water resources development. 4. Bottled water industry. 5. Water utilities. 6. Water security. I. Title.
HD1691.P486 2014
333.91—dc23   2014019914

Printed in the United States of America on acid-free paper

The University of Minnesota is an equal-opportunity educator and employer.

21 20 19 18 17 16 15 14   10 9 8 7 6 5 4 3 2 1

For Vimla Bahuguna

It is given to her to teach the art of peace to the warring world thirsting for that nectar.

—Gandhi

CONTENTS

ACKNOWLEDGMENTS

WITH A BOOK as (some said crazily) ambitious as this, which took almost a decade of travel and research to write, it is hard to thank everyone who helped along the way. I will do my best.

First, I thank the people who made themselves available for interviews, sometimes when I showed up on their doorsteps. These include Sunderlal Bahuguna, Vimla Bahuguna, Kris Tompkins, Juan Pablo Orrego, Patricio Segura, Patrick Bond, Jon Parker, Lalo Franco, Halwest Shekhani, Hukam Chand, Shipra Keswani (of Jal Bhagirathi Foundation), and Maude Barlow. They are really responsible for this book, as well as the nameless others who spontaneously invited me into their homes, especially in Kurdistan (in both Turkey and Iraq). The kindness of these strangers gave me hope for the world. I especially owe a debt to those who acted as translators and guides for me, Halwest Shekhani and Hukam Chand. I would not have survived without Hukam, and I will never forget Halwest's Saddam Hussein imitation. I thank my eighty-year-old mother for accompanying me on so many journeys, partly because she thought I might need protection along the way and partly because she is a born adventurer. I came to recognize that it is the resilience of women and mothers that carries much of the world through times of crisis. For this reason, I dedicate my book to Vimla Bahuguna, in honor of tough old ladies everywhere.

Next, I appreciate the organizations and people who had enough faith in my work to fund my research: the University of Missouri's South Africa Exchange Program and Global Scholars Program, the University of Missouri's Research Council, the National Endowment for the Humanities, and the Carnegie Mellon Foundation. I particularly thank David Shumway, director of the Global Humanities Center at Carnegie Mellon University, for providing me with the year of silence and isolation I required to finish this book. Also, the University of Missouri's Global Scholars Program made this book happen by sending me out into the world before I quite knew what I was getting into.

Jeffrey Williams of Carnegie Mellon offered endless advice, mentoring, and pleasant conversation during my year in Pittsburgh. At the University of Missouri, folklorists Anand Prahlad and Elaine Lawless provided moral support; Luanne Roth did fieldwork with me in South Africa. Postcolonial scholar Kavita Pillai read my India chapter and offered important advice. Geographers Soren Larsen and Mike Urban invited me to work with graduate students on water policy and climate change. Geographer Farhana Sultana and sociologist Joanna Robinson read drafts of this book and pointed me in the right direction to find the nuance I needed in my arguments. Nancy Levinson and Josh Wallaert of *Places* magazine are genius editors who helped me with my Egypt chapter.

At the University of Minnesota Press, editor Jason Weidemann had a vision for this book and has been my biggest cheerleader. Danielle Kasprzak helped pull everything together.

Finally, I thank Patrick Clark and my mom for dealing with my despair about water inequality and climate change—and helping me laugh anyway.

INTRODUCTION

The Colonial Origins of Global Water Inequality

BEDOUIN TENTS fluttered in the breeze, looking like a caravan stop in the African Sahara. The tents were large and spacious inside, with traditional Moroccan symbols painted on the exteriors. Next to them, a safari-style jeep was parked adjacent to a well in the desert sand. Behind the tents, the impressive three-story Grand Palace sported white columns and a wall of windows, and alongside this was the Palace of Europe. For a moment, I thought I was in a nineteenth-century French colonial city in North Africa. Or I might have been at the French Colonial Exposition of 1906, which showcased the colonies at pavilions erected in this exact spot. At that event, a Tunisian village and Bedouin camp had been built next to fifty palaces and pavilions representing locations from throughout the French colonial world. At the popular "human zoo," people from the colonies performed their "primitive" lifestyles, often seminude. But this was Marseille, France, at the World Water Forum in 2012. I was staring at the *Drylands & Oasis* exhibit at the Parc du Chanot Convention Complex.

The World Water Forum is an international event held every three years, allegedly for the purpose of solving the world's water problems.

Attendees include U.N. representatives, international development specialists, water ministers, and heads of state from around the world. In one of the palaces, this forum opened with a ballet in which dancers performed the movement of water dressed in blue bodysuits resembling water drops. It was followed by a champagne-and-caviar reception where heads of state mingled with CEOs of water multinationals. The king of Morocco chatted with Mikhail Gorbachev, who had given the opening address. Security was tight, with airport-type scanners for bags and people, badges read by laser pen, and men in suits who looked like Secret Service agents milling around. This is the future of the global water industry.

"There's Money in Thirst," a 2006 *New York Times* headline read. Estimating the global water market's worth at hundreds of billions of dollars, the article stated, "Everyone knows there is a lot of money to be made in oil. But a fresh group of big businesses is discovering there may

Bored men in suits on the main stage of the World Water Forum.

be even greater profit in a more prosaic liquid: water."[1] Today, a small number of multinational corporations are banking on the fact that the world is entering a global water crisis. These corporations include Suez, Veolia, Thames, American Water, Bechtel, and Dow Chemicals—though the players are always shifting. They are chemical companies, soft drink companies, construction companies, mining companies, engineering companies, and—most recently—banks and equity funds. These are the people who attend the World Water Forum. And now they are mining our water, quietly gaining control over the world's water supplies, with the help of national governments and institutions like the World Bank and International Monetary Fund (IMF). Suez and Veolia are the main private contributors to the World Water Forum.

In 2001, five water companies—Suez, Veolia, Saur, Agbar, and Thames—controlled 73 percent of the world's "privatized" water, or water supplies managed by multinational corporations for the purpose of making profit. By 2025, the proportion of people worldwide served by private water companies is predicted to reach 21 percent. In the United States, it will reach 39 percent. Since 2001, Chinese water companies have also moved up the list of the world's top ten water operators, with Beijing Enterprises Water in the third slot. Nevertheless, the French still dominate the water world. French companies Suez and Veolia receive the majority of foreign contracts, covering 57 percent of the population served by the "top ten" water contractors. In 2012, approximately 90 percent of Suez's customers were in countries outside France; in contrast, Beijing Enterprises Water operates 100 percent within China.[2] But while Suez and Veolia, which operate in the United States as United Water and Veolia Water North America, respectively, are still the water powerhouses, in the future you may be just as likely to be buying your water from China as from France.

Since 1996, the World Water Council, which organizes the World Water Forum, claims it has been "working to ensure that access to water and sanitation all over the world becomes a right for everyone." In the effort to do so, the Water Council supports "facilitating, restoring and reinforcing dialogue on water issues."[3] Since more than one billion people in the world lack access to clean water, and waterborne diseases are the number one killer around the world, there is certainly a dire need for "ensuring access to water and sanitation" for all. The World Water Council claims that it finds this fact "no longer bearable." But who is the World Water Council, really?

According to the Constitution of the World Water Council, its three "Founding Members" are René Coulomb, Aly Shady, and Mahmoud Abu-Zeid. René Coulomb was previously the president of Suez. Abu-Zeid was the Egyptian water minister under former president Hosni Mubarak. Shady is part of the elite "Club of Tokyo," an invitation-only neoliberal think tank started in 2000, whose mission is to promote "water pricing" and "cost recovery." Currently, the president of the World Water Council is Loïc Fauchon, head of the Marseille water subsidiary owned by Veolia. In 2012, both Suez and Veolia had their own exhibits in the World Water Forum pavilion designed for national exhibits, demonstrating their standing and their influence both globally and at the Forum.

Along with its corporate members, the World Water Council's membership list has a distinct ex-colonial flair. In fact, it reads like a veritable who's who of engineers trained in French colonies or former colonies, particularly in North African countries like Algeria, Morocco, and Tunisia. World Water Council governor Pierre-Frédéric Ténière-Buchot explained the reason for this at a meeting for the secretive water think tank (Re)Sources in 2012. He said, "In 1962, at the dismal end of the French–Algerian war, there were numerous French civil servants who had been committed to water works in Algeria—an arid country—and who were looking for jobs, preferably in the public sector of metropolitan France." These men, along with "colleagues from Morocco and Tunisia," were forced out of Africa by anticolonial movements, and so became the heads of newly created French water agencies. Today, these same agencies operate with "revolving doors" to Suez and Veolia.[4] According to Jean-Louis Oliver of the World Water Council, the institutions and water laws that emerged in France were "inspired by people who started their careers . . . in North Africa, or black Africa, or Indochina where there were a lot of water problems."[5] (Oliver is head of the French Water Academy, where Ténière-Buchot is treasurer.) As North African countries gained independence, hundreds of water specialists returned to France and trained today's generation of water specialists, who are now considered experts on "development" in North Africa.

As I was enjoying caviar after the ballet at the 2012 World Water Forum, I could not help but think of the Saharan tents outside in the parking lot and what was next to them—the "Slum." Inside a large tent clearly labeled with this four-letter word was a replica slum of wooden shacks with tin roofs furnished with beds, fans, and even clothes. A dirt road separated two rows of shacks, and on the road were two choices for water. One was a dilapidated metal cart full of plastic jugs with a sign that read "public water" in French. It did not look safe or appealing. Next to it was a shiny, new, person-high box labeled "Veolia," with a slot where it looked like you could put in a coin. A brochure explained that this machine "was conceived as an alternative to free open-access stand-pipes, which are costly to local authorities [and] are often monopolized by intrusive customers who use . . . [them] abusively."[6] At the new Veolia standpipe, the brochure explained, users would insert a prepaid card to release the right amount of purchased water, and so water would be "fair-ly" distributed.

The surreal "Slum" tent: inside is a maze of dirt walkways, filthy mattresses in one-room shacks, and a "public water supply" consisting of a broken-down wheelbarrow filled with plastic water jugs.

The alternative to public water: a Veolia water fountain. *Saqayti* means "my fountain," and such standpipes have already been installed in Morocco.

Next to the standpipe was a basket labeled "Peepoo," or "a self-sanitizing personal toilet, turning feces into fertilizer." It was designed by the for-profit company Peepoople. (Suez is developing its own competing system called Tenant's Toilet.)[7] Peepoo customers would buy a bag lined with urea to defecate into and then return this bag to the larger basket, where it would be stored until it turned into fertilizer. The company brochure said that the bags could be sold by "women micro-entrepreneurs" at parties "similar to the well known Tupperware home parties."[8] One critic of Peepoo said that in India, where there is a strong taboo against handling waste, it might be hard to get people to walk around carrying bags boldly labeled "Peepoo." But this was the new "collective vision of solutions for water and sanitation in slums," according to the "Slum" brochure. It also happened to make money.

To say the World Water Forum is exclusive would be an understatement. Inside, predominantly white men in blue suits drink champagne and eat caviar while deciding the future of these imaginary slum dwellers.

Though the World Water Council claims to be open to "any organization with an interest in water issues," its members are vetted by the Board of Governors to ensure they "accept the missions and objectives of the World Water Council."[9] (Representatives from five countries—France, Turkey, Korea, Japan, and Brazil—dominate the Board of Governors. Tunisia and the United States are a close second.) This vetting, or what some might call censorship, was also ever-present at their Forum. Every day, the Forum put out a newsletter produced by college students, but with clear constraints. "What we write has to fit the objectives of the Forum," a journalist from Pennsylvania told me. And though a website was set up (http://www.solutionsforwater.org) to collect "proposals of concrete answers to water and sanitation issues," the Forum's newsletter explained that all proposals must accept "the constraints of the exercise," including "adequacy with the Forum's targets."[10] Finally, during the closing ceremony of the Forum, a Twitter feed ran on a large screen behind the speakers. Though we were told the feed was open to the public, I watched as the person sitting in front of me was actively modifying it using his iPad, deleting controversial tweets before they went public. He did not realize that I could see his tablet's screen.

Meanwhile, outside the Forum, grassroots activists were complaining about their exclusion from the Forum. Antiprivatization activists have long complained about the activities of the Forum, particularly its corporate sponsorship. In response, the Forum created a "grassroots" component to its program and set up a commission to vet these groups and "guarantee the projects will conform to the objectives and spirit of event."[11] The 2012 World Water Forum organized "grassroots" events into four categories: youth, women, ethics and culture, and nongovernmental organizations (NGOs).[12] The ballet that opened the Forum with the water-drop dancers was part of the "ethics and culture" grassroots subset, which is perhaps the first time ballet has ever been categorized as a "grassroots" movement. Children were also ever-present at the World Water Forum, allegedly further evidence of grassroots organizing.

Outside the Forum gates, the real grassroots organizers were holding their own conference: the Forum Alternatif Mondial de l'Eau (Alternative World Water Forum), or FAME. Unlike the World Water Forum, FAME was not supported by the French government. According to a FAME press release, "The French government, while providing four million Euros out of the 16.5 million of public financing toward the World Water Forum (not counting 6.9 million Euros from Veolia, Suez, EDF and CCIM), decided to refrain from financially supporting FAME."[13] The FAME conference was hard to find, on the outskirts of town in a graffiti-covered warehouse made of corrugated tin. Inside, the building was alive—full of happy people of all colors and genders. Their posters advertised this diversity, showing hands of all colors reaching out to collect a water stream, with the white hand positioned as the last in line to receive water. Unlike the World Water Forum, with its entry fee of $1,500, the price of admission to FAME was $5. Servings of the main food sources at FAME, hot dogs and pizza, were $4 each. There was no free caviar. On the street, a whimsically decorated bus offering transport to and from FAME sported the conference's slogan, "Water for life, not for profit." A march was arranged to start the conference in which marchers carried buckets down the street and at one point created a line from the public fountain and passed a cup of fountain water down the line.

At the opening ceremony of FAME, the president of the Marseille Water Association, Michel Partage, said, "There is a wall separating the two forums, and this wall is money. The foundations of this wall are also laid by corruption. The foundations of this wall are based on the lack of global institutions and laws to protect the people. . . . We are working with much less financial resources but much more conviction and belief."[14] Next, the deputy mayor of Paris, Anne le Strat, said, "It's a much nicer environment here because there are more women. I'm sorry, but over there, it's all men. It's also a nicer place because we have values." (At the time, le Strat had just won an election for the position of president of the Seine-Normandie Water Basin Committee; her opponent was Andre Santini, a French politician convicted of "embezzlement, forgery and illegally charging interest." After le Strat won with a vote of seventy-three to sixty-nine, the election was mysteriously "canceled.") Cheers followed both speeches. A standing-room-only crowd attended, including the water minister of Bolivia, who, like me, had defected from the World Water Forum.

Canadian activist Maude Barlow next explained the history of resistance to the World Water Forum, which she said began when she and one other person decided to take bells to the first World Water Forum in Marrakesh in 1997. There, she claimed, people opposed to the Forum just "found each other in the hall." They watched the speakers and rang

A celebratory FAME march in Marseille. The women in this "water caravan" are demonstrating that women suffer most from water shortages since they are forced to carry water for miles every day to meet their families' needs.

bells when they lied. "If they lied a little bit," she explained, "we'd ring the bell a little bit. And if they lied more, we'd ring the bell more, and at one point, when the former head of the International Monetary Fund was giving a statement on public funding for private finance, we really rang a lot of bells, and he said, 'I hear your bells, but I will not stop speaking.'" By 2006, an official alternative water forum had emerged in Mexico City. There, Barlow said, "We had a march with fifteen thousand people," nearly as many people as were there for the Forum. By the time of the 2009 conference in Istanbul, she said, "we were so powerful and so organized that they had to have water cannons—what a beautiful image [she laughed ironically]—to take care of our protest."

In contrast to the World Water Forum, FAME promotes the idea that no one owns water. "We say that it belongs to the earth, it belongs to all species, and it belongs to future generations," Barlow explained. "It is a common heritage, a public trust, and a human right." FAME asserts that it is against water "privatization"; in response, corporations have argued that they are *not* buying and selling water, only managing water delivery through "public–private partnerships." While this is correct, it does not mean that corporations would not sell water like eggs or bricks if they could. But water is an "uncooperative commodity," as geographer Karen Bakker calls it, because (1) it moves and is not easily contained, (2) it is dense and therefore heavy and difficult to move, and (3) it often does not have just a single user.[15] Of course, water can be bottled and shipped around the world, which is a more direct kind of privatization. There is also a form of privatization that involves buying and selling water *rights* for profit, referred to as "water marketing," which occurs in Chile, Mexico, and California. But to claim that water is not privatized unless it is bottled and sold is to ignore the larger picture. After all, plenty of things are privately owned that cannot be stored on shelves, such as intellectual property, copyrights, futures, and goodwill (i.e., the value of a corporation's reputation). And FAME would argue that even if water is not bought and sold, profit is made from delivering it. In water contracts between corporations and municipalities, corporations are actually guaranteed set profits, generally between 15 percent and 30 percent.[16]

In this book, I use the term *privatization* to refer to the introduction of the "profit motive," both practically and theoretically, to transactions involving water. Practically speaking, privatization means charging higher water rates or redistributing water to make personal profit. Theoretically speaking, privatization means applying a new market paradigm to our water systems, one that sets up the "free market" as the regulator for water distribution. *Privatization,* for my purposes, refers to both profit-making water enterprises and a shift in language to support these enterprises. This new language defines water in economic terms rather than in social, ecological, or religious terms, and it is a necessary component, even a catalyst, for water sales. Perhaps most important, applying the profit motive to our water supplies means drought for those who cannot pay. A tree or a fish, for instance, cannot pay for water, and neither can the world's poor, who often live on the equivalent of less than a dollar a day.

FAME defines water as a "human right," while the World Water Forum defines water as an "economic good." Between the two, there has been little room for compromise. Battles over how we define water have therefore become quite heated. At the second World Water Forum, held in The Hague in 2000, two protesters jumped onto the stage, tore off their clothes, and handcuffed themselves together. On their bodies were the words "No to Water Privatization" and "Yes to Water as a Human Right." In the audience, protesters handcuffed themselves to their seats and began shouting antiprivatization slogans.[17] They were fighting for the *definition* of water as a human right, a definition they wanted recognized by the United Nations.

At the World Water Forum, in contrast, a kind of exclusive technocratic language is spoken; it is the only language recognized as legitimate, and it is a language largely not understood outside the Forum. An example of this would be a 2012 Forum newsletter story about an agreement between the Water Commission of Mexico and the international Organization for Economic Cooperation and Development (OECD). The agreement, Framework Conditions for Private Sector Participation Infrastructure in Mexico, was signed during the Forum, and the newsletter reported: "The agreement consists of implementing a set of benchmarks and information and activity exchanges to improve development of the water sector in Mexico. The emphasis of the work under this agreement is focused on governance and political reform."[18] In simple English, this means "Mexico has agreed to make a series of small steps to allow for greater water privatization." In the agreement, the OECD applauds Mexico for becoming "an important laboratory of innovative private sector participation experiences" and encourages greater legislative changes to "enable" foreign companies to invest.

The Forum community relies on the repetition of certain words and phrases—*benchmarks, efficiency, stakeholders,* and *reform*—that have become a kind of business-speak in global governance circles including the IMF, World Bank, and OECD. In short, we have entered the banker's world of water. At the 2012 World Water Forum, one could sense the anxiety about outside interference that might question this seamless internal language. Question periods after panels were always awkward, since the organizers seemed leery even of their own audience and feared infiltrators. After one panel, audience members who had questions were asked to approach two microphones in the aisles. I quickly noticed that the woman at one of the microphones was being completely ignored as audience members tried to point her out to the moderator. As she stood there patiently, the moderator took questions only from people at the other

Wenonah Hauter of
Food & Water Watch
joins FAME's "clown
brigade" at the World
Water Forum to draw
attention to the circus-
like nature of the
Forum.

microphone. Finally, when there was no one left at that microphone, he actually handed his microphone to someone in the audience rather than let the woman speak. When she tried to say something, her microphone was turned off. Somewhat baffled by the rudeness of the moderator, I found out later that the woman he had ignored, Wenonah Hauter, was from FAME. Ironically, when I read about the incident on the website of the private water consortium AquaFed, I was surprised to see a completely different version of the same event. The website reported, "After the moderator had closed the debate, Wenonah Hauter took hold of a mike rudely and asked a question in an infuriated manner."[19] Indeed, it seemed like parallel realities existed at the World Water Forum.

At another Forum session, FAME activists put on clown noses during a speech by the director of AquaFed, Gérard Payen. Afterward, I asked what he thought of the clown noses, and he said simply, "I knew that Food & Water Watch was here," referring to an organization headed by Maude Barlow and Wenonah Hauter. When I asked if he had a problem with the organization, he replied: "Go to their website and you will see. Their only activity is antiprivatization, against agrobusiness and water companies. They use propaganda against private companies, and we are a federation of private companies."

While activists in clown noses and handcuffs may not seem that threatening, today even prominent international figures are questioning the motives of the World Water Forum. Former Soviet president Gorbachev, a Nobel Peace Prize winner, was asked to give the opening remarks after the ballet at the 2012 Forum. Surprisingly, he questioned the whole basis for the Forum. "During the fifteen years of its existence, the World Water Forum has helped to put water problems on the international political agenda," he started, but then he went on to complain, "Unfortunately, however, it has still not gone beyond general discussion between representatives of government and the business community, nor has it produced breakthrough solutions to the water crisis. That is why, parallel to the forum, alternative discussion platforms are emerging. . . . The voice of the public must be heard." He then closed the opening ceremony of the World Water Forum by reading a quote from one of these "alternative discussion platforms" that sounded very much like the mission statement of FAME.

The Water Players

Since the emergence of the World Water Council, books about the corporate takeover of the world's water have proliferated, but none has examined its colonial history. Leading thinkers on water corporatization include activists such as Maude Barlow and Vandana Shiva and academics like Karen Bakker, Joanna Robinson, and Veronica Strang.[20] (Noticeably, women seem to thrive in this field, though they are underrepresented on the World Water Council.) Their works range from detailed histories of water "privatization" to call-to-arms manifestos against the water multinationals; my book would not have been written without the grounding these authors have provided. However, few scholars have delved into the impact of colonialism on water privatization, even though inequitable water distribution first became the norm under European colonialism, when a global "water elite" began to emerge in places as far ranging as

British India and South Africa. Considering the history of this global water elite can help us better understand the precarious position of global social stability today.

So who are the players behind the World Water Forum? Let's start with the two largest water corporations in the world, Suez Environment and Veolia Water. Suez began as the Universal Suez Ship Canal Company in 1858, headed by Ferdinand de Lesseps. Historian David McCullough describes Lesseps as "both the most daring of dreamers and the cleverest of back-room manipulators. He was the indestructible optimist . . . and he was perfectly capable of deceit and of playing to the vanity and greed in other men."[21] Before joining Suez, Lesseps was an officer during the military occupation of Algeria and then a colonial administrator in Tunisia and Egypt.[22] After he left Suez, he led the first attempt to build the Panama Canal, which failed in scandal and disgrace when Lesseps was tried and convicted for perpetrating a massive corruption scheme involving bribery and deceit. He was also involved in Belgian King Leopold II's International African Society, which was responsible for a slave and ivory trade that killed eight to ten million people in the Congo over the course of twenty years (1885–1905).[23] Lesseps called the conquest of the Congo "the greatest humanitarian work of this time," claiming it was bringing civilization to the jungle by bringing it "development."[24]

After Lesseps retired, the Suez Canal Company continued to be headed by a series of vice consuls and colonial officers from North Africa. In 1880, Suez moved into water and electricity, claiming that the company's goal was to "obtain, purchase, lease and run, in France and abroad, all concession and companies linked to water and lighting."[25] Slowly, its operations moved abroad, at first to colonies or former colonies of the French. Today, many of Suez's advisers and employees once worked in colonial Africa and now have key positions at the World Water Council. For instance, Pierre-Frédéric Ténière-Buchot is on the Board of Governors of the World Water Council as well as on Suez's Water Resources Advisory Committee. He also cofounded the French Water Academy and (Re)Sources think tank. So who is he? In 1991, he published a book titled *The ABC's of Power* modeled on Machiavelli's *The Prince*. It contains a "chart of powers" for mapping "influence" versus "dependence" for decision-making purposes in any situation, but especially for "overcoming or managing crisis." In 1992, he applied this model to contemporary

Europe–Africa relations, arguing that Africa needed Europe for its military support and financial aid, while Europe needed Africa for a sense of adventure and space—and for sex. He explained: "One cannot stress enough the reasons that whites, that is to say Europeans, went to work in Africa during recent decades. Dedication and a taste of adventure, certainly, but there were also the social considerations, like an easy life and sexual ease, which formed a complex set of comparative advantages in comparison with Europe."[26] He further suggested that Africa could provide an outlet for Europe's overcrowding, explaining that while African cities are "horrible socially and economically, [they] may still be suitable for those Europeans qualified as marginal, but more and more numerous, who refuse to accept the world in which they live." For him, Africa functioned both as the dark unconscious of European desire, a notion straight out of *Heart of Darkness*, and a political prison for "bad" Europeans. Because Africa was "dependent" while Europe was "influential," he argued, Europe maintained the upper hand. Africa's only power was in "making Europe feel guilty."

Perhaps more unsettling than Buchot's ideas about Africa is his prestige. He has been asked to publish numerous reports about Africa for the World Water Council and World Bank, and has even coauthored a book with the head of the IMF, Michel Camdessus, titled *Water*. He is also a major spokesman for the water corporations, even though he is ambivalent about creating better "hygiene" with water in Africa. He writes: "Africa needed Europe to bring hygiene and a bit of medical care to its territory. As with any progress, the consequences are not always positive. Lack of employment, training, and qualifications are the consequences of a lack of population control." Imagine arguing that we should withhold medical care in the United States as a form of "population control." Yet this is precisely what he is saying about Africa. And while there is perhaps a subtle element of sarcasm in this article, the World Bank in fact made the same argument in 1966. An internal memo warned: "More attention should be given to the possible unfavorable side effects of improved water supply. The usual studies tend to emphasize better health, longer life, and greater productivity management. The negative effects of the resulting higher rates of population growth . . . are seldom brought out."[27] Complaining of Africa's overpopulation, Ténière-Buchot wrote, "Europe is supposed to solve this inconvenience by either being directly involved with it in

Africa, or by regulating the fluxes of immigration on its own territory." One has to wonder how someone who questions the value of supplying water in Africa was tasked with ensuring "water and sanitation for all" for Suez and the World Water Council.

Ténière-Buchot is not the only Suez employee and World Water Council member with connections to the old French colonial world. For instance, Ivan Chéret and Claude Lefrou worked in colonial Africa, an experience they describe with pride in *The Civil Engineers in Africa: 1945–1975*. Chéret relates being struck with a feeling of excitement and adventure at the scale of the problems he is allowed to solve, but his awareness of his surroundings seems quite limited. Chéret states, "No one ever told me, before I left for Dakar, about Africa, or about Africans, or about our role in the 'colonies.'"[28] He appears not to talk to the locals on his own, but instead "sends out geographers" to study them when, for instance, he wants to develop an enormous hydropower and irrigation system in their valley. When the geographers inform him that the project will basically starve out all the Africans living there, he complains, "Ah, the human factor!" Sociologist Sara B. Pritchard describes the tone of engineers working in Africa at the time: "Overall, hydraulic experts in France framed North Africa as an innovative laboratory where significant advancements were being made by French water specialists."[29]

Now jump to twenty to thirty years later, and these same men are not only the proponents of water privatization but also international experts on water, working together at Suez, the World Water Council, and the French Water Academy. Perhaps part of their colonial legacy is that they associate "development" with the goals of multinationals and governments rather than with people, whom they are more likely to see as irritants ("Ah, the human factor") hindering their vast schemes. Chéret coauthored *Water* with Michel Camdessus and Ténière-Buchot, a book that argues, "We all need to pay more for water." He has been vice chairman at Suez and has written numerous publications on water as an "economic good" for both the World Bank and the World Water Council. Claude Lefrou also works for Suez.

Today, Suez is known as the longest continually running multinational corporation in the world; its main office is located in Paris, next to the Arc de Triomphe. In 2011, the corporation's profits were $6 billion. The combined earnings of Suez and its parent company, GDF-Suez, which remains the majority shareholder of Suez Environment, make them together the twenty-fourth most powerful corporation in the world, two spots below Bank of America.[30] And Suez continues to promote Lesseps as its founding father, with his portrait hanging in the president's office. A Suez chairman has stated: "I see this as a continuation of the work that was commended by Ferdinand de Lesseps and passed down to the Group. . . . By supporting practical solutions around the world, the Foundation is paying tribute to his engineering and continuing the work of this tremendous humanist in a most dignified manner. Heartfelt thanks to its founders and long life to its work!"[31]

Suez's main competitor is Veolia Water, which emerged in France through an imperial decree of Napoleon III in 1853. Formerly Compagnie Générale des Eaux and then Vivendi, Veolia's first major shareholders included the Rothschilds, the wealthiest family in Europe at the time, and Charles de Morny, the emperor's half brother, as well as many other members of the imperial nobility. The company's founder, Count Henri Siméon, from an important aristocratic family, described his enthusiasm for the water industry at that time: "In the new times ahead, be certain, sirs, that millions will be allotted to the supply of water, just as millions were allocated to railways previously."[32] The report of the first board was clear about the company's intentions: "We shall be opening up a mine, the wealth of which has not been explored, as the first occupants of this mine, it will be our privilege to select and exploit the best seams."[33] Profits in the first year were 25 percent.

In short, the wealthiest men in Europe started Veolia with the goal of making more money.[34] One of the more infamous of Veolia's founders was John Sadlier, a notoriously corrupt British financier who went bankrupt and ended up in prison. He became the model for Charles Dickens's Mr. Merdle in Little Dorrit, a man who walked around "clasping his wrists as if he were taking himself into custody." Dickens describes him: "Mr Merdle was immensely rich; a man of prodigious enterprise. . . . He was in everything good, from banking to building. He was in Parliament, of course. He was in the City, necessarily. He was Chairman of this, Trustee of that, President of the other. . . . All people knew (or thought they knew) that he had made himself immensely rich; and, for that reason alone, prostrated themselves before him."[35]

The ambitions of the twenty-first-century leaders of Veolia have not changed much. In a *New York Magazine* profile, journalist Michael Wolff observed that Messier "seemed to see himself as some combination of religious figure and maestro—his idea, I suppose, of an American mogul."[36] Messier used the money that the water business earned for him to purchase media conglomerates and to build an empire in waste management, roads and railroads, electricity, and construction. Today Vivendi is one of the top five media conglomerates in the world, which together own 80 percent of the world's media. Besides cable TV stations, Vivendi owns Universal Music, whose artists include Eminem, Justin Bieber, and Lil' Kim. In 2006, the company was sued for bribing radio stations to play its artists' recordings; the suit resulted in a monetary settlement. In 2000, Veolia Water spun off from Vivendi as Vivendi Environment, with Vivendi holding 70 percent of the stock. It then changed its name to Veolia. Today, Veolia operates in sixty-nine countries. Together, Veolia and Vivendi would rank in the top one hundred global corporations, in the slot above Sony and below Freddie Mac—but Vivendi has sold most of its shares in Veolia due to financial troubles. Though Messier was forced to resign due to corruption scandals in 2002, his goals are clear from the title of his biography alone, *The Man Who Tried to Buy the World*—or from his nickname J6M, for Jean-Marie Messier Moi-Même-Maître-du-Monde, which means "Jean-Marie Messier, Myself, Master of the World."

Like most multinationals, water corporations are notoriously hard to track due to acquisitions and mergers, shareholder fluctuations, and different subsidiary names from country to country. In 1989, for instance, Prime Minister Margaret Thatcher privatized the British water supplier Thames Water—actually selling the water supply infrastructure (including property, plants, and equipment) on the open market. The company was then acquired first by German RWE and next by Macquarie of Australia, a global banking and investment firm. Today, China owns 9 percent of Thames Water, and another 10 percent is owned by Abu Dhabi.[37] The company supplies water in England as well as in Indonesia, China, Turkey, Australia, and Thailand. In 2001, Thames Water purchased American Water, a U.S. corporation that was then sold to German RWE. Within a few years, RWE decided to dump American Water on the open market.

In the United States, Suez is called United Water and is in competition with American Water in the race to acquire U.S. public utilities.

Veolia Water North America is in third place. Though their assets are often held abroad, these companies have direct impacts on the lives of millions of Americans, not only through water rates but also through their investment portfolios. For instance, today the top three shareholders of American Water are U.S. pension fund managers, including my own university's pension fund manager, Vanguard. If American Water loses money, I do too, and so do millions of other Americans who have invested in Vanguard. As banks and equity funds become more deeply entrenched in the water industry, the worry is that this has created a "water bubble" that might be bursting. Many water companies are now facing unexpected trouble, and the water market is increasingly seen as volatile—perhaps even "uncooperative."

The Language of "Development"

If Napoleon and a set of bankers and aristocrats once convened at the emperor's palace offices to draw up a decree to privatize France's water, today at the World Bank offices similar decrees are being signed. There, loans with "conditionalities" are approved that force countries to privatize their water supplies. The World Bank Group occupies about two city blocks of Washington, D.C., two blocks from the White House. It is headquartered in an impenetrable glass-and-steel skyscraper nearly one-third the size of the Pentagon. Inside, the building has the feeling of a greenhouse—or a prison—with a glass ceiling and walls separated by steel bars. In the circular multilevel atrium, the flags of the world are displayed just above eye level, drawing your attention upward to the ceiling. At the Infoshop, you can buy World Bank–produced data and books about developing countries, or your own World Bank piggy bank, golf shirt, or flag.

The World Bank claims to be "working for a world free of poverty," a slogan displayed throughout Bank headquarters. Started after World War II along with the International Monetary Fund, the Bank was initially tasked with aiding in postwar reconstruction, including in the European colonies, by providing nations with low-interest loans. Until 1957, more than 50 percent of Bank loans went to industrialized countries, with no particular emphasis on "poverty reduction." The Bank's primary goal was to establish its creditworthiness by providing loans for large-scale projects with little risk.[38] The IMF, in turn, made sure that countries could pay back these loans, and, for those that could not, had its own funds for "emergency loans" and "bailouts."[39]

Like the executives of the water corporations, the original World Bank members were often former colonial officers from Europe's overseas offices, who were rebranded as experts on global trade. Ironically, the history of colonialism is rarely mentioned at the World Bank, despite the institution's connections to the colonial past. The Bank's primary ideology is economics, specifically "development economics," an academic field that changed its name from "colonial economics" after Europe lost its colonies. For instance, Oxford professor Herbert Frankel simply changed his title from "professor of colonial economic affairs" to "professor of the economics of underdeveloped countries"—but his ideas were essentially the same. In 1947, India and Pakistan became independent. In the 1960s, numerous African countries gained their independence. But in these new countries, development economics promoted the same kind of export-oriented economies as a means to "growth."

"Development" was once a colonial concept directly linked to avoiding unrest among the "natives." Europeans knew that they were in the minority in the colonies and that military strength would go only so far if people were starving. The French Algerian Development Fund was designed "to reduce economic inequality" and "maintain control of the colony."[40] In French Algeria and elsewhere, the World Bank provided loans for colonial "development" projects—primarily roads, railways, and dams. Postindependence, the Bank continued to support the same projects but began to justify its loans in the name of ending "world poverty." Sometimes all that changed were the names of the colonial offices overseeing these projects. For instance, the French Ministry of Colonial Affairs was first renamed the Ministry of Overseas Departments and then the Ministry of Cooperation, and the ministry's colonial officers were renamed "development specialists." During the period of transition to independence, the Bank claimed its goal was to shape for each new nation "a sound over-all development program."[41]

In reality, the creation of the World Bank signified a shift in global power from European to American interests following World War II. The Bank president has always been an American citizen, and the United States holds sole veto power at the Bank. Lawrence Summers, chief economist of the World Bank from 1991 to 1993, once stated, "For every dollar the U.S. contributes to the World Bank, U.S. corporations receive $1.30 in procurement contracts."[42] This high profit margin is due to the fact that contracts for World Bank projects are often granted to U.S. corporations. On top of this, the Bank earns interest that ends up in the coffers of the biggest bulk bond purchasers, large U.S. and European banks. When World Bank projects fail and loans cannot be repaid, the IMF provides taxpayer-funded bailouts so the World Bank can maintain its AAA credit rating. This means that the World Bank and IMF are essentially redistributing funds to banks and large corporations from both middle-class taxpayers and debtor nations.

Even as the Bank was helping U.S. corporate interests, the U.S. military began fighting "communism" around the world after World War II. Conveniently, communism was the ideology behind many wars of decolonization. For the United States this meant that postcolonial dissent against continued Euro-American corporate domination could be sold as "communist" and linked to American Cold War fears of a Soviet threat. A growing U.S. military and its increasing involvement in "hot wars" around the world made it safer for postcolonial nations to work with the World Bank and thereby prove their loyalty to Euro-American "development plans." According to Mike Davis, "This quasi-absolutist centralization of military power by the United States . . . proved highly accommodating to the residual imperialist pretensions of the French and British."[43] For example, when the French were forced out of Indochina, the United States took over their war in independent Vietnam. The Vietnamese believed they were fighting against colonization; the United States said it was fighting against communism.

The World Bank's continuing colonial attitudes are clearly demonstrated in its policies on water. In the European colonies, clean water networks were built to supply water only to areas where the white settlers lived. As Karen Bakker notes, "Unequal access . . . was literally hardwired into the city's network by colonial powers."[44] For this reason, there was an enormous need to extend water networks more equitably following independence, particularly in Africa. But by 1975, only fifty to sixty World Bank loans out of thousands were approved for water supply upgrades, and most of those were approved after 1970. (Only two projects were initiated between 1961 and 1970.)[45]

Though the Bank consistently funded the building of large dams, these were for irrigation and not for urban water supplies. In fact, these dams made life far worse for "dam-affected" poor people. In 2000, the World Commission on Dams found that large dams had displaced forty to eighty million people worldwide. The commission recommended that in the future, people who would be affected by a proposed dam should be informed in advance of the project and have the opportunity to reject or give their consent to it. The Bank, however, concluded that this would "infring[e] on the right of the State to make decisions which it judges to be the best solution for the community as a whole."[46] The Bank did promise to "document" the views of affected people—before they were flooded out. Through its intransigence, the World Bank spawned a massive global antidam movement led by people who had been ousted from their lands.

One of the reasons the World Bank neglected urban water was that the Bank's economists argued improving water supplies would create population growth, which might lower income per capita. (Literally, clean water would allow too many people to live.) The other, related, reason was that the Bank was unable to see any economic benefits from an investment in healthier *individuals*. What mattered to the Bank was the growth and health of industry, not individuals. In 1968, a Bank study demonstrated this ambivalence: "The evaluation of urban water supply projects suffers . . . from the difficulties of assessing the benefits that result from them."[47] In short, drinking water was not a primary concern because improving drinking water supplies offered no obvious return on investment that would allow loans to be repaid. Building a dam to grow food for export generated immediate revenue. Healthier human beings did not.

In the 1980s, economic theory shifted in favor of deregulation and privatization. It was only then that the Bank began to fund drinking water supplies through a program called "full cost recovery," in which the public was charged for the construction and operation of the utilities. In the 1990s, the Bank made water supply privatization an explicit condition of its aid packages, which meant that nationally or municipally run water utilities were forced to hand over management to corporations.[48] In 1992, the "Dublin Principles" on water were also established, declaring, "Water has an economic value in all its competing uses and should be recognized as an economic good." Water privatization had begun, fast and furiously.

The neoliberal thinking of the Reagan–Thatcher years had spilled over into the water sector.

Ironically, private water companies had long been waning in power before the World Bank jump-started them again. Powerful in the nineteenth century in Europe and the United States, private water companies were failing by the early twentieth century due to poor and inconsistent management and regular outbreaks of cholera and typhoid. According to global water policy analyst Shiney Varghese, "Private water companies that had dominated the U.S. water supply for most of the 19th century were unable to make universal access to clean water a reality, and cities were ravaged by epidemics."[49] Because of the massive health emergencies that followed in the wake of large-scale urbanization and industrialization, governments began to regulate and buy out private water contracts. By 1900, more than 53 percent of U.S. water services had been taken over by the public sector. Then, in 1935, private water companies were regulated nearly out of existence in the United States when the Public Utility Holding Company Act broke up water monopolies. In France, Suez and Veolia were able to hang on to assets with the help of the French court system, but today 90 percent of the U.S. population gets its water from public supply systems.

The reemergence of a powerful water industry, therefore, could occur only through deregulation and force. In 2008, David Hall and Emanuele Lobina studied the resurgence of water corporations and concluded that institutional policies such as "lending conditionalities" have been the "key drivers of privatization," even "where historical experience indicates it is an inappropriate solution."[50] In short, cholera killed the private water industry until neoliberalism popularized it again. In 2011, the World Bank lent $7.5 billion for water supply projects, a figure that has been climbing since the 1990s.[51]

At the same time, the private-sector arm of the World Bank has been quietly purchasing shares in water multinationals, and so in essence funding its own growth. In 2008, the Bank purchased 14 percent of Veolia AMI, a subsidiary working in Africa, India, and the Middle East. In 2010, it purchased 9.5 percent of Veolia Voda, a subsidiary in Eastern Europe. The European Bank for Reconstruction and Development has also invested 27 percent of its holdings in water corporations.[52] According to *Global Water Intelligence*, these shareholdings enable these banks not only "to influence decision-making, but also to accelerate physical activity in the sector." Basically, the World Bank wants to encourage water corporations to move into poorer countries and so is taking part of the risk. Bank economist Usha Rao-Monari stated that private companies are "looking to share their equity risk, and in emerging markets, they want to share it with someone who they think can look after them."[53] But the danger of the Bank taking on these risks is that by doing so it is actually transferring risk to the average U.S. citizen. Since the Bank is funded primarily through bonds sold to large banks, a World Bank failure would cause a cascading failure in the global banking system. The Bank sees such a failure as impossible because of the backing of the taxpayer-funded IMF, which promises to step in to bail out problematic loans. But given the number of water contracts that have actually failed around the world—such as in Bolivia, Argentina, and the United States—this risk is frightening. The Bank is aware of the risk, but, as Rao-Monari claims, it is still willing to "leverage private capital with public funds." *Our* funds.

At the World Water Forum in Marseille, debt collectors, development agencies, water corporations, and government ministers all came together. The atmosphere was dismal, despite the ballet. Bank representatives behaved like loan officers, lecturing African water ministers about bettering their credit. (More than 50 percent of the water ministers who came to the Forum were from Africa.)[54] Water companies threw around money, pamphlets, and gifts stamped with their logos. Water ministers either prostrated themselves before both of these groups by asking for investment or loans, or looked depressed and cynical. They were lectured about their problems with "poor governance" and handed a pamphlet that explained they "must demonstrate their 'willingness-to-collect.'"[55] Water executives liked to repeat that if Africans could afford cell phones, they could afford water. President of AquaFed Gérard Payen tried to sloganize this idea at one point, shouting, "No money, no water!"[56] He obviously thought this was clever, inviting the audience to laugh with him. No one did. Overall, there was a feeling of dissatisfaction, even anger, at the Forum. Perhaps no one likes being lectured by a loan officer.

After the Bank's decision to mandate privatization in the 1990s, the idea that the "poor" must be educated about what they *should* pay for water quickly followed. Thames Water executive Peter Spillet said, "Clearly people do not understand the value of water and they expect it to fall from the sky and not cost anything."[57] Corporations began massive campaigns with World Bank funds to educate the public about what water should cost. Seminars and training workshops were held around the world on the "value of water," trying to sell the idea that if people did not "value" water, it would be wasted. Their motto was that raising water prices would lead people to conserve water, though poor people use very little to begin with. Instead, raising prices forced poor people to drink from rivers and streams; cholera outbreaks followed. At the World Water Forum in Kyoto in 2003, one of the talks was titled "How Will the Poor Become Customers?" By 2012, corporations had funded numerous studies on both the poor's ability to pay and their "willingness to pay."[58] Indeed, a great deal of energy is put into "making them pay."

Ironically, not one of these corporations publicly supports "water privatization." On the contrary, Veolia's website claims: "Water taken from the environment is a public good. . . . Its conservation, protection and regulation fall under the purview of public authorities. We have supported and lent our expertise to all types of public authorities."[59] Rather than privatizing water, these corporations claim they are working to achieve the United Nations Millennium Development Goals of halving the amount of people in the world who do not have access to clean water by 2015. Or they claim to be environmentalists; as Suez says, "If we had to define our mission, it would only take four words: working for the planet."[60] Publicly, their goals are saving the planet and helping the poor. But behind closed doors, the meetings are all about making the poor pay and raising water prices. And while water corporations claim that raising water prices leads to conservation, this is not the case. If anything, privatization has increased the corporate search for "customers." In one contract, the corporation was even allowed to raise water rates if people conserved water, in order to offset the corporation's "losses."[61]

During the opening ceremony of the 2012 World Water Forum, "the poor" were actually brought out on stage in traditional dress to explain what it felt like to be thirsty, while audience members, dressed in suits, ties, and pearls, were most likely dreaming of the free champagne that would follow. I thought of the "human zoo," where the well-heeled had also once gawked at the poverty of the colonies. Loïc Fauchon, president of the World Water Council, introduced Maï Walette and Sid Ahmed Ag Ahmouden as "brother and sister, young, poor, living in an insecure region suffering permanent water stress . . . from the Imrad ethnic tribe of Mali." He said that they would speak of their "hope for water." Bizarrely, I happened to know that there is no "Imrad ethnic tribe" in Mali, or anywhere. (*Imrad* is a class or caste distinction, not an ethnicity, in Tuareg culture.) I wondered if they were even from Mali.

Nevertheless, the teenagers were happy to explain their suffering. Sid Ahmed Ag Ahmouden said, "Do you know what thirst is? . . . I am referring to the fire burning your throat after three hours spent waiting to collect water from a well under a stifling sun. I am referring to that terrible feeling and need to vomit after you have drunk dirty water from a stagnant pond." He pleaded with the people in the room to provide his region with drinking water, ending with thanks for their "kind and noble endeavors." Fauchon followed this speech with a moment of self-congratulation, saying, "Let us take pride in the cause of water in which we all believe. For this is truly a marvelous and most noble cause." He then promised that the Forum would remain committed to the "implementation" of the solutions proposed in the "Village of Solutions," including the coin-operated water fountain in the "Slum."

How to Profit from a Water Crisis

Scientists like to point out that there is exactly the same amount of water on the planet now as there was in the time of the dinosaurs. The same number of drops exists today as existed billions of years ago—in fact, we all drink the same water that dinosaurs drank. In this sense, "water shortage" is a misnomer of sorts. The only shortage is in the amount of water that reaches our bodies, or the bodies of other plants and animals that need it to survive—and in the amount of *clean* water.

There are in fact three main problems facing the world in regard to water: pollution, groundwater loss, and climate change. Only 1 percent of the world's water is drinkable, while the rest is stored in the ocean or ice caps, and within the past generation, most of that 1 percent has become unfit to drink without increasingly expensive forms of treatment. Since most of the world still relies on well water and untreated surface water, the world entered its first "global water crisis" when those water sources became too polluted to be drunk safely. Today, polluted water is the number one killer in the world, and children die in record numbers from dysentery and other waterborne diseases. They may be drinking from the same sources their families have used for generations, but when those sources went bad, they began to die. One of the reasons for the increasing incidence of waterborne diseases and deaths is out-of-control urbanization. As more people crowd into cities without adequate sanitation, the rivers and streams become severely polluted, but sometimes no other source of water is available.

The next problem is groundwater overextraction. To understand the problem, imagine you have a reservoir bigger than the whole state of California beneath your feet, which is the actual size of the Ogallala aquifer in the United States. You use it for irrigation, drinking water, and so on. You think it will be there forever. After all, groundwater that is pumped to the surface does not disappear from the environment—it eventually runs into streams and then oceans, then evaporates to form clouds, and finally falls back to the earth as rain, which seeps back into the ground. But groundwater around the world is being pumped faster than it is being recharged—and so the stored water in *certain areas* is being lost. So one day your well stops producing. What do you do? You start drilling deeper and deeper, but eventually there is no drill that will go deep enough, or your drill hits the brackish water that pools at the bottom of an aquifer. This scenario is what experts call "peak water," when groundwater becomes prohibitively expensive to extract and treat (similar to the "peak oil" situation happening with our oil reserves). After that point is reached, all you can do is move. As groundwater stores are depleted, the populations that rely on those sources, such as 75 percent of American cities, will have to relocate. This is obviously a serious impending crisis.

Groundwater comes in two varieties: fossil water and replenishing. Fossil water is as ancient as oil, trapped underground for thousands or even millions of years. When it's gone, it's gone. In contrast, replenishing groundwater basins can refill over time from precipitation. Unfortunately, when water is overextracted, the earth's weight can actually cause that open space underground to collapse or subside. When that happens, it is like blowing up a multitude of dams. There is no place for the water to be stored, and when it falls as rain, it runs out to sea instead. (In parts of California's San Joaquin Valley, the earth had sunk approximately thirty feet by the 1970s. It has sunk even farther in India.) Besides this problem, underground reservoirs near coastlines fill with saltwater if they are pumped too low. Like freshwater estuaries, these reservoirs must maintain certain water levels in order to keep ocean water out. As we deplete these aquifers, saltwater rushes in to fill the void; this has happened in both Los Angeles and the Gaza Strip.

Finally, the melting of glaciers and ice caps significantly decreases the amount of freshwater available in the world. While one might think that this would create *more* freshwater, polar ice melts directly into the ocean and immediately becomes salty. Melting glaciers on mountaintops do temporarily increase the flow of rivers, but once these glaciers are gone, the rivers will be gone too. We have already begun to see a pattern of extreme flooding in glacial areas, which will eventually be followed by never-ending drought punctuated by devastating flash floods. In fact, some climate change specialists are already recommending building massive dams to capture glacial water before it is all lost. Glaciers are our aboveground reservoirs. They regulate the flow of rivers as predictably as dam spillways do. And they are disappearing more quickly than anyone predicted they would.

Of course, all these problems could have devastating impacts on the future of our species. But too often corporations are found celebrating rather than lamenting, uncorking the champagne bottle as the ship goes down. For them, water shortages are stimulating investments, and so the impending water crisis is potentially profitable. Investment companies describe water as "the new oil" or the "new gold." In 2006, a Bloomberg News headline read, "Water Outperforms Oil."[62] *China Daily* recently ran a front-page story on the water crisis with a positive spin: "Water will emerge as the 'new gold' and an integral part of future global security, considering there is tremendous pressure on water resources from climate change, urbanization, and economic growth. . . . Private equity and venture capital firms have been spearheading the 'green gold' rush."[63] According to investment specialist Jim Powell, water is an even better commodity than oil because, "unlike oil, there is no substitute for water."[64] And Rainer Otteman, head of fund sales at KBC Bank Deutschland, said, "Water may be the most underestimated resource in comparison to traditional resources, because it has much more significance to humans."[65]

So how do corporations profit from the water crisis? The primary way corporations "sell" water is by treating and delivering it. For this reason, increased water pollution means increased profit. Corporations are brought in to build and/or manage water treatment plants and to extend existing urban water networks. After acquiring a contract, there are four ways a corporation can make profit: by raising water rates, by cutting spending on infrastructure and labor, by receiving government subsidies, and by selling more water. Corporations are known for doing all four.

First, corporations will raise water rates as high as they can, up to 400 percent in Manila and 300 percent in Bolivia. To be fair, they are forced to do this to some extent because their costs are higher than those of public utilities. Unlike public utilities, corporations have to pay taxes. They also do not have access to federal low-interest loans as city utilities do. Finally, they have high advertising costs, which public utilities do not have. But whatever the reasons, rates have never *not* gone up after water management has been transferred to a private company.[66]

Second, corporations can lower the amount they spend on infrastructure and labor. An example of this would be Atlanta, where Suez acquired a contract to run the city's water and immediately began firing employees. Unfortunately, this backfired when the new employees could not locate the piping connections. Water turned brown as frozen and broken pipes went unrepaired, and residents received five "boil water" alerts in the first year.[67] Nevertheless, it remains common practice for corporations to lay off utility workers after an acquisition. One might even say this is the main reason for privatization.

Third, corporations can require that governments provide subsidies for poor people who cannot pay their bills. This is a policy called "transferring risk," since many early water contracts failed due to price increases for the poor. AquaFed is now asking governments to raise rates through the "3 Ts"—taxes, tariffs, and transfers. Tax revenues are now used to subsidize low-income customers, tariffs are charged monthly to customers, and transfers are made from "national budgets" to corporations.[68] Ironically, these same corporations once argued they would "streamline" water delivery by eliminating government inefficiency, removing bureaucratic hurdles, and relieving the government of its water operating expenses. The reality, instead, is that cities are not only losing a permanent income stream from water bills but are also having to pay corporations extra money out of pocket.

Finally, the latest trend has been for water corporations to coinvest in real estate developments (or vice versa) and thereby sell more water. This trend is occurring throughout the world, as "private towns" become popular alternatives for the wealthy. In the U.S. Southwest, PICO Holdings, a water and real estate conglomerate that focuses on buying "bargain-priced developable land," supplies its new housing projects through its own subsidiary, Vidler Water. In turn, Vidler Water chases down new water sources by buying cheap property for its water rights, then transferring that water to its housing projects through water markets. Vidler now owns water rights in Colorado, Idaho, Nevada, and Arizona. Similarly, J. P. Morgan Asset Management, with $46 billion in real estate and infrastructure assets, recently acquired Southwest Water Company and so can now codevelop real estate projects in the American Southwest. For water corporations, these mergers mean they can avoid municipal regulations regarding water pricing and quality and can seek out (and literally house) the highest-paying customers.

As investment banks are snapping up water corporations, we have to wonder how much power these banks will acquire in the global marketplace. And what will become of our water? According to John Hayward, a water executive at the World Bank, "Water will be moved around the world as oil is now."[69] Already, we can see water being moved to the highest-paying customers, with whole new cities being built for them. In the future, will the poor inhabit only "public" cities, the ones without clean water? Even in industrialized countries, public investment in water infrastructure has been bled dry for decades. In the United States, it is estimated that we need $1 trillion to upgrade our water supply system. Besides this, the more polluted our waterways become, the more power we hand over to water corporations developing new treatment technologies for precisely this reason. Soon, we may be asked to demonstrate our "willingness to pay" if we want to continue to receive clean water. "No money, no water!"

Your Tap

The 2008 James Bond movie *Quantum of Solace* shows an uncanny presentiment about the shadowy world of water corporations. In the film, a multinational corporation, Greene Planet, gradually starts buying up the world's water supplies while posing as an environmental organization buying land for "a global network of eco-parks." The CEO of the company, Dominic Greene, explains to the board, "This is the world's most precious resource. We need to control as much of it as we can." Starting its machinations in Bolivia, Greene Planet first purchases an enormous underground aquifer, then dams the outlet to "create a drought" and raise the price of water. Next, Greene funds a military coup (using a Bond-worthy assortment of bad guys) to topple the socialist Bolivian government and install a president who is privatization-friendly. In return for this favor, the new president must sign a contract to use Greene Planet as "utilities provider."

When Bond stumbles upon this organization by chance, his boss, known as M, says, "What the hell is this organization, Bond? How can they be everywhere and we know nothing about them?" At the World Water Forum in 2012, I sometimes felt this way, thinking I had stumbled into a fund-raiser for Greene Planet, surrounded by oil magnates, bankers, and water barons, with millions spent on duck pâté and undulating water fountains spelling WWF. How could I have known nothing about them? In this world, bribery and corruption seem to be the industry standard, as one water executive explained, "If one company is not corrupt, another one will get the money . . . and they know that."[70] He was actually *defending* the payment of bribes, explaining that it was inevitable. This was indeed a new world to me.

Suez officials once bribed the mayor of Grenoble, France, with $3 million to have the city's water supply turned over to them. Suez then proceeded to recoup the cost of the bribes by charging the customers. In 1994, Grenoble's mayor received a five-year prison sentence for this crime; two Suez water executives and a Suez lobbyist also received prison time.[71] In another case, consultant Jacques Michel began investigating overbilling practices in the French water corporations at the request of French municipalities. Mysteriously, his house then burned down in a case that was later determined to be arson. Later, two thugs were arrested on the way to Michel's house with "two bags containing wigs, gloves, handcuffs, a roll of tape, a sawed-off shotgun, a 9mm pistol, shotgun shells, brass knuckles, sunglasses, a truncheon or blackjack, smoke and tear gas grenades." They admitted to having been hired to intimidate him and, upon further investigation, were reported to be working for Veolia. Michel argued in court that a "city should not allow a mafia-like exercise of power by companies no matter how great their political or financial powers." In response, Veolia sued Michel for libel for calling them "the mafia." Veolia lost the case when the judge ruled that Michel was simply describing "his own experience as a victim of mafia-like crimes."[72]

For decades, the World Bank and IMF have handed out water contracts like candy to these corporations. Now we may find it hard to extricate ourselves from their influence. As pension plans are invested in water corporations, a downturn in the water industry might affect your retirement. Besides this, water rights and utilities are being bought up at bargain-basement prices in the United States, thanks to the housing market crash in 2008. "Water markets" and transfers are also in full swing, a situation of which few are even aware. Finally, gas and oil companies are using hydraulic fracturing, or fracking, to get at hard-to-extract supplies, a method in which millions of gallons of water, mixed with sand and toxic chemicals, are forced through rock to push out natural gas. Not only does the process waste an enormous amount of water, but it also pollutes underground aquifers. Yet at the World Water Forum, fracking was not even mentioned, except in a "side event" with Wenonah Hauter. In the Forum newsletter, I found the probable reason for this exclusion: "A significant number of gas and oil representatives joined the discussion here."[73]

By now, I hope you can see how these issues reach your tap. In this book, I look at different forms of water privatization around the world, describing the corporate–government collusion that is creating a "water bubble." In the first section, I begin in the Americas, comparing two kinds of "water marketing" in Chile and the United States. Chile has privatized 100 percent of its water supply, while the United States is investing in "water banks" in the Southwest. I will show how large corporations are monopolizing water resources in these countries and how the so-called free market in water has been linked to a military dictatorship, water billionaires, and even Fox News. In California, water billionaires hoard water in "water banks" that have been quietly gifted to them by the government. In Chile, dictator Augusto Pinochet privatized the nation's water, handing 80 percent over to one hydropower company, Endesa. In both of these cases, privatizing water meant gifting water to the already rich and further removing it from indigenous populations; in a later chapter, we will see how the same thing led to a revolution in Egypt. I focus first on Chile and the United States because the World Bank considers each a "model" for successful water marketing. "Water marketing" is generally not included in books about privatization, though it is perhaps an even more insidious form of commodifying water than the corporate control of urban utilities; the water itself is bought and sold, rather than the water treatment plants. Water marketing has also not received nearly as much public scrutiny or resistance as the large water multinationals; it has therefore been deemed more "successful."

The next section of the book looks at two former British colonies, India and South Africa, and introduces the international network of colonial dam builders. Today, the water diversion systems built for the colonial elite are being used to send water to private corporations. For instance, the Ganges River is now being diverted to Suez in Delhi, and water from the Lesotho Highlands is being diverted to Johannesburg, a municipality whose water was once run by Suez but is now run by utility managers trained by Suez. In South Africa, the postapartheid constitution once enshrined water as a permanent *right* for everyone and was the first constitution in the world to do so. But pressures from the IMF forced South Africa to ignore its constitution and privatize its water supplies, bringing up questions about national sovereignty. We will look at the way people in postcolonial nations are pushing back against the water corporations and have sometimes succeeded in chasing them out with tactics based on earlier anticolonial strategies of resistance.

Finally, the last section turns to the Middle East, specifically Egypt and Iraq. Both were also once British colonies but more recently have been affected radically by the United States. In Iraq, the destruction of the water infrastructure by the U.S. military was followed by pressure to hand water management contracts over to European and American companies during Iraq's subsequent occupation and "reconstruction." I will show how this privatization strategy backfired, leading to a growing insurgency in Iraq. In Egypt, riots turned to revolution in Tahrir Square after President Hosni Mubarak handed vast quantities of land and water over to his friends. While the American media closely followed this revolution, few were aware that Mubarak was following U.S. and World Bank directives to privatize national holdings. In both countries, the push to privatize or "liberalize" the economy led to a growing Islamic insurgency, from the Muslim Brotherhood in Egypt and al-Qaeda in Iraq. I will show

how failing water infrastructure directly contributed to the rise of these groups, which have now spread to Syria, Israel, and elsewhere. The World Bank has also supported massive dam projects that have cut off water supplies to Syria and Iraq, directly leading to this unrest.

In each of these regions, resistance has varied more than the corporate blueprint for water privatization. In the United States and Chile, minority indigenous groups have fought for but often failed to achieve greater control over their water supplies. Environmental and antiprivatization organizations have had more success. In India and Africa, majority indigenous and anti-privatization groups have followed the traditions of their anticolonial predecessors in destabilizing corporate control, sometimes with great success. In Iraq and Egypt, antiprivatization movements are often co-opted by Islamic extremists. In all of these instances, the pushback by the people over water supplies cannot be ignored.

Besides seeking to cover water problems around the world, I chose the nations that I examine in this book because their water problems could affect the life of the entire planet and, therefore, your life. For instance, southern Chile is located next to the Antarctic Circumpolar Current, which fuels all the world's ocean currents. Today it is moving south due to climate change; without it, the world's oceans would die, and Europe could be plunged into an ice age. Dam construction by private companies exacerbates this problem by warming inland glacier-fed seas. In India, the Himalayas border Asia's largest freshwater bank, the glaciers of the Tibetan Plateau, which provide water to a quarter of the planet but are quickly disappearing. California and India are also running out of water, even as much of the world depends on the food they grow for survival. And Egypt and Iraq are embroiled in bitter water battles that are creating an international refugee crisis and fueling Islamic extremism. By visiting every continent in the world except Antarctica, I demonstrate not only the scope of the problem but also how all these stories are interconnected. This is truly a planetary problem.

As I visited each of these countries, my goal was to compare the rhetoric used about water in international governance institutions to the reality on the ground. The World Bank now makes available most of its archival materials, and these provided a wealth of information, as did engineering journals, explorer narratives, and water agency records. In each country, my primary goal was to read the landscape, unobtrusively visiting dam sites, resettlement villages, and watersheds to see the impacts of the infrastructure on the land. Traveling as a journalist with a press pass, I ended up meeting environmental activists, water engineers, and city utility officers along the way. But more important to me than prearranged interviews was simply seeing an area and finding out whether or not a dam had been finished or if people were actually drinking from the water taps. I wanted to "ground truth" what I had read, to see what was actually true and not true.

In the end, I hope to reveal the competing languages vying to define our water. One kind of language is scientific, economic, and international; it is spoken in corporate boardrooms, academic halls, and government meeting rooms. But there is also the language of the "antiprivatization" groups, who focus on water as a "human right" or a "right of nature." While the fight for water rights has been strategically successful in many regards, there are also potential pitfalls to viewing water as a "human right," not the least of which is the easy co-option of this language unaccompanied by fundamental changes in practice. Co-opting the language of their adversaries was clearly one of the tactics at the World Water Forum, as described by activist and author Arundhati Roy: "Every speech was percussive with phrases like 'women's empowerment,' 'people's participation,' and 'deepening democracy.' Yet it turned out that the whole purpose of the forum was to press for the privatization of the world's water." She concluded, "[It was] the ritualistic slaughter of language as I know and understand it."[74]

Finally, if there is an agreed-upon language of "development" in global governance institutions, there is also another global lingua franca, one that is potentially more powerful—the language of water. The former language contains terms like *benchmarking, scaling up,* and *best international practices.* But the latter language is evasive and a trickster. It is smarter than those in power. It will turn to steam and then to clouds when it is hot. It will fall to the earth when it is cold and turn solid when it is colder. It flows from mountains down rivers to the ocean. It seeps into underground reservoirs and becomes "fossil water" that sits for thousands or even millions of years. It seeps into the bodies of plants and animals. It is 90 percent of each of us. In every country I visited, I met people who spoke the language of water. I found that those who had intimate relationships with rivers or streams were most likely to have the best solutions. They provided the models through which we can rethink the dominant attitudes presented at the World Water Forum. But these are the very people whose water is being taken from them.

In 2002, the people of Bolivia threw out the U.S. water company Bechtel in a revolution that led to the election of the country's first indigenous president, Evo Morales. I was surprised to find that Evo Morales had been invited to speak at the World Water Forum in Kyoto in 2003. "We are all in favour of cultural diversity," he said at that meeting, "but what do we see? There is one model—of privatization and generalization—that is spreading and pushing out the others. . . . So we have to speak clearly: the World Bank and IMF are against cultural diversity, and are opposing indigenous rights." Complaining that only 2 of the 350 World Water Forum sessions addressed indigenous issues, he said, "Do you suppose that we are only one half of one percent of the world population?" In fact, he insisted, "we are over half the world population. . . . But how many societal, rural, and indigenous populations are on the World Water Council? None."[75] Similarly, at the World Water Forum in Marseille, members of the Tsilhqot'in Nation of British Columbia circulated a handout complaining that indigenous peoples are "not informed, nor are they included in the establishment of policies, or agreements that involve the sale of their water sources." They further argued that "the establishment of water as a commodity violates the basic human right to water and sacred principles of water," concluding, "water is a right of nature." Though they had submitted a formal solution to be included in the "Village of Solutions" at the Forum, it apparently had been rejected.

My goal in writing this book is to help return cultural diversity to the management of the world's water supplies. Since colonial times, our understanding of water has been shrinking, mapped out for us by colonial and economic forces that see one way of doing business for the entire planet. At the same time, the solutions to the world's water problems are already out there; they just need funding and legitimacy. For instance, Evo Morales has said that all we need to do to have water for all is take money out of military budgets and put it into water budgets. Costa Rica has followed this model. Others believe in rainwater harvesting or simply allowing people to remain on their land rather than pushing them into cities where supplying water infrastructure is a nightmare. Another easy solution would be to create laws against the chemicals that pollute water.

Unfortunately, most books on water privatization have focused only on urban water supplies, avoiding both the larger structural problems of internal migration and the solutions offered by indigenous peoples. The truth is that the solutions are often up in the hills, among guerrilla insurgents, Gandhi-inspired activists, and indigenous peoples who live close to the sources of water.

Of course, finding these solutions is not always easy. Though hardly a Bond-like figure, I did face obstacles and suffer injuries during my investigation. In Iraq, my plane had to evade missile strikes as we landed—my first realization that the war was far from over. In India, I just missed a glacier collapse that killed more than a dozen people on the trail I was hiking. In Turkey, I went to sleep to the sound of gunfire battles between people fighting over water, and I woke up to witness mass arrests. In Egypt, revolution was in the air. In South Africa, I drove through rioters and burning tires to get to the airport before it was shut down. But everywhere I went, I heard the most amazing stories from people who would sacrifice their lives and freedom to protect their water supplies. Those stories made it all worthwhile. As I traveled, I sometimes felt I was diagnosing a patient, scanning the globe for the worst injuries to its precious circulatory system—its rivers and streams. I was drawn ever forward simply by a need to understand how and why these injuries were being inflicted and what could be done to stop them. Ultimately, I did find the answers I was looking for. But in the end, you may want to sit down before you hear the prognosis.

I

WHEELING AND DEALING WATER IN THE AMERICAS

ONE

Water Hoarding in a California Drought

I GREW UP IN SOUTHERN CALIFORNIA, in a part of the country hit by the nation's worst dust storms, deadly storms full of heavy metals that blow from dry Owens Lake. Studies have shown that I will not live as long as others because of this. I have accepted this, while at the same time hoping that these studies are wrong. Where I grew up, the city of Los Angeles diverted water away from Owens Lake, slowly draining it starting in 1913. It took more than ten years for the lake to dry up and turn into a toxic dust bowl, when naturally occurring heavy metals like aluminum and cadmium that had concentrated in the salt lake over centuries became airborne. This dust has been shown to cause cancer and respiratory failure, among other ailments. I grew up experiencing water inequity in my own body.

So when I saw Sean Hannity on Fox News broadcasting from another California valley allegedly drained of its water, I must admit I became curious. In September 2009, Hannity broadcast from Huron, California, in a weeklong special titled "The Valley Hope Forgot." He was broadcasting from the poorest congressional district in the nation, in California's San Joaquin Valley. According to the 2009 U.S. Census, 39 percent of Huron's close to eight thousand residents live below the poverty line. It is a migrant labor town, a cotton-picker town, and is 98.6 percent Latino/a. Huron has no medical services, no high school, and no voting booth during elections, because most of the residents are undocumented. Some 80 percent of Huron residents have not finished high school, and children who are born there have more birth defects than children anywhere else in the country—most likely due to pesticide exposure. One resident of Huron said she shut the windows when the wind blew. "What good is the wind?" she asked. "It's all poison."[1] The water quality is no better, ranking 490 out of 502 cities in California, with fecal coliform bacteria, *E. coli*, and nitrates found in dangerous levels.[2] The water system is built and run by Tri-City Engineering and owned by a former manager of Bechtel.

I could certainly see why Hannity would call it "The Valley Hope Forgot." Ironically, these were not the problems that Hannity had come to discuss. According to Fox News, Huron had only one problem: "environmental extremists" had turned off the water to save a "two-inch fish" in the Bay Area. According to Hannity, both the winter-run Chinook salmon and the delta smelt had been listed as endangered species in 1994, an event that wreaked havoc on local farms. It had been determined that water pumped for farming in the San Joaquin Valley was destroying the fishes' habitat up north. In an area known simply as "the Delta," an ecologically unique inland estuary exists between San Francisco and Sacramento. Through this Delta, much of the state's water supply passes, as do its endangered fish species. It turned out they were all competing for water.

Of course, the farmers were not happy about the endangered species listing. From a stage draped in American flags, Hannity reported that in order to save the delta smelt, pumps that had once brought water from the San Francisco Delta area to the San Joaquin Valley had been shut down. Behind him, a rally of thousands periodically cheered, "Turn on the pumps!" They carried American flags or signs that read, "Stop Eco-Tyranny." They wore identical baseball hats. But what surprised me most was that it looked like at least 90 percent of them were white. Hannity said they were "family farmers." It was surreal.[3]

From the stage, Governor Arnold Schwarzenegger promised to turn the pumps on as soon as he could, claiming the president was stopping him. (Strangely, the pumps were actually on at the time and had been for two months. According to Secretary of the Interior Ken Salazar, "The temporary pumping restrictions that were required under the Endangered Species Act ended on June 30th."[4] The rally was held in September.) Congressman Devin Nunes compared President Barack Obama to both Saddam Hussein and Robert Mugabe for withholding water from "his own people."[5] The one environmentalist on Hannity's show was shouted down by the crowd, and Hannity said, "The water has been turned off because wackos and environmental extremists like you care more about fish than about people. And I just want to know, how did you get your priorities so screwed up in life . . . what happened to you?"

Of course, Fox News is known more for its politics than for its veracity, but the surreal nature of this show took even me by surprise. It seemed that Fox News counted on nobody visiting Huron, which may have been a safe bet since it is not exactly a tourist destination. But whom was Fox News fighting *for,* and *why,* if not the residents of Huron? I decided to go to Huron to find out. What I discovered on the way was a story of collusion, corruption, and water privatization spreading across the United States.

The Road to Huron

Getting to Huron is like taking a trip into a postapocalyptic future. It is not surprising that the town is not well visited. California's San Joaquin Valley is dotted with prisons and landfills. Dust storms regularly close the freeway. On the way to Huron, I ran into a dust "blackout" and had to stop the car, unable to see even a few feet ahead. As I waited for the storm to clear, I began to notice strange objects pelting the car. At first, I could make out only plastic bags and cardboard boxes, but then a diaper hit the windshield, and the smell told me it was trash. As the storm passed, I realized I had been forced to stop next to an uncovered landfill in Wasco, California. Ironically, this is the "rose capital" of the nation, growing 65–75 percent of U.S. roses. Next to the landfill is Wasco State Prison, where six thousand inmates were waiting out the dust storm, too.

Dust storms now close Interstate 5 (the I-5), the main freeway from Los Angeles to San Francisco, several times a year. They are a frequent cause of multicar pileups. Once considered the "bread basket" of the nation for its surfeit of nut, fruit, and vegetable crops, today parts of the San Joaquin Valley are wasteland. Health experts have warned that increasing temperatures and more intense dust storms are also leading to higher transmissions of "valley fever," a fungal disease that can target organs, joints, and the nervous system. The spores are spread through the blowing soil—something that becomes more likely when there is little ground vegetation. In ten years, the number of cases of this disease has nearly quadrupled.[6]

Before settlers arrived in the San Joaquin Valley, a person would have needed a boat to get across it; now sometimes crossing it is impossible because of Sahara-style dust storms. Huron was once on the shore of the largest freshwater lake west of the Mississippi, Tulare Lake, which was fed by three large rivers, the Kings, Kawea, and Tule. John Muir once wrote that the valley was "one smooth, continuous bed of honey-bloom, so marvelously rich that, in walking from one end of it to the other, a distance of more than 400 miles, your foot would press about a hundred flowers at every step."[7] A forest of tule reeds up to twelve feet high surrounded the lake, which was brimming with freshwater mussels, turtles, fish, and waterfowl.

One of the early settler families in the area was the Boswell clan, and today they still own the land surrounding Tulare Lake. The Boswells are one of the richest families in California, another being the Resnicks. These two families also control much of the water in the San Joaquin Valley. According to historian Mark Arax: "The Boswells own, if you can own a river, they own 15 percent of the Kings River, which is in the middle of California, coming down the Sierra and emptying in what was Tulare Lake. The Kings River irrigates more farmland than any river in the world except for the Nile and the Indus."[8] The Boswells are also the largest single grower of cotton in the world, with cotton farms in California, Arizona, and Australia.

The founder of the Boswell enterprise was Joseph Boswell, a Confederate soldier who amassed enough of a fortune from his cotton plantation in Georgia to allow his son, James G. Boswell, to head to California. In California, J. G. Boswell did what he knew best. He planted cotton, replacing slave labor with immigrant labor, first Chinese and then Mexican. Soon, his brother Bill and Bill's wife, Kate, came out as well and brought along Maggie and Will, "a dear old Negro couple." But it was not long before Kate was complaining that this couple had become "impudent," doing things like entering through the Boswells' front door, rather than the back as they did in the South. Apparently, the Boswells had trouble adapting to the more tolerant social mores of California. Kate described what happened to this poor couple: "I can never forget when Bill went out one morning, and . . . said, 'Nigger, you get yours and Maggie's things packed. There's a train that leaves here at four o'clock this afternoon. I've got your ticket, and you be on that train or else I'll have a dead nigger on my hands."[9]

Besides controlling their servants and laborers, the Boswells spent most of their time trying to control the lake. Since the 1850s, farmers had been setting up diking and irrigation systems to grow wheat and other crops, thereby draining Tulare Lake. As the lake shrank, the bottom was used for growing crops. This was encouraged by the state of California, whose brochures still call this the "reclamation of swamplands."[10] In 1905, as the lake dried up, millions of gasping fish were found dying in the lakebed. The *San Francisco Chronicle* lamented, "Tulare Lake is gone. . . . Once the largest body of freshwater west of the Mississippi is a grain field."[11] Farmers torched the remaining tules and started building massive levees to straighten and contain the rivers. Unfortunately for the farmers, the lake kept coming back, bursting through their levees to drown their fields.

Eventually, the Boswells and other growers convinced the federal government to stop this "flooding" of their land by damming the rivers that fed Tulare Lake up in the foothills. In 1928, the Flood Control Act passed, allowing dam construction for the purpose of keeping water out of the San Joaquin Valley. Ironically, only a few years later another law was passed to bring more water *to* the San Joaquin Valley. In 1933, the Central Valley Project Act was passed to sell bonds for a project that would eventually encompass twenty dams and five hundred miles of major canals that would bring water from Northern California to the San Joaquin Valley. The U.S. Bureau of Reclamation, created to construct "irrigation works for the reclamation of arid lands," took over the project when state funds ran dry.

The U.S. Reclamation Act of 1902 had been designed to relieve population pressures in the East and help end poverty by moving Americans westward onto small family farms of no more than 160 acres. The Bureau of Reclamation would build the facilities—dams and canals—to irrigate these properties with the proceeds from the sale of federal lands.[12] Farmers were supposed to pay back the costs of the facilities with their profits over a period of ten years, which failed to happen when crop yields were

not as high as the bureau had expected them to be.[13] Initially, the Central
Valley Project was modeled after the British irrigation system built in India, which had six thousand miles of canals by 1900. In fact, the British
engineer who oversaw construction of the Indian project was actually
hired in California to help design the Central Valley Project.[14]

Despite the massive water engineering, Tulare Lake continued its
. cycle of flooding and drying. In 1941–42, the sport of "dry-land fishing"
was taken up as residents clubbed to death fish in receding floodwaters.
In 1969, J. G. Boswell Jr. built a levee out of junked cars to keep floods
from invading his property. The *Corcoran Journal* bragged in 2009, "Like
the war in Vietnam, our famers are embattled, alert and doing everything
possible to prevent and minimize flood losses."[15] Until his death, Boswell
liked to talk about his heroic struggles against the lake. He even hired a
film director to make a documentary about it called *The Big Land* in 1967.
The film opens with an aerial shot of lake, as the narrator explains, "This
is Tulare Lake. . . . Once it ranged over 600 square miles, the uncontested
master of the valley. Now it's become the lake that was; its waters controlled, its bottom reclaimed. Once master, it's now servant. Once deso-
late, it's now fertile. The difference is man."[16]

In 1960, the State Water Project was approved, promising to bring
even more cheap water from the north. This project includes thirty-four
dams and more than seven hundred miles of canals and pipelines; it claims
to be the nation's largest publicly built and operated water and power conveyance system. Unlike the Central Valley Project, this project got around
the 160-acre restriction because it was funded by the state. According
to journalist Robert Gottlieb: "The deal set the stage for a whirlwind of
activities that changed the shape of the region. Major corporate interests took over some of the big landholdings in the area and aggressively
moved into the land-development business. . . . The amount of irrigated
acreage shot up by more than two hundred thousand acres in less than a
decade." At the head of this massive land acquisition were companies like
Houston-based Tenneco and Prudential Life Insurance. And then there
was Boswell. "King Cotton," Gottlieb writes, "came to dominate the valley in ways inconceivable just two decades earlier."[17] The state had been
bitterly divided over the State Water Project. Residents in the north questioned the damage that would be done to the Delta. The California Labor
Federation claimed the project would aid agribusiness and not workers.

Ultimately, the Burns–Porter Act, which authorized $1.7 billion in state funds for the project, passed by a very narrow margin in 1959. By 1973, Justice William O. Douglas noted that Boswell had created a "corporate kingdom undreamed of by those who wrote our Constitution."[18] Today, Californians are still fighting over the same issue, taking sides on protecting the environment versus protecting agribusiness. The difference is that agribusiness is a much more powerful force in politics, aided by the water attained from the State Water Project.

The State Water Project was supposed to be 100 percent paid for by the "project beneficiaries," the farmers. But this has not been the case. The costs of construction were supposed to be recouped through water rates, but due to pressure to keep water rates low because of low crop prices farmers went tens of millions of dollars into arrears on the state debt. Today, farmers in the San Joaquin Valley pay about a tenth of what someone in Los Angeles would pay for water, and they have not paid for the last 30 percent of the State Water Project. In 1994, the Monterey Accord canceled the remaining debt, which means that taxpayers will pay that extra 30 percent.

An added complication is that farming operations are now in trouble on the west side of the San Joaquin Valley—and not from lack of water. If fighting with the lake was once the Boswells' greatest problem, today it is preventing salt buildup in their fields. Beneath the topsoil on that side of the valley, there is a clay layer that prevents irrigation water from sinking into the ground. Because of this, water sits on the surface, evaporating and leaving a layer of salts and minerals behind. In the 1970s, federal officials tried installing piped drainage to divert water away from the fields and into ponds to solve the problem. Then, at one of these ponds scientists began to notice that the concentrated pesticides in the water were killing or disfiguring birds. In 1985, the drainage program was stopped, but the drainage issue is still being litigated between farmers and the federal government.[19] It is estimated that by 2040 approximately 160,000 to 225,000 acres of farmland in the San Joaquin Valley—nearly as much land as the State Water Project had supplied in its first decade—will be ruined for farming due to salinization. Now it appears that the State Water Project will not only remain unpaid for but will also no longer serve its purpose of irrigation. It may become a ghost relic of U.S. ambitions to "make the desert bloom."

One solution proposed by the Bureau of Reclamation has been land retirement, in which willing farmers sell their land and/or water rights back to the state. Unfortunately, not enough farmers have been willing to sell to make this a feasible alternative, and farmers are still fighting for more drainage ponds. In 1987, it was found that bird killings from these ponds were far worse on the Boswells' property than had been seen elsewhere. Joe Skorupa of the U.S. Fish and Wildlife Service went to the Justice Department with allegations that the preventable bird deaths on Boswell land were criminal acts. "We were told we had an excellent case," Skorupa told *Audubon*, "that they had every confidence that it was winnable, but that until we went and got someone at least at the secretarial level in Interior to give a clear policy directive, the Justice Department would not pursue it."[20]

Today, Tulare Lake is home to some of the world's biggest cotton farmers, with water subsidized by the state. Throughout the American West, farmers have become the largest water consumers, using about 85–90 percent of the total water consumed in each state. According to Gottlieb: "These agricultural interests have . . . benefited from a special relationship not only with the Department of Agriculture, which implements a variety of crop subsidy programs, but the big federal agencies as well. They have developed strong ties with key congressional leaders."[21] In short, large landowners have demonstrated enough political clout to have water directed their way.

If the Boswells brought a bit of the Old South with them to Southern California, their billionaire farming neighbors are Los Angeles socialites. Stewart and Lynda Resnick own Paramount Farms, the largest supplier of pistachios in the world, as well as POM Wonderful juices, Fiji Water, Teleflora, and the Franklin Mint. Stewart Resnick makes over $2 billion in revenue. While the Boswells like to tour their property in pickup trucks and cowboy hats, the Resnicks prefer to manage their operations from their Beverly Hills mansion. Stewart Resnick attended law school at the University of California, Los Angeles, and made his first fortune in security alarms and services. With that money he bought the Franklin Mint, which is known for making model cars, souvenir plates, figurines, and Civil War–inspired chess sets. Only after he had earned hundreds of millions of dollars did Resnick decide to buy land in the San Joaquin Valley. Besides pistachios, he grows almonds and pomegranates. He is also the biggest grower of citrus in the United States. In 2000, he acquired Dole Food Company's citrus business for $55 million, along with a citrus packing plant in Huron.[22]

Today, the Resnicks are perhaps the wealthiest couple in all of Los Angeles, and their Beverly Hills mansion has been called a "West Coast Versailles." Lynda Resnick has described her house as "topped off on all four sides with rows of balustrades through which a queen might peek out and utter, 'Let them eat cake.'"[23] Christina Aguilera has sung at their parties, Arnold Schwarzenegger has called them "some of my dearest, dearest friends," and they have a wing of UCLA's hospital named after them, as well as a wing of the Los Angeles County Museum of Art. They also happen to be friends with the owner of Fox News, Rupert Murdoch, who wrote a blurb for Lynda Resnick's memoir. Located between the Boswell and Resnick properties, Huron was in fact the perfect place for Fox News to host a weeklong special. After all, Fox was fighting for the water supplies of the Boswells and Resnicks, who were friends of the Murdochs.

Today, the road to Huron is littered with signs every half mile that read, "Congress Created Dust Bowl," placed there by agribusiness. One hand-drawn sign says, "Owens Valley II." You might mistakenly think you are approaching a city full of angry activists. But until you are right on it, Huron is hidden in the dust and haze; it then jumps out at you like a lost city. It is full of one-story concrete buildings with signs in Spanish and men sitting on curbs wearing cowboy hats. It feels like a Mexican town, but one full of unemployed people. Since I arrived just after picking season, I figured that most of the people had left. The others sat around, bored, telling stories to pass the time on the two city blocks that constitute Huron. Farther down the street, the Dole packing plant dominated the landscape, enclosed in chicken-wire fence topped with barbed wire. Across from it was a collection of portable toilets waiting to be hauled to the fields, though many of them looked trashed or abandoned. Huron is a company town, a Resnick town.

Resnick was once asked how many of his farmworkers were employed illegally. He replied, "If not 100 percent, then the majority. If they had their papers in order they would get other jobs. Do you really think that someone with the proper papers is going to be killing themselves for $8 when at least they'll get $11 at another job?"[24] Mexican labor contractors bring workers across the border to the United States. How Hannity

In 2009 signs like this one were put up all over the Central Valley by Russ Waymire of Families Protecting the Valley. Waymire is a paid "consultant" for the pistachio industry (i.e., Stewart Resnick) who also works in real estate development with Doug Anderson. Resnick, Anderson, and Waymire are all "farmers" in the Lost Hills Water District, which is active in the Kern Water Bank.

had found so many Anglo farmers was beyond me. I did not see any in Huron. Huron had become my red herring—undocumented, forgotten, underrepresented, poisoned. The town was dead, the fields were dead. Fox was not around.

The Boswells versus the Yokuts

Leaving Huron, I stopped at an Indian reservation twenty miles outside town. There, I met a Yokut historian, Hector "Lalo" Franco, with an ax to grind against the Boswells. He worked at the Tachi-Yokut Indian reservation, a small property surrounded by salt-encrusted fields with its headquarters on Alkali Street. Franco, a kind and fast-talking man in his forties, welcomed me at headquarters, the newest-looking building on

Residents of Huron, California, bide their time outside a supermarket.

the reservation. Inside the front door, portraits of famous Yokuts lined the walls of the reception area. When I asked about the street name, Franco shrugged and explained, "This land out here is very hard to grow anything on because of the alkali." Ironically, everything about the history, language, and even place names of the Yokuts signifies water. So where was the water?

In 1800, approximately twenty thousand Yokut Indians lived around the lake, the highest density of Native Americans in the United States. They lived in huts made from tule reeds, foraged for food in canoes made of tules, and stored their food and cooked in watertight baskets made from tules. Franco described the area: "The marshes were incredible. It was just literally a water world anywhere you went. . . . Water was important for processing the acorn, for washing, well, for everything. Water is life."[25] The village where the reservation now stands was called *tachi,* or "mud hen," because of the large numbers of mud hens that once lived along the shores of the lake. Yokut villages were spread throughout the valley; before the land was leveled and drained by farmers, it was full of

hills and water. "Everything was done by water. Our world here was literally a water world," Franco explained.

For the Yokuts, Tulare Lake represents the actual beginning of the
world. "Tulare Lake is the focal point for our creation stories," Franco
said. "Basically, our world was all water. Eagle and the sacred beings that
existed in the early days of the world created the land. What was left over
as the water was receding was Tulare Lake. That's why Tulare Lake is considered a sacred place." Geologists confirm that Tulare Lake was once part
of the ocean, as evidenced by the minerals and shells found in the area.
In Tachi legend, animals got together and decided to give parts of themselves to create humans, who then spread across the valley.

Of course, the Yokuts are no longer spread across this land. First, the
Spanish came to the valley to chase down coastal Indians who had fled
to Tulare Lake to escape the brutal Spanish mission system. According to
geographer William Preston, "Expeditions were sent to capture renegade
soldiers and mission Indians who had sought refuge in the 'labyrinth of
lakes and tules.'"[26] Gradually, Anglo-Americans also arrived in the valley.
By 1852, Franco said, "We were faced with a tsunami of Europeans from
all over the world." Americans came with the Gold Rush, and San Francisco mercantile companies mined the valley for food by traveling down
the San Joaquin River to Tulare Lake.

The region was abundant with a wide variety of food sources. As
Preston notes, "Smoked or dried fish—not only freshwater species but
also salmon and steelhead caught 'by the ton' in Tulare Lake and the Kings
River—was stored in great quantities as an important Yokut staple."[27] This
became a draw for mercantile companies, which gathered thousands of
pounds of turtles, pelicans, and carp; they also found beavers, river otters,
minks, pronghorn antelope, and grizzly and black bears around the lake.
Franco told me, "The huge elk herds that existed on both the west side
and the east side—two distinct herds—almost disappeared overnight to
feed the hungry town of San Francisco. . . . I lived in San Francisco for
a while, and I just never really enjoyed it, I guess because of the history."
When these supplies were decimated, the Yokuts began to starve. On top
of all these problems, in 1853 California's first governor, Peter Burnett,
issued an order for the extermination of all Indians in the state, offering a
bounty of fifty cents for each Native American scalp. By 1880, the population of Yokuts had dwindled from twenty thousand to just six hundred.[28]

Slowly, the Tachi-Yokuts were confined to the tiny piece of land they live on now and prevented from traveling outside that land in search of food or warmer weather. Franco said of the settlers who invaded the valley: "They didn't find a lot of gold here, but what they did find was water. And of course they found a lot of open ground to develop their farms, that was the gold that they found over here." Trapped on the reservation with no food, Franco's grandmother would cross farmers' fences to gather food—until she was shot at one day.

In the 1950s, the Yokuts were paid an insubstantial amount for the loss of their lands, but Franco's father sent his part of the payment back with a note that read, "I'm not selling my portion of California." The tribe has survived by building a casino, but the reservation still shows obvious signs of poverty. It does indeed look like a miserable place to live, with dirt yards and small houses and blowing salt. And the Boswells, who own almost all of the Tulare lakebed, as well as the water from the lake, surround the Yokuts. In fact, the reservation today is like a little Boswell-created prison. Cotton from the Boswell fields blows onto Yokut land. And the Boswells' relationship with the Yokuts has not been good.

If Boswell history is about combating "flood" waters, the Tachi-Yokuts' history is about having their water taken away from them. On the reservation, there is a waterway called Mussel Slough that once emptied into Tulare Lake. It is now dry. "That was a very valuable waterway," Franco explained. "From here, the Native people kept a connection with the tribal people up in the Kings River and up higher. . . . Well, the water from that canal was diverted for agriculture. . . . They took the water away from us. They didn't want us to have it." Franco described the Boswells: "All of a sudden they owned the valley. So we were like, 'How can you own that valley?' 'It's real simple,' they said, 'we have an army and you don't. It's that simple. We have more might than you do, so it's our valley. Case closed.'"

Today, Franco is trying to ensure that Indian artifacts on Boswell property are protected, but he has had trouble gaining the Boswells' cooperation. He explained: "They have an attitude. They said, 'It's our land! It's our country.' And we said, 'Well, okay, but . . . work with us, you know. Dignity, respect.' But you're talking to people who could care less about that." As for getting any water back from the Boswells, Franco dismissed this as an impossible request, given the political climate. "When we try to sit down with our Congress people to discuss it," he said, "they say, 'Oh, can't we talk about something else? Can we talk about gaming or bingo or education? Do we have to talk about water?' Because who are the people who are most powerful here? It's the ranchers and the big farmers like the Boswells." (Today, J. G. Boswell Jr.'s son, James Boswell, runs the business.)

At the Tachi-Yokut headquarters, I toured a small museum filled with artifacts including watertight baskets made from tule reeds, fishing spears, and tule mats. On the walls were photos of people fishing from reed canoes. I had the feeling I was touring the artifacts of an old Polynesian village built for people living out over the water, not for people living on a desiccated salt flat. When asked who has benefited from Tulare Lake, Franco replied, "Certainly not us, and yet we lived all around that source of water. But the Tachi never benefited from it. So that's been a sore subject for us for a number of years." Indeed, whenever Franco spoke, he spoke of water—and yet he worked on Alkali Street.

Leaving Tachi reservation, I passed J. G. Boswell's hometown of Corcoran, which has the distinction of having half its population consist of prison inmates. Its prison holds forty-five hundred inmates, including Charles Manson and Juan Corona, who killed twenty-five people in 1971. It was also home to Senator Robert Kennedy's assassin, Sirhan Sirhan, before he was moved to another valley prison in 2009. The guards at Corcoran State Prison have shot and killed more inmates than the guards at any other prison in the United States. Corcoran Prison is tucked behind electrified fences and guard towers in what looks like a hellish suburbia of diamond-shaped windowless gray barracks. It also happens to be in the middle of Tulare Lake.

Besides being the serial murderer capital of the world, Corcoran is known as one of the unhealthiest places to live in the United States. The EPA ranks its water quality as 1 on a scale of 1 to 100. So it was surprising to me that J. G. Boswell and his wife, Ruth Chandler, chose to remain in Corcoran, living on ten acres in a mansion with Italian-carved bannisters until his death in 2009. Of course, their house was the epitome of luxury. Scenes for the 1968 movie *Funny Girl* were filmed there, and Barbra Streisand exclaimed upon walking in, "It must have cost a fortune. . . . It's the perfect house for a millionaire!"[29] Surrounded by prisoners, immigrants, and Indians, perhaps the Boswells felt the security of a plantation home. J. G. Boswell certainly lived in a landscape of his own creation. His

New York Times obituary read: "He re-engineered the landscape, much to the consternation of environmentalists. . . . There was an antiseptic cleanliness to the whole operation. He pushed the industry in terms of modernizing, from seed to field to gin."[30] Though nothing in the area seemed to me to have an "antiseptic cleanliness," perhaps in Mr. Boswell's mind it did.

California's Water Banks

My visit to the valley seemed to confirm what Sean Hannity had said on Fox News—the area was bone dry and needed water, especially the Yokut reservation. There were almond trees pulled up and stacked alongside the highway in places, and Huron did look like "The Valley Hope Forgot." But I had one last place to visit, the Kern Water Bank. I had heard that the water was going there. I wanted to see if I could find it and find out who controls it.

An hour south of Huron, the Kern Water Bank feels like a watery oasis in the desert, almost a hallucination or mirage. Marshland filled with flocks of birds goes on for miles—the birds were initially my only clue that I had reached the bank. Occupying thirty square miles, the Kern Water Bank has no entrance. I had arranged to meet its general manager, Jon Parker, on an unmarked dirt road in his (also unmarked) white pickup truck in the middle of the marsh. I felt like I was doing a drug deal, planning a secret prearranged meeting in a deserted place. As I hesitatingly approached Parker's truck, I noticed he was looking at birds through binoculars. I was relieved to see that Parker looked like any Audubon Society bird lover. He was thin, gray-haired, soft-spoken, dressed in khaki, and never without binoculars. But in reality, he is more banker than bird lover. The Kern Water Bank has been called one of the top five freshwater wetlands in California, but it is also a "bank."[31] In fact, that is its primary purpose. Parker explained his job: "I hate to use this analogy because people twist it and make it sound like water is money. But we are a bank. People bring their water to us and we store it and then we deliver it back. . . . When it's wet, we put water in the basins and it infiltrates into the aquifer just like water when you put water in a flowerpot. Then we pump it back out when it's dry."

The United States is the first place in the world to support "water banking." Practically speaking, a water bank is simply a belowground reservoir in which water is "deposited" and from which it is "withdrawn." Deposits involve filling large open-air ponds with water, then letting that water filter into the ground, where it is stored in aquifers until it is pumped up as withdrawals. One of the benefits of this system is that it allows states to avoid building new dams for water storage. One of the detriments is that it has turned water into money. Since beginning in earnest in the 1990s, water banking has come to be used in Arizona, California, Colorado, Idaho, Montana, Nevada, New Mexico, Oregon, Texas, Utah, Washington, and Wyoming. It is particularly suited to the American West, where large water conveyance systems facilitate water "trades."

In the late 1980s, the state of California developed the twenty-thousand-acre Kern Water Bank to store water for times of drought as well as to recharge badly depleted groundwater systems.[32] In the 1950s, it became clear that the valley was sinking as the result of the overextraction of groundwater, and this was recognized as a "serious concern." In 1977, a study by the U.S. Geological Survey (USGS) found that land in the valley had sunk thirty feet in the preceding fifty years. Since then, estimates are that it has sunk another ten feet. Today, the USGS is calling this problem "the largest human alteration of the Earth's surface." The subsidence, which is caused both by groundwater loss and by the weight of irrigation water on the surface, has caused millions of dollars in damage to irrigation canals, dams, roads, and buildings, and it is turning the once-flat land of the valley into rolling hills in certain places. House foundations have cracked, buildings are leaning, and some residents have even been forced to leave.[33]

While the state was investing $74 million in building the Kern Water Bank infrastructure, including pumps and canals, the idea of water "trading" was also beginning to emerge. In 1986, the California legislature passed a statute giving Californians the right to "wheel," or move, water through state conveyance systems. Farmers realized that, under the statute, they could move their water out of the valley to Los Angeles or other places. The idea of "banking" water for sale was starting to look attractive, but farmers realized they would need to own the Kern Water Bank in order to do so. To force the state to transfer the bank to them, they refused to supply water to the bank, turning the state's investment into an enormous boondoggle.

In 1994, a severe drought occurred, which brought the conflict to a head. During periods of drought, the state was allowed to cut back on supplying irrigation water, but farmers were still required to pay back the costs of the State Water Project as per their contracts. This situation had long caused tensions between the state and farmers. According to Parker, the farmers were "having such issues with the state water contract, not getting any water but still having to pay for it. I mean, they didn't have to pay for the water, but they had to pay for the facilities." Ultimately, the farmers threatened to sue, and the state could not afford to fight. Losing a lawsuit worth tens or even hundreds of millions of dollars would have been disastrous for the California Water Resources Department, with its annual operating budget of $1 billion. The state was forced to the negotiating table.

The farmers wanted two things: the Kern Water Bank and something called paper water. *Paper water* is the term critics use for water that *would have been* delivered to the farmers if the last phase of the State Water Project had been completed—an extra 2.5 million acre-feet of water. The last phase of the State Water Project was supposed to divert water from the Feather River north of the Delta, but in 1970, the Wild and Scenic Rivers Act protected rivers north of the Delta, and so the project was never finished. And even though farmers had contractually agreed to give up their rights to this water if the project could not be completed, they later changed their minds. Although there was no way this water could be delivered to the farmers, they wanted the rights so they could sell them on the open market. The emergence of water marketing was providing new opportunities to these farmers even as their land was becoming infertile.

The farmers got everything they wanted during these negotiations, which took place behind closed doors in Monterey, California. They were given the Kern Water Bank in exchange for 45,000 acre-feet of water rights. Those who contributed 10 percent of the 45,000 acre-feet became 10 percent shareholders in the bank, and so on. And because Stewart Resnick contributed the most water, he gained control of the bank.[34] The irony is that the water they gave up was not real—it was part of the paper water farmers also were granted in Monterey.[35] Theoretically, this water was worth about $1,000 per acre-foot at the time—but the key word is *theoretically*, because it did not really exist. Since there was no actual water to go along with these rights, they were essentially *future* claims on any water provided by new infrastructure.[36] The reality is that farmers gained an estimated 2.2 million acre-feet of paper water less 45,000 acre-feet through the Monterey amendments. These water rights can now be used on the water market—bought and sold *as if* they were real water. Farmers like Resnick knew exactly what they needed to make money from water: a bank and some "deposits."

At the Kern Water Bank, Jon Parker was obviously defensive about paper water. "This isn't paper water," he said at one point, pointing at the vast wetlands filled with ducks, cormorants, and seagulls.

"Excuse me?" I replied.

"In case there's any question about the water that comes on the water bank or leaves the water bank, it's real water, it's wet water. There's no paper water. People will say we're banking paper water but we're not. It's all an open book. All the numbers are out there for anyone to look at. There's no secrecy."

In fact, Parker was telling the truth. Obviously, one cannot "bank" paper water because there is nothing to bank. Buying and selling paper water does not require a storage facility of any kind. Owning paper water is like owning futures on the stock market, though there is no specified date of delivery. Owners have a prior claim on any water that *does* become available, and they can sell these futures to anyone they like. It is the ultimate abstraction of the meaning of water. But the water held in the bank is the water that farmers have chosen to sell or hoard rather than use for irrigation.

In 1995, the bank opened for business. Today, when a bank shareholder sells water to someone farther north, the purchaser takes water out of the California Aqueduct upstream. "If we want to send water to these guys, we can't make it go up the aqueduct," Parker explained. "They take water out up there, and we put it in down here. That's how it works." In this way, water is moved, or "wheeled," all over the San Joaquin Valley today. At first considered a risk due to uncertainty about water market values, the water-banking concept has become so popular that, according to Parker, "people are coming up here from Southern California trying to build water banks." Banks have since been started with the express purpose of selling water to Los Angeles, like Rio Bravo Water Storage District and Buena Vista Storage District, but the Kern Water Bank is not among them.

To solidify the legality of these transactions further, State Senator Jim Costa from California's Twentieth Congressional District introduced a bill that the state legislature passed in 1999. It read, "Water, or the right to the use of water . . . may be sold, leased, exchanged, or otherwise transferred."[37] Senator Costa's campaign was generously funded by the Boswells and Resnicks, whose lands are in the Twentieth Congressional District. Today, the San Joaquin Valley has perhaps a dozen water banks, some public and some private, hidden underground. The Boswells store water in the combined public–private Semitropic Water Storage District bank. They have enough water to supply a city of three million people, and their water rights alone are worth $1 billion.[38] In 1996, J. G. Boswell Jr. set up a software program, WaterLink, to sell water. Farmers could use the program to post bids or list water sales. This was the first attempt at electronic water marketing in the world. (Today, WaterBank—at http://waterbank. com—is the leading Internet dealer of water in the United States.) Resnick banks even more water than Boswell, controlling 58 percent of the Kern Water Bank.[39]

The Kern Water Bank certainly has the perfect location, at the juncture of the California Aqueduct, the Friant-Kern Canal, and the Kern River. It can pull in water from all over the state. As Parker and I drove into the bank on a dirt levee separating two ponds, I immediately noticed coots and ducks floating in large flocks on the water and red-tailed hawks soaring overhead. Parker noticed the coots and said, "One of the guys who used to work out here called them coyote Happy Meals." He laughed. There were killdeers, meadowlarks, avocets, harriers, egrets, herons, black-shouldered kites, kingfishers, grebes, shrikes, great horned owls, prairie falcons, and pelicans. "We get pelicans by the hundreds, if not thousands, sometimes," Parker said. "It's almost like you could walk across the water on them." Indeed, the number of birds was astonishing. On land once leveled for farming, the Kern Water Bank has rebuilt islands for bird nesting. "I'm telling you, it's raptor city," Parker joked when an owl crossed our path. A fat-looking coyote even ran along beside the truck for a while, outpacing us. "He's going more than thirty miles an hour!" Parker laughed. The coyote ran alongside the tules, cottonwoods, and willows that were returning to the bank.

Parker took me to a canal where he said he likes to swim when the clear water is being pumped out. "When we're recovering water," he said, "the canal looks like water in the tropics where you can see right to the bottom of the canal and it's just beautiful crystal-clear water. So we go snorkeling in the canal. It's really fun because you can see all the fish. That's a highlight for us." He said he also enjoys taking Boy Scouts canoeing in the canals to work on their canoeing badges.

But the bank is not always lush and beautiful. In fact, when PBS came to film a documentary segment with Huell Howser, the bank was completely dry. Parker lamented this fact: "He came when it was bone dry and the rabbits had grazed it to dirt. He had this vision of some kind of Garden of Eden, and it was all dirt and burros. . . . And I was like, 'This is it, man.' It was really sad." One of the problems with the banking model is that it operates as an economic system and not an ecological one. So when the "deposits" are withdrawn, the wetlands dry up and the neighbors' wells go dry.

Though water banks were initially touted as a way to recharge groundwater and create wetlands, people seem to forget that the water is pumped *back out* when the market demands. For instance, the Kern Water Bank pumped hundreds of thousands of acre-feet during the drought in 2007. Neighbor Gaylord Beeson said the water table dropped 115 feet in three years—something that in the past would have taken two decades. People's wells dried up.[40] It seems that the rapid rise and fall of the water table was not foreseen as a consequence of the bank. The image of a dry bank became vivid to me when Parker explained what happened to the fish when the marsh and ponds dried up. When I asked about fish in the lakes, Parker said he knew there were carp, perch, bullhead, and rockfish. But then he added, "The reason I know that is when the ponds dry up you see them." The image of people clubbing fish to death in the drying Tulare Lake came to my mind.

"So when the water dries up do the fish die?" I asked in surprise.

"Yeah." He seemed embarrassed.

"Do the birds eat them?" I asked.

"Vultures will come out here, but there's just too many fish. They can't eat them all." Still, he insisted it was not a problem, at least not for now. "The only problem, potentially in the future, is that homes will move in close to the water bank and it will smell. Closer to town, there's already problems with other banks." I pictured thousands, perhaps millions, of gasping, thrashing fish on the muddy ground, and the bank no longer seemed so utopian.

Parker was adamant about the fact that none of the water in the Kern

Water Bank was sold outside the valley; he was obviously defensive about the bank being accused of selling water to Los Angeles. I had to wonder where its water was going if not to Los Angeles, since the rest of the valley looked so dry. Ironically, I was to find out it was being sold back to the very "environmental extremists" that the farmers and Fox News claimed to be fighting. In fact, they are the primary "withdrawers" from the Kern Water Bank, since the water farmers receive from the state of California is now sold back to the state for environmental protection of the Delta. According to Barry Nelson of the Natural Resources Defense Council, this is "classic arbitrage," or purchasing something at a low price to resell immediately at a higher price on a different market: "What makes this arbitrage so remarkable is they're buying the water and selling the water to the same entity, using water that should never have been pumped in the first place."[41]

Today, subsidized water that Resnick receives from the state for an average of $30 per acre-foot can be sold back to the state for $200 per acre-foot.[42] Jon Parker confirmed this, saying, "Some of the sales that do occur are to the Environmental Water Account, and that was an account that was set up by the state to offset impacts from environmental regulations in the Delta." The Environmental Water Account was in fact the result of a lawsuit by Resnick and other farmers against the U.S. government in 2001. In this suit, Resnick et al. claimed that keeping water in the Delta for the Endangered Species Act was a "taking" of water that should have gone to them. This ultimately led to a curious ruling that stated: "The federal government is certainly free to preserve the fish. It must simply pay for the water it takes to do so."[43] In response to this ruling, the state-run Environmental Water Account was set up, costing taxpayers close to $200 million. A journalist noted, "Roughly one-fifth of all the money spent to buy water for the program went to companies owned or controlled by Resnick, one of the state's largest farmers."[44] In short, it went to the Kern Water Bank.

To summarize, farmers forced the state to give them the Kern Water Bank and more water rights even as their farms were becoming less productive. They then sued to have the Endangered Species Act overturned in an attempt to turn their "paper water" into real water. Their ultimate goal was to be able to pump more water through the Delta. Failing this, they began to sell water to the state to comply with the Endangered Species

Act. As Robert Gottlieb notes: "For the agricultural wing of the water industry, water policy has continued to evolve around the search for a cheap water supply. . . . Once the price of water begins to approach its real cost, then the thoughts of the industry turn to water markets and bail outs."[45]

The question remained, why would the farmers continue to fight the Endangered Species Act when it provided their main source of water income? In 2001, they began to sell water to the Environmental Water Account to implement the Endangered Species Act. But in 2009, they funded a vicious attack on the Endangered Species Act that aired on Fox News. Something still did not add up. But one thing was clear: the so-called free market in water in California is actually an intensely negotiated (and corrupted) system set up jointly by the state, the U.S. government, and San Joaquin Valley agribusiness.

Ghost Cities

Today, California cities and counties are going bankrupt at a staggering rate: the cities of Stockton, San Bernardino, and Vallejo, as well as Orange County, have all filed for bankruptcy. And on May 15, 2012, *USA Today* reported that the following California cities could be next: Atwater, Fresno, San Jose, Mammoth Lakes, Azusa, Compton, Hercules, Monrovia, Oakland, and Vernon. So what has gone wrong? In 2008, when the U.S. economy collapsed under the burden of deregulated banks and bad mortgages, California was hit particularly hard. Since the 1978 passage of Proposition 13, the largest steady revenue stream for California cities has been property taxes, and people began walking away from their houses at an alarming rate after the financial collapse. This national fiasco provided new opportunities for one sector, however: private water corporations. For me, this provided the final clue as to the water plans of the Boswells and Resnicks.

Like much of the world, the United States jumped on the privatization bandwagon in the 1980s. At that time, a growing distrust of "big government" under President Ronald Reagan led to the U.S. government's slow disinvestment from urban public water systems. Over time, legislation was amended to allow privatization of U.S. water supplies. In 1997, President Bill Clinton threw out regulations preventing government from entering into long-term contracts with private water companies, including foreign investors.[46] Soon afterward, Veolia acquired U.S. Filter, which has since been sold to Siemens Corporation and was renamed Siemens Water and then Evoqua Water while Veolia continued to operate as Veolia Water North America. Suez acquired United Water, the second-largest water company in the United States after Veolia. Next, RWE, a German water conglomerate, acquired American Water. In the early 2000s, Atlanta, Indianapolis, and Stockton all sold their water supplies to Veolia or Suez, but all three contracts led to management fiascos and the cities returned to public water systems. Today, bankruptcy is pushing cities again toward privatization, particularly in Detroit but also in San Jose, California. As both international and start-up local water operators have set their sights on the profits to be made from municipal water systems, laws in California have made it easier for farmers to buy and sell their water on the open market. And the Boswells and Resnicks are planning to get into the residential water supply business—by building their own cities.

As California cities drift into bankruptcy, they lose leverage to control their own water supplies. According to the U.S. Environmental Protection Agency, there has been an annual shortfall of at least $11 billion to replace aging drinking water facilities in the United States.[47] (Some say we need $1 trillion.) In 1902, the U.S. government sold land in the American West to fund the country's major water infrastructure. Today, that option is not available. Instead, privatization is being pushed by tea party organizations like FreedomWorks, which claims: "Obama's budget wastefully funds socialized water production that displaces efficient private sector solutions. . . . Government involvement in water quality treatment and production is unnecessary."[48] Meanwhile, the French water companies, facing failures in poorer countries, have set their sights on the U.S. market. Yet very few Americans are even aware this is happening.

Because of California's financial troubles, another trend is also emerging: "private cities" or "planned cities." These are gated communities that are completely privately funded, in which property owners pay fees or dues for services. One Kern Water Bank owner, Semitropic Water Storage District, is banking water for Newhall Ranch, a development scheme adjacent to a Magic Mountain amusement park that will have twenty-one thousand homes, a commercial district, seven public schools, and a fifteen-acre lake. Newhall Ranch is run by Lennar Corporation, a Fortune 500 company based out of Miami, Florida, and the second largest home builder in the United States.[49] Stewart Resnick plans to sell water to Gateway Village, a private town outside Fresno that will have sixty-five hundred houses, four elementary schools, and a town center.[50] Asked by a *Los Angeles Times* reporter about these plans, Bill Phillimore, vice president of Resnick's Paramount Farms, replied, "We honestly don't like to share information with people. It's one of the advantages of being a private company."[51]

A third Kern Water Bank owner, Tejon Ranch Company, is using the water to create its own mountain community. With a 24 percent interest in the Kern Water Bank, Tejon Ranch owns the largest contiguous landholding in California, 270,000 acres. Funding Universe describes the company as a "diversified, growth-oriented real estate development and agribusiness company." Its property runs along the section of the I-5 known as the Grapevine, which crosses over the mountains from the San Joaquin Valley to Los Angeles. It is prime real estate, with acres of oak savanna, enormous wildflower displays, and rolling green hills.[52] In 1853, Tejon Ranch came into being when it was designated an Indian reservation, though it was never used as such. Later, it was purchased by Harry Chandler and held by his heirs, who used it for ranching until the real estate market crashed in the late 1990s. (Ruth Chandler, J. G. Boswell's wife, is Harry's daughter.) Today, its primary owner is Third Avenue Management, a New York asset management firm that specializes in acquiring undervalued properties. Immediately after its acquisition, the Tejon Ranch Company announced that it would build a resort community called Tejon Mountain Village, with thirty-five hundred luxury homes, hotels, two golf courses, and a shopping center.

Another planned city in Tejon Ranch will be Centennial City, which will have twenty-three thousand homes, three fire stations, eight schools, and its own private water supply. The website for the project advertises:

> Centennial will provide diverse and secure water sources. The water plan includes an aggressive recycled water program, a water conservation program, and the combined use of water from the groundwater basin and the State Water Program. In addition, the Centennial Water Plan includes storage of water into a groundwater bank, which will substantially increase reliability during droughts.

The site claims that Centennial will be a "sustainable city": "By employing sustainable principles we were able to [create] walkable village centers and anticipate the full balance of needs that allow people the opportunity to live close to their work, shopping, schools, and recreation."[53]

Interestingly, Centennial City anticipates that "people ultimately will be employed at nearby Tejon Industrial Center," also owned by Tejon Ranch. Now called Tejon Ranch Commerce Center, this industrial foreign trade zone sits at the corner of the I-5 and Highway 99. It is an ugly barrage of giant warehouse spaces dotted with fast-food restaurants and gas stations. Foreign trade zones are usually located next to shipping ports of entry, since they are intended to be duty-free and tax-free environments for import–export activities as well as areas for the loading and unloading of ships. At Commerce Center, one hundred miles from the ocean, companies like IKEA are moving in to store goods, thus delaying or avoiding paying taxes.

Finally, Boswell plans to develop Yokohl Valley into a city of thirty thousand people, with three golf courses and a commercial center like Tejon Ranch Commerce Center. Like the Tejon Ranch property, Yokohl Valley is of enormous scenic and environmental value to the state, since it has remained undeveloped. It contains rolling grassy hills and oak woodlands as well as stands of sycamore. In the spring, it is bursting with color as wildflowers bloom. It is also the location of numerous Yokut burial sites, since Yokuts used to go there to gather seeds. The Boswells waited for water regulations to change so they could develop it, and those changes happened in Monterey in 1994. Now, Boswell remains mum about the source of water for this private town, but a spokesman for his consulting firm said that the firm would try to influence legislation to increase water supply.[54] Thus, Fox News.

In order to gain permission to build these housing projects, the developers had to ensure they had adequate water rights to supply the facilities—and herein lies the real value of the 2.5 million acre-feet of new water rights. Of course, this "paper water" creates an obvious problem, since people actually need real water to live. Ultimately, this problem has the potential to create another housing bubble in California as ghost cities are sold without real water to supply them. For instance, there are billboards near Bakersfield for a housing development called McAllister Ranch. The plans include a golf course, lake, and beach club, but those plans have been in the works for almost a decade and the development has not yet gotten off the ground.[55] The problem is that the farmers who planned this real estate development need more "real" water to be able to build. So while it is true that *some* farmers are not selling water south to Los Angeles, it is not because they want to keep farming or because they disdain urban sprawl. They simply know they can make more money by building private cities, thus forcing the state to create more supply. "By controlling the water bank, they are now poised to profit from water sales to urban development," John Gibler of the nonprofit consumer advocacy group Public Citizen said. "And don't think it won't happen. Look at Newhall and Tejon ranches. Big Ag is becoming Big Sprawl through water trading."[56]

Clever as a Fox

In 2009, Fox News broadcast a fake grassroots rally to help build these new private cities. The rally was organized by the pricey advertising agency Burson-Marsteller and paid for by valley megafarmers. People had to be bused in to be protesters and dressed like "family farmers." Mostly, they were tea partiers from adjacent cities.

Sean Hannity introduced one actual farmer, Jim Jasper, as a "small and independent" farmer, but later bragged that Jasper sold "hundreds of thousands of pounds" of almonds around the world.[57] Hannity praised Jasper for filing a lawsuit through Pacific Legal Foundation, an organization devoted to "protecting freedom from environmental extremism," mainly against the Endangered Species Act.[58] Video images of dead almond trees being pulled from the ground by bulldozers played in the background as Jasper lamented the loss of his prized trees due to a Congress-imposed drought. Yet that same year, valley newspapers reported record sales in almonds. Exports at Paramount Farms went up 100 percent from 2009 to 2010, primarily due to loosened import restrictions from India.[59] After taking over the Kern Water Bank, Paramount doubled its production of almonds and pistachios and became the largest grower and producer of nuts in the world. A study by the Pacific Institute revealed that California farms and ranches had their third-highest gross revenue year on record in 2009. And in the period 1995–2005, Kern Water Bank members sold more than 423,000 acre-feet of water either back to the state or to other interests for millions of dollars. By 2010, the Kern Water Bank had 0.71 million acre-feet of water stored underground. But all that water was never mentioned on Fox.

Congressman Devin Nunes was also featured at the Fox rally as the owner of a small "family farm." Heavily funded by the Resnicks, Nunes was included in *Time* magazine's "40 under 40," a list of the forty most influential politicians under forty years of age, in 2010. The Nunes "family farm" includes twenty thousand acres in the San Joaquin Valley as well as property in Salinas, Ventura, and Yuma, Arizona. The family also has farm property in Mexico, where they were recently accused of using child labor. Tom Nunes, Devin's father, was asked if he would be willing to sell lettuce bunches for one penny more in order to stop the exploitation of laborers in Mexico. He answered, "There's no incentive for us to do that. . . . The power of the market is stronger than all of us."[60]

Devin Nunes is important to the San Joaquin Valley west-side farmers because he has been taking these issues to the U.S. Congress. There, the meaning of water is further abstracted as voting tends to break down along partisan lines. In fact, when farmers lost their case against the Endangered Species Act in the California Supreme Court, they turned to the U.S. Congress for help. Nunes introduced the San Joaquin Water Reliability Act, which would repeal the law that protects the delta smelt and Chinook salmon and declare hatchery fish "legally equivalent" to wild fish.[61] When concerns were raised about financial losses to salmon fishermen, Nunes infamously replied, "The salmon fishermen can still fish, they just can't fish for salmon."

Only Representative Grace Napolitano from California clearly understood that Congress was being scammed. She argued against Nunes's bill:

> The radical changes contained in this bill would ultimately benefit a small group of agricultural users while causing chaos for the rest of California . . . including fishermen, Delta farmers, urban communities, and many others, none of whom were invited to appear as witnesses today. It is unacceptable to exclude these Californians while making decisions about their water supply in Washington, D.C.

Despite her logic, the bill passed in the House, with Republicans supporting it 236–1.[62] The bill also passed on a strictly partisan vote in the House Committee on Natural Resources. On the page about the bill on the committee's website is a link to a video: "The Valley Hope Forgot."[63] Though the bill is now on the Senate calendar, President Obama has said he will veto it. He explained: "It would codify 20-year old, outdated science as the basis for managing California's water resources, resulting in inequitable treatment of one group of water users over another. . . . The bill also would reject the long-standing principle that beneficiaries should pay both the cost of developing water supplies and of mitigating any resulting development impacts."[64] Thus, Fox equates Barack Obama with Saddam Hussein and Robert Mugabe.

California is in real financial trouble because of the massive water infrastructure that it once believed was necessary for "growth." Once celebrated as the first state in the nation to develop a modern transbasin aqueduct, California is now paying a price for the Los Angeles Aqueduct, which was finished in 1913. Diverting the entirety of Owens Lake into a canal and pipe system that feeds Los Angeles, the aqueduct created a giant toxic dust bowl. Today, the city of Los Angeles has to pay $45 million a year to stop the dust by irrigating the dry lakebed, after an initial expense of $1.2 billion for setting up the sprinkler system. To date, the region around Owens Lake still has not met Clean Air Act requirements, which means that Los Angeles is forced to keep pouring money into it.

Further south, another enormous water disaster has taken place in the Imperial Valley. In 1900, the California Development Company, a private real estate and water firm, began construction of an earthen canal at the border with Mexico. The company's intention was to bring Colorado River water to the dry Salton Sea, thus creating new agricultural communities. But by 1905, the canal had filled with silt, which caused it to burst and fill the Salton Sea. Three times larger than Owens Lake, the Salton Sea is now shrinking and creating dust storms similar to the ones at Owens Lake, except these also contain pesticides. No one has quite figured out what to do about the problem, or who will pay the enormous expense of fixing it. Instead, we are today repeating the same mistake of moving water around like money without understanding the consequences.

Finally, a third potential catastrophe haunts the Delta, which houses hundreds of small farms built on land diked and dried around a hundred years ago. Unfortunately, exposure to oxygen has caused the peat soil to compress, with the result that large parts of the Delta have sunk as much as thirty feet below sea level and are now protected from the ocean only by earthen levees. Today, many of these levees are on the verge of collapse, and their failure would be catastrophic to California's water system. If these levees collapse, ocean water will flood into freshwater areas, including the very aqueducts that supply much of the state with water. As with the Salton Sea and Owens Lake, no one quite knows what to do about this problem, or who will pay the enormous expense of dealing with it. Instead, San Joaquin Valley farmers want to give up on the Delta and let it flood in order to get what they really want: water farther north.

The Boswells and Resnicks claim the solution is to move freshwater *around* the Delta through a "peripheral canal," so that when the Delta collapses, it will not affect water systems farther south. This $14 billion project would indeed bring more water south and thereby theoretically complete the last link of the State Water Project. What it would sacrifice, however, is the Delta, including the farmers and fishers who live there. It would flood the Delta with saltwater, making it unusable for farming *or* for fish. By keeping freshwater from flowing into the Delta, it would eliminate salmon runs. Ultimately, the reason Fox News was in Huron was to push for this canal, which is now envisioned as taking the form of tunnels *under* the Delta.

In 2011, San Joaquin Valley farmers (who call themselves "water exporters") proposed the misnamed Bay Delta Conservation Plan, which has little to do with conservation and everything to do with building a peripheral canal under the Delta. It is essentially a reworking of the thirty-year-old peripheral canal model that was earlier voted down by 80 percent of Californians. With this plan, the farmers claimed they were providing "the path towards a secure water supply for California and a healthy Delta ecosystem." They also said they were willing to pay for it just as they once claimed they would pay for the State Water Project. Governor Jerry Brown supports this plan, which means it is getting serious attention. The plan proposes to create 15,000 acres of fish habitat—in a 738,000-acre Delta. It does not deal with the levee problem at all, except to say that Californians will be protected in the event of a catastrophic collapse by the diversion of water around the Delta. It also does not make sense. Citing a study by the National Research Council, the news website ScienceDaily reported that the science on which the plan is based is "fragmented and presented in an unconnected manner, making its meaning difficult to understand." A panel of experts called to review the plan found it to be "disconnected and poorly integrated" and stated, "There are many scientific elements, but the science is not drawn together in an integrated fashion."[65] Clearly, the reason for this is that the plan really has only one goal: to get more water from the north.

Fixing the problems that have already occurred as the result of water diversion schemes will require billions, and perhaps trillions, of dollars, and no one even knows if they can be fixed. The truth is that we are in completely uncharted territory here. At the Yokut reservation, Lalo Franco talked about the scope of these problems:

> So there's a lot of issues surrounding water, and for us, the native people, the main issue is that they've turned the water, which is sacred, and no one can live without, one of our sacred elements, they've turned it into a commodity. They don't treat it with respect, and so look at the problems they're having. So for us, it's like, they get what they deserve. If you don't treat something with respect, it's going to come back at you. It's a basic rule, it's what children are taught. If you kick an ant pile, they're gonna bite you.

Today, the natural world is biting Californians, draining the state of its financial reserves. Rather than building yet another multibillion-dollar canal as a temporary fix or funding private cities and banks through corrupt water transfers, it is perhaps time for the state to admit the scale of the problems and seek a comprehensive solution that involves scaling down rather than scaling up.[66] This means setting limits on urban sprawl, rethinking the state's agricultural system, and redistributing water to small-scale businesses whose goal is ecosystem protection—for instance, permaculture, organic agriculture, or agroforestry businesses—as well as to those who have a deep understanding of the region's ecological history, people like Lalo Franco. Our first mistake, after all, was taking water from people like Franco and handing it to the Boswells.

Of course, all of these solutions would require keeping water in the public domain. It would also mean paying much more attention to how our food is being produced and who benefits. In 2011, California produced nearly half of all the fruits, nuts, and vegetables grown in the United States. The nation's largest exporter of food, California is the fifth-largest food producer in the world, according to the California Department of Food and Agriculture. Ironically, the hungriest place in the United States also happens to be the San Joaquin Valley, where all this food is grown. According to the UCLA Center for Health Policy

Research, "The number of food-insecure adults in California grew by half (49%), five times the increase in California's total population (10%)" between 2001 and 2009. The study defined "food insecure" as not being able to "afford to put food on the table" for part of the year, a status claimed by 3.8 million Californians. "In 2009, the highest rates of food insecurity across California were observed in the San Joaquin Valley," the study determined, and more than half these households were Spanish speaking.[67]

According to the United Nations, food insecurity, globally, is not caused by food shortages; rather, it is a result of people not being able to *afford* food. U.S. agribusinesses regularly dump their excess food on poorer countries at lower costs, something Washington, D.C., calls "food aid" but others call "food dumping." The problem is that this food undercuts local farmers' prices, forcing them out of business. Yes, the food is cheaper, but for people without jobs it is not cheap enough. For this reason, subsidized agriculture in the United States is actually making the *world* poorer, along with people in the San Joaquin Valley. For people dependent on foreign cheap food, even a small rise in prices due to fluctuations in the market can lead to riots. A 2013 report by the U.N. Conference on Trade and Development concludes, "This is bound to increase the frequency and severity of riots, caused by food price hikes."[68] The solution? As Brian Stoffel summarized it, "Though a slew of potential solutions have been proposed, one came up again and again in the U.N. report: sustainable, organic agriculture."[69]

The U.N. report also lists seven companies that are standing in the way of transforming modern agriculture—Monsanto, Dow Chemicals, Bayer, Cargill, DuPont, Syngenta, and BASF—primarily because they are the chemical and genetic engineering companies that control the agricultural market. Dow Chemicals and J. G. Boswell Company together own Widestrike, a variety of genetically modified Bt cotton seed, as well as numerous other cotton strains. Paramount Farms does not grow genetically modified crops, but its exports to India are destroying the almond farming business in Afghanistan, where almond prices dropped 40 percent in one year. "If I sell my almonds at 60 Afghanis [US$1.20] a kilo I will not be able to feed my family during winter," one farmer said.[70] And in the San Joaquin Valley, poverty has long been known to be a fact of life for immigrants who are paid piecemeal for part of every year.

Fox News would have us believe that the food problems in the San Joaquin Valley are a result of the water being cut off in 2009. Hannity said, "We have generations of farmers here. And they are losing their farms. . . . We literally have—I met people earlier that now are on food lines because their farms have been shut down." Fox News showed people lining up at a food bank yet neglected to note that these people were suffering from food insecurity due to low wages, and not because their farms had "been shut down." Meanwhile, those who control the global food market—and thus the world's water—are branching out into nonfood products, like towns and cities. Resnick is adamant that he will never lose the bank. "We paid for it, we built the infrastructure," he told *Bloomberg Businessweek*. "I don't know how we could lose it. We bought it. We own it."[71] The situation in California, as presented by Fox News, reveals only that the wealthiest and largest holders of water rights are able to manipulate both politicians and the media in order to acquire even more water. Those standing in line at the food bank in Huron remain trapped in a cycle of poverty while Afghani almond farmers, pulling up their own trees, are forced to eat Resnick's Blue Diamond almonds instead.

TWO

How a Coup Opened Chile's Water Markets

IN CHILE, September 11 has long been commemorated as the anniversary date of a national tragedy. "Some Chileans were upset that the World
Trade Center attack happened on *our* day," Patagonian river-rafting guide
Rolando told me, "though mainly it just deepened our sense of tragedy."
We were sitting beside the aquamarine Baker River in northern Patagonia,
sharing a local *yerba mate* tea from a gourd with a stainless steel straw,
when Rolando told me how his mother had been brutally tortured following the coup by General Augusto Pinochet on September 11, 1973. Now
on each September 11, thousands flock to the streets of Santiago to remember the death of democratically elected socialist President Salvador
Allende, who committed suicide rather than surrender to certain torture
under the Pinochet regime.[1] Rolando did not look like the typical Chilean, with his blond hair and blue eyes; perhaps in his early forties, he
spoke with the somberness of a much older man. Ironically, the setting
could not have been more peaceful; the river was a blinding Caribbean
blue and, along with the *mate,* put me in a trance. Sadly, Rolando could
not escape Pinochet's legacy even there. It was during Pinochet's regime
that the Baker River was privatized, which means that one hydroelectric
company with close ties to Pinochet has made a fortune from it. In fact,

Chile was the first country in the world to privatize 100 percent of its water supplies, and in a unique way. While the United States experimented with water marketing that is still tightly controlled by the government, Chile gifted the country's water en masse as a commodity to de facto users. Any disputes over ownership are now treated as "property rights" cases overseen by the courts, which has led to a different—and potentially more entrenched—set of problems from those seen in the United States.

In 1980–81, U.S. economist Milton Friedman was invited by the Chilean government to head a group of economists from both Chicago and Santiago in creating a new Chilean constitution and Water Code. Pinochet had come into power during a U.S.-backed coup intended to eliminate socialism in Chile, so the privatization sweep that occurred afterward seemed to many to be inevitable. "Chicago school" economists like Friedman, who believed in a black-and-white struggle between socialism and "the free market," had a great deal of influence both in the United States and abroad in the 1980s. In contrast, Pinochet was hardly an ideologue or an intellectual; what he provided was the military leadership to make this economic transition possible. Called the Chile Project, the economic transformation encompassed a total reform of Chile's constitutional and legal system.[2] In order to shrink "big government," the state had to turn over its properties—water, electricity, banks, real estate, airlines, and so on—to private companies. But the biggest beneficiaries were the commanding officers in Pinochet's army.

Water was turned over at no charge to de facto users, and at the time the largest holder of water rights was the state-owned electric company Endesa. Endesa supplies at least 75 percent of the country's electricity, with 25 percent going to mining interests in northern Chile. The company was granted "nonconsumptive" water rights for the purpose of potential hydropower development, meaning that the water could not be used for drinking or irrigation. The idea behind "nonconsumptive" rights was that hydroelectric companies would control water rights in the mountains in eastern Chile. After water was used for hydropower, it would be reused by farmers in central Chile as a "consumptive" right. But hydropower companies want to store water during the summer, when farmers need it, and no one can use the water that Endesa deems necessary for hydropower. According to philosopher Hans Achterhuis, "The introduction of private property rights in water is a legally and institutionally condoned form of theft," one that "fundamentally challenges the claims that justify privatization reforms: freedom, efficiency, equality and civilized progress."[3] In this instance, the exact same people have benefited in both the public and private water sectors by simply making use of the revolving door between the two. Before they left office, they were handed Endesa as a newly "private" company—after taking the nation's water.

Because Pinochet's officers ran Endesa and knew about the privatization plans in advance, they were able to register water rights before anyone else had a chance. According to activist Juan Pablo Orrego, the timing for privatizing water, and then Endesa, was not a coincidence: "From 1973 to 1981 they registered like crazy all the water rights that were left, because they were already orchestrating the privatization."[4] Meanwhile, small farmers who were never informed of the need to register their rights lost access to water both to Endesa and to large landowners. In 1989, the last year of the dictatorship, Endesa was privatized, thus transferring water permanently to Pinochet's friends and colleagues. Ironically, during Salvador Allende's presidency, several of these same men had been considered terrorists, creating chaos in order to undermine Allende's government. They were part of the ultraright organization Patria y Libertad (Fatherland and Freedom), which had a penchant for blowing up power lines to throw Santiago, the capital city, into blackouts. The leader of Patria y Libertad was Pablo Rodriguez Grez, who became both Endesa's and Pinochet's lawyer after the coup, defending Pinochet until his death in 2006. Other members included José Yuraszeck, who ran Endesa under Pinochet and became known as the "Electricity Czar." Today, he owns one of Chile's top football (soccer) teams, having made a fortune on the sale of Endesa. And Jose Piñera was first Pinochet's labor minister and later vice president of Endesa. He used his position as labor minister to privatize the country's social security, making Chile the first country in the world to do so, and then invested these funds in Endesa. The price these men paid for Endesa was—and still remains—a secret, largely due to an agreement the military government made in exchange for stepping down from power in 1990. Clearly, their goal was to conceal the fortunes they made from acquiring state property for less than it was worth—quite possibly for not even one Chilean peso.

In 1988, Pinochet was forced to hold a referendum on his continued dictatorship and was thereby ultimately ousted from power; but the

Water Code and constitution created under his regime remained in place. One of the authors of Chile's constitution, Jaime Guzmán, openly stated it was always the framers' intent to maintain control of the country even after Pinochet left: "The constitution imposed in 1980 was destined to rule Chilean society in perpetuity. . . . If our adversaries ever come to power, they will see themselves forced to follow an action not so different from the one we would have wished for."[5] By the time Pinochet left office, the top-ranking men in his administration were firmly in control of the country's water supplies.

At the Santiago office for the organization Patagonia sin Represas (Patagonia without Dams), Juan Pablo Orrego told me about his fight against Pinochet's legacy. Tucked away on the second floor of a plain stucco-covered building with bars on all the windows, Orrego's office is as unimposing as he is. A handsome sixty-something man with graying curly hair and an impressive mind, Orrego was honored with the prestigious Right Livelihood Award (1998) and the Goldman Environmental Prize (1997) for his work with the indigenous peoples of Chile along the Bío-Bío River. Before Pinochet's coup, Orrego had been in a band that played with famed folksinger Victor Jara. After the coup, Jara was killed along with many of Orrego's friends, and Orrego fled to Canada. Meanwhile, Pinochet's government destroyed all of the band's recordings. Orrego explained: "They tried to destroy an age, a memory. They destroyed books and audiovisual material, everything they could put their hands on. Like the Nazis."

Orrego spoke hesitantly of that time, explaining, "It was the end of life for us for a good while. My mother was in danger of being shot because she was secretary to the general secretary of the Socialist Party, who was an uncle of mine." In fact, his whole family had to flee: his grandfather to Canada, his uncle to Honduras, his father to Mexico, his mother to Ecuador. Orrego helped smuggle his mother into the Ecuadorian embassy by hiding her in a car under a rug. In Canada, Orrego went back to school to get his master's degree in environmental studies and ultimately returned to Chile, where he is now an activist against water privatization and Endesa.

"Everything about the privatization is under a cloak of secrecy," Orrego said, "including the water rights and how they were transferred at zero cost from the hands of the Chilean state to the hands of these

Chilean gangsters." From 1997 to 1999, Pinochet's friends sold Endesa to investors in Spain for $3 billion; it quickly became one of Chile's largest and most profitable companies.[6] With this acquisition, Spain also gained 80 percent of Chile's water. The Spanish deal was initially lauded as the "sale of the century," but the designation quickly changed to "the theft of the century" and "one of the biggest business frauds in Chilean financial history."[7] According to an official during Allende's government, "These new financial groups are as powerful as the drug lords in Colombia, powerful enough to bring down any government."[8] Today, the constitution and Water Code cannot be altered without the approval of three-quarters of the Chilean Parliament—something that has never happened in Chile's history. As Orrego noted, "If you look at it, it's like a checkmate to democracy. In a very concrete way, it transforms water into a commodity, into merchandise that can be sold freely like anything else, like any other merchandise, like potatoes or socks or cars." In 2009, the Italian company Enel purchased a controlling stake in Endesa for $60 billion, thus transferring Chile's water once again to another country.[9]

Another change in water policy that began at the end of Pinochet's rule—and continues today—was the privatization of municipal water supplies. In general, Latin American countries were the primary targets of privatization in the 1990s. The highest levels of foreign investment in water services occurred during this decade, with more than one hundred water services contracts signed. According to sociolegal studies professor Bronwen Morgan, "Suez, Vivendi and Thames all invested significantly in Chile and Argentina during this period."[10] In part, this was due to debt defaults in the 1980s that forced Latin American countries into "structural adjustment" loans with the IMF. Starting in 1988, Chilean-owned water utilities were required to model their management practices on those of private utilities, gradually raising water rates to guarantee at least a 7 percent return on investment, a process that was done slowly over the course of ten years. In 1998, the Chilean government sold the state-owned utilities to foreign investors. Suez won the bid to take over 42 percent of EMOS (Empresa Metropolitana de Obras Sanitarias), the water company of Santiago. According to one report, the state guaranteed Suez a profit margin of 33 percent. By 2000, three-quarters of Chilean households were receiving water from privately owned companies that had purchased the utilities as permanently titled property.

It is important to note that these purchases did not occur without resistance, which ultimately led to the cancellation of utility sales in exchange for thirty-year contracts in 2001.[11] Yet despite rising protests, privatization of urban utilities was quickly lauded as a success story for corporate management in Latin America, based on the fact that Chile now supplies 96 percent of its urban population with clean water and sanitation. Carl Bauer notes: "Since the 1990s, the fame of the Chilean model . . . has spread among international and Latin American water experts. Much of this fame is due to the World Bank, which has actively publicized the Chilean case as a model of success and an inspiration for water policy reforms in other countries."[12] The World Bank still commonly cites Chile as a success story in contrast to Bolivia and Argentina, where antiprivatization advocates threw out Bechtel and Suez after water rates became unaffordable. In contrast, the World Bank has said of Chile, "The long-term success of the Chilean economy is explained by the continuity of strong macroeconomic policies, an open trade regime and a business-friendly environment."[13] In 1996, José Yuraszeck of the far-right Patria y Libertad was invited to speak at the annual meeting of the World Bank and IMF. His panel was titled "After Markets Succeed: Opportunities in Chile."

However, scholars often fail to note that Chile was far ahead of other Latin American countries in urban infrastructure long before privatization. According to Morgan, "In 1930, the Chilean central government made the provision of water and sewage services (WSS) a developmental priority, and unusually high coverage was achieved as early as the 1970s."[14] Also overlooked is Pinochet, who seems to have never existed, or is treated as an anomaly in an otherwise successful free market program. But according to journalist Patricio Segura, "Pinochet was not a Martian. He was a part of Chile. Many people still think like him."[15] Today, decades after privatization, Chile is the only country in the world that has privatized every aspect of its water, from the companies that supply the water to the rivers and lakes themselves. Suez owns water and wastewater treatment plants in the cities, while an Italian company owns the rest of the country's water. In this sense, Chile provides an excellent case study for the impact of large-scale privatization.

In this chapter, I will demonstrate how privatization of water resources can lead to a corrupt "gifting" of water to government cronies, an issue that will recur in later chapters. I will also examine the environmental consequences of privatization as well as the impact on Chile's indigenous peoples. Finally, I will discuss the failures of the international water experts in both addressing local concerns and creating reliable data. According to geographer Jessica Budds: "Much Chilean writing on water markets contains positive claims and touts the Water Code in Chile as a symbol of neoliberal ideology. Such assessments of water markets contain little, if any, empirical evidence, yet produce sweeping claims that are framed as fact." Budds explains that the World Bank then relies on this bad science in its own reports, and thus "many documents neither provide nor cite field evidence, and are replete with inaccuracies and misleading."[16] The trajectory of this abstract ideological form of water privatization is today leading to some devastating results—and potentially not only for Chile.

Today, Endesa is planning to dam southern Chile's rivers and send electricity two thousand miles north to be used for digging copper out of Chile's northern deserts.[17] But as Endesa begins its massive dam-building programs in the south, the delicate ecological balance of the Southern Ocean could be changed. The Antarctic Circumpolar Current, the northern edge of which flows past this region, is extremely sensitive to changes in ocean temperatures and, due to climate change, has already been moving south. Combined with the impacts of climate change, dams will make the region more ecologically unstable—contributing to glacier melting, changing river temperatures, and affecting ocean salinity—with unpredictable results. I had come to northern Patagonia to see the beauty of the Baker River before it was locked up behind a dam. Once there, I found out that I was also witnessing the delicate balance among oceans, rivers, and ice that sustains the planet—and might be coming to an end.

Nazis, Natives, and Two Dams

After Endesa gained control over Chile's water, the company started building dams. Some of its first large dams (more than three hundred feet high) were on the Bío-Bío River, which flows through the Araucanía and Bío-Bío regions. Located at a transition zone for different ecosystems, the upper Bío-Bío River region has some of the highest biodiversity rates in Chile, as well as numerous endangered species. It is where the dry weather of the north meets the wet weather of the south, and where the steppe system of Argentina meets the Pacific system of the coast. There, the Pehuenche people live, who call themselves "the people of the *pehuén*" after a tree known outside Chile as the monkey-puzzle tree, allegedly because an English gardener once exclaimed, "It would puzzle a monkey to climb that tree!" This tree is also sometimes called a "living fossil" because it has existed nearly unchanged in this region for more than two hundred million years. The Araucanía region is also known as the site of the "last stand" of indigenous peoples against Europeans. Today, it is the site of a different kind of battle, against water privatization.

In 1845, the Chilean government passed the Selective Immigration Act, which specifically recruited and encouraged Germans to settle in Araucanía, "based on the idea of positivist race improvement." According to anthropologist María Jensen Solivellas, "European immigrants were seen as instruments of social progress and development, the only ones capable of economically revitalizing Araucanía and in turn contributing to the improvement of the 'Chilean race.'"[18] The lands of indigenous peoples were opened in a eugenics-style effort to dilute and push out the indigenous "races." As Orrego told me, "At the beginning of the twentieth century, Chile was bringing Germans to push the Mapuche back into the worst land and to 'better the race.' That was public policy." During this period, the indigenous peoples resisted the encroachment on their territories. In response, the government of Chile began a military campaign called the Pacification of Araucanía in the 1860s, which continued into the 1880s.[19] Around ten thousand indigenous Chileans were slaughtered.

The Mapuche who stayed north of the Bío-Bío River eventually assimilated with Chilean culture, but those south of the river continued to defend their territory and culture. Then, in the 1930s, the rise of the German Nazi Party was matched by a Chilean National Socialist movement, which attempted to violently overthrow the government in 1938. Though this attempted coup failed, more German Nazis were encouraged to immigrate through the selective immigration laws following World War II. Thus the racism of Nazi Germany was reinforced by Chilean racism. In 1954, the Chilean Immigration Act stated that its goal was to "increase the population, bring technical improvements, and upgrade the biological conditions of the race."[20] In the 1960s, a labor law textbook used at Chilean universities asserted that "the common people are still too indigenous and need a greater mixture of European blood to give them thriftiness, seriousness, honesty, hygienic habits, etc.; it is indispensable, then, that we stimulate immigration to improve the race."[21] At the same time, in the context of water, indigenous peoples came to be viewed as "backward" in their irrigation practices. According to geographer Margreet Zwarteveen, "In the Andean context, water expertise thus constructed indigenous peasants as backward, uncivilized and irrational. Indigenous peasants were marked and named by irrigation experts, who themselves remained unseen and whose own identity (gender and ethnicity) did not matter in terms of their authority and knowledge."[22]

After Pinochet took over, one of the more twisted collaborations between his army and the German Nazi exiles occurred on the border of the Bío-Bío region. There, the ex-Nazi Paul Schäfer founded Colonia Dignidad, or Dignity Colony. Schäfer had befriended Pinochet, who let him use land tax-free for an "orphanage" and agricultural commune. In reality, Dignity Colony was a Nazi-style cult where kidnapped children were held against their will and camp members worshipped Schäfer. The camp was surrounded by barbed wire, guard dogs, and armed guards, preventing curious outsiders from knowing what was happening. Before Pinochet's coup, Patria y Libertad trained there. Afterward Pinochet sent his opponents there. Those who survived "spoke of electric-shock torture in underground dungeons from a German who turned up the volume of his Wagner music as he increased the electric current." At the same time, Schäfer raped, drugged, and tortured orphans and other abducted children, actions that ultimately let to his arrest and conviction on twenty-five charges of sexual abuse in 2005.[23] In January 2013, sixteen more perpetrators from the colony were convicted. Today, international Mapuche organizations still call for protests at the site, which is said to contain a mass grave where more than one hundred Chileans are buried.

While men like Schäfer were protected under Pinochet, indigenous peoples were treated as terrorists. According to a report published by the U.N. Working Group on Indigenous Populations: "On the day of the coup, the big landowners, the land barons, the military and the carabineros started a great manhunt against the Mapuches who had struggled and gained their land back. . . . The counter-revolution hit the Mapuche populations even harder than most other sectors."[24] Pinochet supported this "manhunt" by privatizing indigenous peoples' lands in 1979 through a law titled For the Indians, Indian Lands, the Division of Reserves and the Liquidation of the Indian Communities. When the Mapuche resisted, Pinochet passed a 1984 antiterrorism law that allowed illegal land occupations to be treated as terrorism. Prosecution under Chile's antiterrorism laws meant detention without due process, the withholding of evidence from the accused, anonymous witnesses, and, upon conviction, harsher sentences.

Today, many of the changes that occurred under Pinochet are still in place, including the antiterrorism laws. According to Human Rights Watch: "The unjustified use of terrorism charges keeps Mapuche leaders in pretrial detention for months. Investigations conducted by the public prosecutor can be kept secret for up to six months. At the trials themselves, key evidence may be admitted in oral hearings from 'faceless' witnesses whose identity is withheld from the defense." Individuals who have been accused of violence against the police may also be tried in military courts by the same paramilitary police organization, the Carabineros, that accused them. Human Rights Watch states that the U.S. antiterrorism push globally has "become a cover for governments who want to deflect attention away from their heavy-handed treatment of internal dissidents."[25] By linking Mapuches to "terrorist" activities, the Chilean government can appear to be fighting the "Global War on Terror."

It is important to understand this regional history mainly because the current water regime is so deeply tied to the abuses of the Pinochet era. The economic model promoted by the World Bank conceals a history of violence. One reason that Pinochet's terror has been left out of discourses surrounding water privatization in Chile is simply that the language of economics pretends to be neutral, rational, and separate from any political considerations. Unfortunately, this pretense makes it possible for repressive regimes to mask their oppression by associating their "free market" practices with "freedom" and thus receiving support from the United States. Chile is the clearest example that this pairing not always accurate. The alleged neutrality of the economic model has instead erased land and water rights, particularly for indigenous peoples, and is hardly free from systematic violence. According to Zwarteveen, "Such systematic exclusion of context, or of the specifics of the cultural, social and political environment, allows sustaining the façade of a universal and generic 'water expertise,' which can be applied the world over with only minor adjustments."[26] Pinochet reveals most clearly the dangers of excluding context. In fact, I would argue that choosing to overlook this regime of terror, as the World Bank has done, makes one complicit in it.

Today, Chile's indigenous peoples are still facing "terrorism" charges for protesting against the taking of their rivers. In 1990, Orrego and the Pehuenche people began their fight against Endesa on the upper reaches of the Bío-Bío River, and their Mapuche neighbors downstream joined the battle. Endesa was building two dams—the Pangue and Ralco—on Pehuenche land. The post-Pinochet Concertación government had promised it would not take "one millimeter" of indigenous land and would even give state-owned land back, but even the Chilean government did not have authority when it came to Endesa's water. It was now private property, and disputes over property could be settled only in the courts. As Orrego explained, "Once a water right is granted to you . . . it separates water from the land, totally. So an indigenous community, or any community, can have the dominion over their land, but that doesn't mean they control the water rights." In short, the Pehuenche people no longer owned their water, even if they owned the land along the river.

The decadelong battle against the dams became a battle between Endesa and "terrorists" in which hundreds were arrested, beaten, and harassed by the police. In 2003, for example, Mapuche leader Victor Ancalaf Llaupe was arrested for setting fire to four trucks owned by Endesa. Tried as a terrorist, he received a ten-year sentence. Even as indigenous individuals were confronted with secret evidence against them in the courtroom, they had to deal with the fact that the entire water privatization process remained top secret. When Orrego asked to see the documents supporting the privatization of both water and Endesa in order to make a legal argument against it, he was told they were classified. "But the amazing thing," he said, "is that there is a lid that has been put on top of this operation. It is a taboo. What happened with the energy and the water sector cannot be touched."

Meanwhile, the World Bank supported the whole operation, providing funding for Endesa's first dam, the Pangue, through its International Finance Corporation, an arm of the Bank that funds only private enterprises. But as the dam protests gained international attention, the World Bank faced harsh criticism and, in 1993, Bank president James Wolfensohn announced that the Bank was pulling out of the project.[27]

In turn, Endesa simply returned its World Bank loan and secured other financial backing to continue with the dam.[28] It seemed that the Pehuenche could not beat Endesa. In 1996, the Pangue Dam was filled, creating a reservoir 14 kilometers long and 360 meters wide in a valley that had been full of old-growth *pehuén* trees.

Next, the Pehuenche turned their attention to the second proposed dam, the Ralco. They set up roadblocks, held marches, and sometimes set equipment on fire. In 1999, thousands of protesters, including Mapuche and Pehuenche, walked 395 miles from Temuco to Santiago.[29] At the helm of these protests were seventy-four-year-old Berta Quintremán and her sister Nicolasa, arrayed in colorful Pehuenche head scarves and dresses. Nicolasa said of her home, "I was born here and so were my parents and their parents. If they want me to leave this place, they'll have to carry me out dead."[30] The elderly Quintremán sisters later took part in a demonstration where, according to Human Rights Watch, "Carabineros indiscriminately hit children, women, and old people and arrested about fifty protestors, who were presented to the military prosecutor in Chillán."[31] Despite the determination of people like the Quintremán sisters, Endesa ultimately prevailed once again. After twelve years, the last to leave the area were the Quintremán sisters, who had spent their old age fighting the police and ultimately lost.

In 2004, the Ralco dam filled, flooding the homes of twelve hundred people and an indigenous cemetery. Orrego explained where the people went: "Some of them were resettled, but I want to give you one little piece of information: today the highest suicide rate in Chile is in the upper Bío-Bío, and it's triple the national average. Shocking. I mean, you don't need to say much more." The dam-affected Pehuenche were moved to two main unsettled areas that had both been deforested and had no rivers or streams. For people used to living by a river under the shade of the *pehuen*, the culture shock was enormous. One community was called El Barco, "the boat"; a reservoir was built into the hills there to provide drinking water, but the water was untreated and full of silt. "It's awful. They can't drink it," Orrego said. The other community was called El Huachi, "the rabbit trap." According to Orrego, this land was allotted to the Pehuenche because the power lines from the dam passed through it. He commented, "It's worth nothing. It doesn't have running water or sewage or forest cover. So of course the people are just dying there, alcoholism is widespread. It's nightmarish, seriously." The World Rainforest Movement has also noted the people's dire circumstances: "A few families who have already been relocated to the El Huachi and El Barco areas . . . are suffering due to their livestock's miserable conditions during the heavy winter snows, lack of technical assistance, shortage of firewood, and lack of medical assistance."[32]

If the Bío-Bío River was the place of the "last stand" against invaders, the Ralco dam was the "last straw" that broke the relationship between indigenous peoples and the Chilean state. Since the dam was built, a group of Mapuche have renounced their Chilean citizenship and declared war on the state.[33] Protests across the country have only intensified, as have arrests on terrorism charges. In 2006, Mapuche activist Juana Calfunao was convicted of making "threats to police officers on duty" and sentenced to four years in prison. Prosecutor Alberto Chiffelle requested "the preventative detention" of Calfunao, alleging that "her freedom was a danger to society" and calling the Mapuche community a "gang" and Calfunao its "leader."[34] Previously, Calfunao's house had been burned down three times (her uncle died in one of the fires), and she had been beaten by the police to the point of miscarrying. From prison, she said, "Should the government finally kill me, they will never in reality manage to eradicate me, for the roots of my spirit are entwined far and deep within Ñuke Mapu (mother earth) and I will continue to return for eternity, my strength fortified manifold."[35] Calfunao's treatment is symptomatic of the way the indigenous population is considered merely a group of criminals, gangs, or terrorists. Because its antiterrorist laws are used only against indigenous peoples, Chile is now being prosecuted in the Inter-American Court of Human Rights for racist application of these laws. And when I asked Orrego how the resettled Pehuenche were surviving without subsidies, he simply said, "They're not really surviving, Karen."

Flooding Patagonia National Park

After defeating the Pehuenche on the Bío-Bío River, Endesa moved south to Patagonia and the Aysén region, where the Baker River flows. Orrego described the Baker River: "It's the largest river in Chile, in terms of water flows, but nobody can touch the river. Why? Because Endesa says, 'Eventually when I want to use that water for a dam, it might not be there.' So

the river today is a monopoly of Endesa." Endesa holds "nonconsumptive" water rights, which means that anyone who reduces the flow of the
river and thus lessens potential hydroelectric power is considered a thief.
Orrego explained, "When somebody in Aysén requests even liters of water, which has happened, immediately Endesa's lawyers show up and say,
'No. Because eventually Endesa might want to exercise its nonconsumptive water rights for its dams.'"[36] Essentially, Endesa is hoarding the nation's water. In fact, Endesa controls *more* than the average flow of the
river, since it was granted rights even to the eventual flows from spring
surges and melting glaciers.

Leaving Santiago, I took the four-hour flight south to the Aysén region of northern Patagonia to see the Baker River. To say it is hard to get
there would be an understatement. The only way to get to the Baker River
is to take a five-hour bumpy drive on a two-lane gravel and dirt road built
across northern Patagonia by Pinochet. He had the road built to ensure
military access to this remote region, where dissidents once hid, but in
so doing he created a unique Patagonian culture. This part of the world
runs at a very slow pace—owners of restaurants sit outside their shops
and wave at passing cars. The highway itself forces this slowness upon
you, since going even thirty miles an hour could be dangerous. People
from Aysén have a saying, "He who rushes loses time." Distances grow
in this environment. The landscape ranges from dense forests and rivers
bursting with wildflowers to rocky, arid canyons. Bathroom breaks are
taken on the side of the road, or even on the road, since the chances of
seeing another car are slim. The last part of the road was blasted through
a cliff overhanging Lake General Carrera, the source of the Baker River.
The lake, which is the second or third largest in South America, is a stun-
ningly bright aquamarine; it is surrounded by mountains with glaciers
that feed into it and cause its brilliant color.

When I finally spotted the Baker River, I hit the brakes and gasped
in delight. The Baker River is a very fast river; but unlike other fast rivers, it has no rocks jutting up through its surface, no dramatic twists and
turns. It is like a brilliant blue Missouri or Mississippi River. The reason
for this is that it is a relatively new glacial river. It has not had time to develop deep canyons, corners, and recesses full of rockfall. It is just getting
started. Just over one hundred miles long, it is unlike any other river in
the world.

A breathtaking view of Lake General Carrera, on the border of Argentina and Chile, which feeds the Baker River.

A few miles downstream from the headwaters, the river enters a desertlike landscape called the Patagonian steppes. This is where Doug and Kris Tompkins live, on a large former ranch called Estancia Chacabuco. The Tompkinses are also fighting Endesa; in fact, you can tell you are nearing their property by the increasing number of antidam billboards lining the highway, paid for by the Tompkinses. Their property, which they are turning into a nature reserve, is perhaps the only place where you can see flamingos and mountain lions (called pumas) together. Here, guanacos (wild llamas) and numerous other "steppes" wildlife meet the deep-forest wildlife of Chile. Here, the glacial waters of the Baker meet the brown rapids of the Nef, then the Chacabuco and Colonia Rivers; the river gradually becomes less bright until it drains into the ocean as milky gray. Unfortunately, their land is also adjacent to a prospective HydroAysén dam, which will be built across the road. Financed by Endesa and the Matte Group, which is run by a rich Chilean family who were once major supporters of Pinochet, the dam will have a direct negative impact on the Tompkinses' dream of turning their land into Patagonia National Park.

Doug Tompkins created the North Face and Esprit outdoor-gear labels. Kris was once the CEO of Patagonia, Inc. In 1990, Doug sold his share of North Face for $150 million and decided to invest in Chile, working with Kris to purchase land from the ocean to Argentina for ecosystem restoration.[37] Eventually, they hoped to donate the land to the Chilean government, but with a strict mandate that the land would be used only as a national park—free from power lines, mining, or other forms of development. Ironically, though the land is worth hundreds of millions of dollars, the Chilean government seems uninterested in this donation. In 1995, the government politely suggested that the Tompkinses stop buying property in the region, citing national security concerns and a fear that their property would split Chile in two. The government even accused the Tompkinses of threatening national sovereignty. Former defense minister Edmundo Perez Yoma said that Doug Tompkins was "irritating and out of place."[38]

The reason for the anti-Tompkins sentiment in Chile is complex. At Chacabuco, neighbors were angered when the Tompkinses started taking down fences, removing sheep, and restricting the hunting of mountain lions on their property. Neighbors thought that allowing mountain lions to live would endanger the sheep on neighboring properties. For many Patagonians, sheep are an emblem of the region, even though the British brought the sheep there. In the 1880s, London-based sheep companies began to establish farms in Patagonia, primarily on Tehuelche lands. The Tehuelche were soon confined to reservations and killed by British settlers. Travel writer A. F. Tschiffely described being shown a riding harness made from the skin of an Indian in the 1930s. He wrote about the shooting parties that British sheep farmers organized against defenseless Indians in his book *This Way Southward* (1945).[39] Today, the Tehuelche are extinct, but sheep still provide the livelihood for Patagonian residents and absentee landlords. For this reason, the Tompkinses are seen as a threat to that income stream because they provide a refuge for mountain lions.

In Chile, there are even stranger conspiracy theories about Doug Tompkins, some showing signs of old German-influenced anti-Semitism. In 1998, *Outside* magazine described these ideas:

> Over the last four years he has been accused in the Chilean press
> of an increasingly implausible litany of offenses—from throwing

impoverished settlers off his land to planning a dumping ground
for nuclear waste, from spying for the United States and Argentina
to establishing a new Jewish homeland (Tompkins is not Jewish).
Anti-Tompkins graffiti have appeared in Puerto Montt, the closest
city to the park, and there have been death threats against him and
his wife.[40]

Endesa employees have made fun of Tompkins for having "sentimental
problems" and being obsessed with "beauty" rather than with people. But
according to Orrego, the real reason Doug Tompkins is harassed is quite
simple: "It's because he is a conservationist, and Chile is for exploiting."

For other Chileans, Tompkins is a hero. When I stopped at a restaurant in the region, the owner proudly showed me something Doug Tompkins had scrawled in his guest book. "When the people and the region
wake up to the consequences of dams, then it will be time to rethink the
economic model," it read. "Without . . . a solid ecological understanding,
we are all on board a rudderless ship, heading to the abyss."[41] Whatever
criticisms might be wielded against Kris and Doug Tompkins, they are
certainly a couple obsessed with implementing a rather selfless vision of
ecological health, one that can serve as an educational model for future
generations.

As I turned off Pinochet's highway into Estancia Chacabuco, I immediately noticed large herds of guanacos that were surprisingly unafraid of
the car. Rather than moving out of the way, they stared at the car as if a
curious beast had invaded their territory. The dirt road that runs through
Chacabuco goes all the way to Argentina and is visited by numerous endangered wildlife species, including *huemules* (south Andean deer), rare
creatures that look like elk but have thick fur like dogs. The *huemul* is the
national emblem of Chile and is on the verge of extinction. As I drove
along the road, I saw volunteers pulling out nonnative plant species in
an effort to bring back the plants that preceded the sheep. The discarded
plants covered the road like flower petals on a wedding aisle.

Turning a corner, I saw what looked like a midwestern-style fortress on a hill, a large stone house seemingly transported from a wealthy
St. Louis suburb, with a twin-engine plane parked outside. Further down
the hill was a cluster of trailer-like buildings under construction, where
I pulled in to park at the main office. There, I found out that Kris wanted

to meet me at her house on the hill, but in the meantime an enormous black-faced ibis had blocked my car in the driveway and was refusing to move. I was gradually beginning to think the animals around here had as much gumption as the Tompkinses. "Nope, I'm not going anywhere," the ibis seemed to say. I had already adjusted somewhat to the Aysén notion that "rushing loses time," and it seemed the animals were aware of this principle too. Luckily, though completely unflustered by the car, it did not want to be physically moved by me when I got out of the car to deal with the situation.

"Let's talk out here," Kris greeted me at her door and led me to the porch. "It's nicer." Glancing inside her house, I saw an enormous living room with wall-to-wall windows overlooking the park. A man in a suit was waiting to continue a business meeting. Kris looked like a New Yorker to me, a fit and attractive forty-something woman who was unsmiling and businesslike. I could tell she was short on time, so I quickly asked her how she felt about the dam that was going in across from her property.

Immediately I sensed I had asked the wrong question. "I thought she was here to talk about the park," she said to her assistant, who had joined us outside. Then, turning to me, she said, "I work on the park. The dam issue is my husband's thing."

"Well, won't the dam impact the park?" I asked.

"I have no official position on the dam," she replied. "That's not our business. I mean, we contribute to the antidam movement, but we work on parks."

It was clear to me that she had a political reason for not wanting to go on record about the dam; perhaps doing so would lead to further harassment. This made perfect sense to me, given the bizarre criticisms she had received already. So instead we talked about her plans for Estancia Chacabuco and her home in California, which she said had inspired her to buy this property. She began to brighten up. "It looked the same, the rolling dry hills, the open sky," she explained. "Yes, I sometimes miss the landscapes of home." Meanwhile, she said, her husband was working at his own park farther north, called Pumalín, which made it sound like Kris and Doug had "his-and-hers" parks in the middle of the Chilean wilderness. "But I have work to do here," she explained. "When this is done, we will have trails for hiking and wildlife viewing. It will be spectacular."

Kris is clearly a tough, no-nonsense hardworking woman who seems determined to leave a legacy of ecosystem health on nearly two million acres in Chile. Her dream is to join the property she and Doug own to the Chilean national reserve system and turn it all into a national park. But her bigger goal is to save a planet threatened with mass extinctions. In an article on the Patagonia, Inc., website, she states: "Private wildlands philanthropy, mixed with political will, can create wildlands restoration and preservation on a grand scale and swing the pendulum of extinction back on wavering species."[42] In fact, her park could be Chile's last hope for the *huemul* by providing it safe habitat. It could also create a tourism circuit to Argentina and back, which would be one of the world's most beautiful loops. But the dams might destroy it all. In fact, I later discovered that the last piece of land the Tompkinses needed to join the two sections of their projected national park was secretly sold to Endesa.[43] Leaving Kris behind that day, I could only hope that the dams would not destroy her dreams altogether. If the Baker River were dammed, it would not flood her property but would bring in massive construction equipment to tear up the land and crisscross it with electrical wires. And that would be only the start of the problems.

Evacuation and Ocean Death

After leaving Kris Tompkins, I followed the river downstream, heading into a dark and dripping old-growth acacia forest that eventually opened into an estuary full of fjords, looking a bit like Norway. The last stop on the Baker River is the tiny logging village of Caleta Tortel, which is built entirely on stilts and boardwalks over the bay, as if the villagers had simply become overzealous in chopping down trees. The hills behind Caleta Tortel are actually too steep to build upon, pushing the village out onto the sea. Located at 47 degrees latitude South, Caleta Tortel sits within the boundaries of the Antarctic Circumpolar Current, though the village is set far back from the sea at the end of a long fjord.

The Circumpolar Current, which circles Antarctica, is the only current that runs through the Pacific, Atlantic, and Indian Oceans, affecting global ocean life.[44] It is considered the main driver of global ocean circulation. At Caleta Tortel, the Circumpolar Current hits land and breaks into two new currents, one going north and one going south. Of the southward Cape Horn current, oceanographer Marcus Sobarzo

Bustamante has written, "The local influence of freshwater originating from the continent modulates the temporal variability of this coastal current."[45] It is difficult to separate river and ocean dynamics. Scientists of this subantarctic zone tend to talk about "sea–ice" interaction, and a good part of that ice is inland, in the second-largest nonpolar ice field in the world, the Patagonian Ice Field. In short, rivers dramatically change the ocean in this region, with global impacts, and HydroAysén plans to build five dams in the ice field watershed

So what happens if you dam the region's rivers? Besides interfering with ocean–river temperature interaction, the dams would block the silt that once flowed into the ocean, which supports the food chain on which krill depend and, in turn, much of the biodiversity of the Southern Ocean. Damming rivers would also cause massive algae blooms, which are shut down only by predictable freshwater flows; at the same time, dams could stop the world's largest "carbon sink" from functioning, where ocean currents pull algae blooms and phytoplankton down to deep levels and thus "sequester" carbon, protecting the atmosphere from excess carbon dioxide (CO_2). Finally, disruptions or shifts around the Antarctic Circumpolar Current would be even more catastrophic, potentially causing mass ocean extinctions and abrupt shifts in the earth's temperature.

The ice sheets in Patagonia and Antarctica play a significant role in climate change moderation and ocean health, but the outflow of the former may soon be blocked behind dams. Of the fjords, oceanographers Jose Luis Iriarte, Humberto E. González, and Laura Nahuelhual write, "The factors affecting freshwater dynamics would impact nutrient load and water circulation on a local scale; they would also affect ocean productivity and climate from the regional to the global scale."[46] In short, dams affect freshwater dynamics and thereby climate at the "global scale." The Southern Ocean is not only the world's most biologically productive ocean but also its coldest ocean, and both aspects make it critical for climate stability. Its cold, dense waters help create the trade winds that drive the Antarctic Circumpolar Current.[47] As the ocean warms, scientists are unsure what will happen. Bustamante writes, "Little is known of the coastal dynamics in this region."[48] This is in part due to its remoteness but also due to fact that only in the past decade have scientists begun to realize the seriousness of the global feedback loop for this region. (Previously, it was believed that the Antarctic was more immune to climate change than the

Arctic.) Climate change scientists in the Southern Ocean are only starting to catch up to their Arctic colleagues. The question is whether or not we want to mess around with the process before we know exactly what will happen. Theoretically, if the Circumpolar Current were to stop, all ocean currents would follow suit, and the world's climate would be permanently changed. Europe would most likely enter an ice age and Antarctica would abruptly melt.

Just as the flapping of butterfly wings is said to create ripples around the world, it has been said that damming the Baker River can have impacts on ocean life hundreds of miles away. At least that is what Bernardo Reyes, head of the NGO Etica en los Bosques (Forest Ethics), told me. I met with Reyes, a witty and brilliant man, at a jazz club in Santiago to talk about Caleta Tortel. "The dam will keep silica from the glaciers from being washed down the river," Reyes said. "This will kill tiny ocean phytoplankton called diatoms that need silica to survive. That means that krill will be in trouble."[49] The nearly microscopic Antarctic krill, a crustacean that looks like a shrimp, is one of the largest protein sources on Earth. The quantity of krill swimming in the Southern Ocean—feeding whales, seals, penguins, fish, and squid—is enormous. As the diatoms disappear, toxic blue-green algae blooms that grow in warmer, silica-free waters will eventually replace this rich ecosystem. Ice in the region cools ocean water down, making it sink and thus keeping organic matter in the deep oceans from rotting and producing toxic blooms, or giant methane bubbles. If this vertical mixing stops, our oceans will die, meaning the end of a good portion of the global food supply. And methane gas, which is already being released into the atmosphere from Arctic lakes and permafrost, is twenty times more potent than CO_2 as a greenhouse gas. Climate change would be unstoppable.

"If you want to hear a really frightening story," Reyes continued, "these dams could also impact the Circumpolar Current, which feeds the ocean currents for the entire planet. Nobody knows what will happen." It turns out the Baker River is the outlet for the Northern Patagonian Ice Field, second only to the Tibetan Plateau in size, and the region is considered a global driver of climate change.[50] If this ice-cold glacial outflow were trapped behind a dam, it would gradually warm and thus cause the glaciers feeding the reservoir to melt faster. "The dams heat the rivers," Reyes explained, "impacting this balance." This is called a negative feedback loop between climate change and dams.[51] Today, 70 percent of Chile's freshwater is held in glaciers or ice fields, which are melting at an alarming rate.

Ironically, Bernardo Reyes told me a strange story about Chilean businessmen actually *wanting* to melt glaciers.[52] Under the Water Code, glaciers cannot be bought and sold and are not defined as private property. But this was recently challenged when the Canadian mining company Barrick Gold claimed it *owned* the glaciers on its land and intended to melt them in order to mine underneath them. After the local population protested· that these glaciers fed the river that supplied them with water, the company's plan to "relocate" the glaciers was overturned in the courts. The battle over these glaciers became so huge that in 2006 Chilean presidential candidate Michelle Bachelet campaigned on the promise that she would not allow glaciers to be moved or damaged.

But while glaciers cannot be melted intentionally, the question remains as to who owns the water or other resources made available by "inadvertent" melting due to climate change. In short, a gold rush has begun around the world for the resources that are beneath the melting glaciers, whether it is gold in Patagonia or oil and gas in the Arctic. As the Barrick Gold case demonstrates, corporate interests can view melting glaciers as opportunities. And, as mentioned earlier, Endesa has already registered future glacial melt for ownership. This issue may enter the courts again if, as Reyes believes, the intention behind the building of HydroAysén is to open up Patagonia to mining interests. The dams would provide the roads and electricity necessary for mining interests to move in, and the gold is there.[53] According to Víctor Formantel Gallardo of the NGO Ecosistemas, "Once they've come here and built a 1,000-kilometer high tension line that stretches to Puerto Montt, and then reaches from there through the valleys and foothill areas all the way to Santiago, at that point there really will be no reason for them not to come and extract the region's very real resources." Interestingly, during a battle over Water Code modification, "the mining sector was among those that opposed any significant changes to the law."[54]

Reluctantly leaving the beauty of Caleta Tortel to head back to Santiago, I stopped on the Baker River one last time to go on a rafting trip with Rolando. From the raft, Rolando encouraged me to jump in the river and take a swim. So I did. The water was cold and swift, but I held on to the raft and floated there for a while, looking at the snow-covered peaks while contemplating the loss of this serene beauty. I could understand why the Tompkinses wanted to protect it. I asked Rolando what would happen to him after the river was dammed, and he said he might switch to guiding mountaineering expeditions. But then he explained a new employment opportunity caused by the melting glaciers.

"Have you heard of GLOFs?" he asked. "It is when an ice dam breaks. It happened here in 2008. The water rose up to there," he pointed at a mountain across the river. "About eighteen feet. Luckily, everyone survived, except for the roads and sheep and cattle. But who knows if the HydroAysén dam would be able to withstand that force." An "ice dam" occurs when glaciers crack and melt, forming unstable lakes whose outlets are blocked by chunks of ice. A glacial lake outburst flood (GLOF) happens when the building pressure of the water causes the ice dam to burst. GLOFs are occurring more frequently around the world, Rolando said, because of climate change. In fact, records show that GLOFs once occurred about every fifty years in this region. Between 2008 and 2011, they occurred seven times. Recent reports show that more than 87 percent of Chile's glaciers are melting, and faster than expected. Scientists have discovered Patagonia's glaciers have melted enough to cover the entire United States with more than an inch of water since 2000.[55] Ironically, this might help Rolando find a new job. An early warning system called the Sentinel Project has been set up in the valley to warn residents of coming glacial floods due to breaking ice dams. One person with a satellite telephone is posted at each ice dam twenty-four hours a day to warn of a collapse. Rolando thought that maybe he could do that.

A bigger problem is that a GLOF could cause HydroAysén dam to collapse. In fact, GLOFs are the biggest threat to dam safety—even more worrisome than the earthquakes and volcanic eruptions common in the region. A study from the Massachusetts Institute of Technology demonstrated that, under pressure from a GLOF, HydroAysén dam could break in as little as 7.6 minutes as water pouring into the reservoir causes the dam to overtop.[56] If this were to happen, Caleta Tortel would suffer "catastrophic consequences" within an hour.

Despite these problems, many along the Baker River believe it is inevitable that the dams will be built, given the sanctity of private property in Chile. Nevertheless, Endesa still faces a major obstacle. The land it needs to build transmission lines from the dam to the north are in part owned by the Mapuche and the Tompkinses. Ironically, Endesa's current problem is caused by the very privatization that its owners once skillfully enacted. Because a privately owned company cannot declare "eminent domain" over someone else's property, as the government once could, there is no clear path for establishing an easement for these power lines. And obviously, Endesa has not exactly made friends with either set of landowners. So the situation may end in a stalemate, with Endesa hoarding water endlessly.

As the case of Chile shows, a "free market" in water rarely means that. A "free market" can easily be linked to an undemocratic, even despotic, government. It can ultimately erode state authority and create roadblocks to development. As has happened in other countries, water privatization has been an excuse for cronyism and corruption in Chile, and the water market has also opened up the country for foreign speculators. Today China is looking to purchase vast amounts of Patagonia's water, as Saudi Arabia has already done in Egypt. According to investment banker James Rickards, in a world of unstable currencies, the "leading investment—and the one Chinese now favor—is commodities . . . [including] the most valuable commodity of all—water." He explains China's interest in the water market: "Special funds are being organized to buy exclusive rights to freshwater from deep lakes and glaciers in Patagonia."[57] It is not clear what the Chinese government intends to do with this water.

As the harmful by-products of the Water Code manifest themselves, a growing movement to renationalize water has emerged. Far from a "model" for the world, the situation in Chile reveals that a free market in water leads to monopoly control, water hoarding, violations of indigenous rights, and environmental catastrophe. Orrego observed, "You know, some people say that [the Water Code] 'deregulates.' . . . I say it regulates very precisely for corporate takeover. It's not a deregulation; it's a regulation. It's all wordplay, but it's very interesting." In 2008, politicians, church leaders, environmentalists, indigenous groups, and labor unions formed a coalition called Recuperemos el Agua para Chile, or Let's Get Chile's Water Back.[58]

One of the obstacles to renationalization is that the state may not even be able to *afford* to buy back Chile's water, even if it could find a way around the Water Code. In 2010, when right-wing billionaire Sebastian Piñera was elected president, many lost hope that the dams could be halted or the water renationalized. After Piñera's victory was announced, his supporters ran into the streets of Santiago carrying Pinochet signs and chanting, "General Pinochet, this victory is for you," and "Long live Chile and Pinochet." Neo-Nazis marched in formation down the streets of Santiago, performing the Nazi salute. Soon afterward, Piñera announced it was time for the "second pacification of Araucanía," referring to the slaughter of the Mapuche people. In June 2012, a historic theater in Santiago screened a film honoring Pinochet produced by the Corporation on September 11, which has a completely different view about that day than the majority of Chileans. Thousands attended. Augusto Pinochet Molina, grandson of the dictator, introduced the film: "In the year 1973 this country gave a strong cry and that cry was 'Freedom.'" The Wi-Fi signal in the theater was named "Viva Pinochet," or "Pinochet lives," and the crowd jeered whenever ex-president Salvador Allende appeared on the screen. To them, he represented the evils of socialism. "Drunk, degenerate, homosexual," they shouted at the film. Outside the theater, families of Pinochet victims carried signs with photos of their missing loved ones that read simply, "Where is he?" or "Where is she?"[59] Police used water cannons to disperse the hundreds of protesters outside the theater.

Chileans are clearly still divided between "socialism" and the "free market," which perhaps should not be surprising. After World War II, this polarizing rhetoric swept the world, forcing newly independent countries to choose sides between the Soviet Union and the United States. Today, this language remains entrenched long after the Soviet Union has crumbled, revealing itself recently in tea party diatribes against "socialism," in China's hypocritical praise of "communism," and in neoliberal policies of the IMF and World Bank. It is unfortunate that water has recently been forced into this old divide. Perhaps the lesson to be learned from both Chile and the United States is that the polarizing "public versus private" model is not adequate for thinking about water, since this false dichotomy tends to delimit political thinking. Perhaps instead we need to think about decolonizing the political imagination, particularly in settler nations with alternative indigenous knowledge systems. In the conclusion to their edited collection of essays on water rights titled *Out of the Mainstream*, water scholars Armando Guevara-Gil, Rutgerd Boelens, and David Getches note that "Andean states have often undermined the subsistence means and strategies of indigenous and rural societies, marginalizing local rights, effectively denying that multiple cultures and identities can coexist, and oppressing local people's management and self-determination."[60] Allowing "multiple cultures" to flourish and provide alternative viewpoints would help to counteract the consolidation of water according to a centralized orthodox position controlled by those in power.

New Zealand has provided one model for how to allow "multiple cultures and identities" to coexist. Since the 1980s, New Zealand has been gradually introducing biculturalism into its public-sector services, recognizing both European immigrant (Pakeha) and indigenous Maori cultures.[61] Some have suggested that this biculturalism does not go far enough, but a few accomplishments have been quite significant, such as the implementation of a bicultural early childhood education system, the funding of a Maori TV station, and negotiations to revise the constitution in accordance with Maori treaties. Even when it is only "window dressing," this approach would still be a significance advance for countries like Chile, where Pinochet's government infamously declared, "Today there are no indigenous people in Chile, only Chileans."[62] While Maori represent a larger segment of their national society (15 percent) than do either Mapuche (5–10 percent) or American Indians (1.7 percent), the principles of biculturalism can be applied to any settler society whose founding documents include treaties with the indigenous population. According to Justice Eddie Durie of the High Court of New Zealand, "Biculturalism is about the relationship between the state's founding cultures, where there is more than one. Multiculturalism is about the acceptance of cultural difference generally."[63] Influential political theorist Will Kymlicka has described the legal implications of this concept in Canada, using the term *multination state* (rather than *bicultural state*) to describe Canada, with its three founding cultures (First Nations, Francophone Quebecois, and Anglophone Canadian), in contrast to its *polyethnic* or multicultural state status.[64] He argues that the three cofounding cultures should be accorded group rights to territory and land management while at the same time not infringing on individual rights to property, cultural practices, and state protection in a multicultural society. New Zealand implemented biculturalism in part to right the wrongs done to Maori and to acknowledge the contributions that Maori knowledge can provide to the country.

In response to legislation addressing biculturalism, the Centre for Resource Management released a report titled "Water: Towards a Bicultural Perspective" in 1990. It not only outlines Maori values regarding water but also offers suggestions for incorporating these values into water management decisions. It also attempts to educate public-sector workers about Maori language and etiquette, above all suggesting that knowledge of and respect for Maori values are crucial elements for successful working partnerships in New Zealand's bicultural environment.

Unfortunately, New Zealand's turn to biculturalism is today threatened by water privatization, owing to the ways in which transnational water companies violate Maori values. Maori water experts G. Raumati Hook and L. Parehaereone write:

> Delivery of fresh water requires unity of purpose and it is important that all those who are engaged in that activity, both the deliverers and the delivered to, behave accordingly. Cronyism, lying, intimidation and secrecy threaten unity of purpose leading to dissension and eventually rebellion. . . . Transnational corporations have uniformly demonstrated poor leadership, questionable honesty, corrupt behaviours and little tendency to help those in need. Their breaches of rangatiratanga [chiefly qualities] make transnational corporations ill-suited for any kind of leadership especially in the service industries.[65]

Because foreign corporations do not operate according to the principles of biculturalism, they remain threatening to the legal status of Maori water claims. According to New Zealand politician Winston Peters, "It is astonishing that Government ministers and officials did not realise that announcing plans to use this water for private, commercial profit would be like poking a stick into a wasps nest."[66] Interestingly, the Maori do not necessarily favor either public or private water vendors, acknowledging the necessity for small-scale private vendors in some cases. The *ethics* of whoever is providing water is the primary issue.

As Maori experts have suggested, water delivery requires transparency, honest leadership, and help for those in need. And the most important ingredient is trust between deliverers and receivers. In the cases of Chile and California, water markets have led to the opposite—secrecy, deception, and collusion. Large-scale transfers of water from public to private hands have occurred behind closed doors in negotiations that have both enriched the private sector and empowered the public sector through campaign donations and revolving doors. Hook and Parehaereone argue that when the balance of power between the deliverers and receivers of water is heavily tilted toward the deliverers, "by Māori principles that balance must eventually be restored." "In the days of the ancient Māori," they conclude, "this might take the form of a punitive raid or even war, but those days are gone and the principles remain; nevertheless, hostility will remain until balance has been restored."[67] While the days of war may be over for the Maori in New Zealand, they are not over for the Mapuche in Chile, who have recently declared war against the state. Nor are they over for the people of Bolivia, who overturned the government because of Bechtel's water contract. This might be a lesson to transnational corporations that have been forced to retreat from countries around the world because of hostility from local populations. In ongoing battles around the world, the balance of power is perhaps slowly being restored.

II

POSTCOLONIAL WATER
INSURGENCIES

THREE

South Africa's Water Apartheid

NELSON MANDELA, during his presidential inaugural address, famously said, "Let there be work, bread, water, and salt for all." While Pinochet's government turned Chile's water into private property for electric and mining interests, President Mandela chose to do exactly the opposite, enshrining the right to water as a public good in the new South African government's constitution. In 1996, South Africa became the first nation in the world to include in its constitution the mandate that "everyone has the right" to "sufficient food and water." Access to water came to symbolize the end of forty-six years of brutal segregation under apartheid law, when water was inequitably distributed in a system that heavily favored white people. The country's first "White Paper on a National Water Policy" (1997) opened with words by the poet Antjie Krog: "We want the water of this country to flow out into a network—reaching every individual—saying: here is this water, for you. Take it; cherish it as affirming your human dignity; nourish your humanity. With water we will wash away the past, we will from now on ever be bounded by the blessing of water."[1] After apartheid ended, water became a symbol of hope, equality, and renewal; but then economic apartheid emerged.

Given that he had lived without sufficient access to clean water for nearly thirty years while imprisoned on Robben Island, it is no wonder that President Mandela would include equal access to water as a goal for the postapartheid nation. Thrown into prison as a "terrorist" for fighting apartheid, Mandela found that freshwater was scarce on Robben Island, which is located a few miles off Cape Town's coast. Initially, water was transported from the mainland and rationed; later, wells were dug that supplied brackish water. One former prisoner, Billy Nair, told an interviewer in 2002 that every morning at the prison there would be "four pails of water against one wall and another four used as toilets against the other"—to be shared among sixty prisoners. "Because the water had to last the whole day, men rationed their water supplies—a mug full was all that was allowed for morning ablutions." For a full shower, there was saltwater. Nair said that in the 1960s, "you actually had to bathe in salt water . . . pumped right from the sea."[2] Another inmate claimed that "five liters per day" were allotted to each prisoner, less than what it takes to flush one standard toilet in the United States.[3] Navanethem Pillay, who was appointed U.N. high commissioner for human rights in 2008, expressed her horror at the conditions she found at the prison when she was an attorney: "On my very first visit to Robben Island prison, the warders told me not to drink the water from the taps provided for the use of the detainees and handed me water from the mainland. I immediately drank from the taps and found that the water was brackish. It was causing health problems for my clients."[4]

If Mandela experienced water scarcity, he was well aware that all black South Africans were having similar problems. In 1913, the colonizing British began implementing the Native Lands Act, forcibly moving rural black Africans to designated areas, similar to Native American reservations. This land was in the water-scarce and least productive parts of the country. More than 80 percent of land went to white people, who were only 20 percent of the population. Under British riparian water law, only those who owned property adjacent to the rivers had legal access to water, and blacks were moved away from the rivers. In 1923, it also became illegal for blacks to live in urban areas. Those who worked in cities were moved to the peripheries, or "townships"; those who could not verify employment were deported to the reserves. In the black townships, government dormitory-style housing was built for workers, but residents had to pay back the building costs as well as electricity and water costs.

Rents and services were all bundled into one monthly payment, a practice intended to conceal the costs of individual services, which could be raised at any time. Residents found that these payments continued even after building costs had been paid back. Many of the people, unable to afford the cost of government housing, erected shantytowns, or "informal settlements," supplied with only the most rudimentary of services, usually a standpipe for drinking water.[5] Women often had to walk miles get to the single standpipe in their area.

In contrast, the cities' white areas were filled with lush lawns, large swimming pools, and golf courses—even though South Africa is one of the most water-scarce countries in the world.[6] In 1948, when the Dutch-based Afrikaner government took over, this inequity only intensified under the segregation policies of apartheid (the Afrikaner word means "apartness"). According to the 1997 white paper: "Apartheid was an inefficient racial spoils system under which the distribution of water-use was racially biased, and access to water and the benefits of its use a privilege of those with access to land and political and economic power."[7] By the time apartheid ended in 1994, 70 percent of South Africa's population received only 11 percent of the country's water.

In 1994, Mandela's Reconstruction and Development Program (RDP) was unveiled, promising "water security for all." The program's framework document stated, "The fundamental principal of our water resources policy is the right to access clean water." Specifically, the RDP promised that "in the short term" all households would be supplied with twenty to thirty liters per capita per day, with access no farther than six hundred feet away. In the "medium term," households were promised an on-site supply of fifty to sixty liters of clean water per capita per day, with a "subsidy" for the poor. City limits would also be redrawn to include black townships and thus make cities' tax bases and services available for all, ending preferential treatment for whites. (Previously, water and electrical services in black townships were funded in part by "Native Beer Accounts," which designated profits on beer sales in townships for this purpose.)[8]

The start of democracy and the end of segregation laws in South Africa was a time of high hopes for black South Africans. Yet exactly a decade later, the South African Cities Network reported, "All surveys show that the perceived quality of life is declining amongst black residents, while increasing among white residents."[9] Part of the decline in satisfaction among blacks was linked to rising unemployment, which more than doubled in the decade after apartheid ended.[10] Income inequality was also growing. *The Nation* recently reported, "Since 1994, the number of South Africans living on less than a dollar a day has doubled, but so has the number of South African millionaires." Statistics reveal that infant mortality also rose during that decade, with the number of deaths highest in children under four years old. Between 1997 and 2005, child deaths increased 90 percent. The leading cause of death was intestinal disease. In short, these children had been drinking dirty water.[11]

In 2007, when I arrived in Cape Town, the face of the "new" South Africa had become the urban riot—often sparked by lack of water, housing, and sanitation. Since then, the numbers of protests and riots, which are called "service delivery protests" in South Africa, have only increased every year. During two weeks in May 2008, more than fifty people died in riots across the country. Much of the violence was directed at immigrants from other African countries and so was blamed on racism, but the underlying causes were clear. "We have no running water, no electricity and we use the bucket system," one resident said. "That is why we are angry and want to fight."[12] In 2008, President Thabo Mbeki ordered the army to back up the police against the rioters. A recent survey revealed that lack of clean water ranks second (after lack of housing) as the reason people protest.[13] Bloomberg News reported that in 2012 South Africa had a record 173 "major protests over poor delivery of municipal services," including water. This was more than double the number of protests the year before.[14] The phrase "ring of fire" has been used to describe protests in the poorer areas surrounding South Africa's cities that threaten to close in on nation's city centers.[15] So what happened to the heady first years of Mandela's presidency, when "water for all" was the slogan of the day? According to South African politician Ronnie Kasrils, "We were entrapped by the neoliberal economy—or, as some today cry out, we 'sold our people down the river.'"[16]

In 1991, the World Bank and IMF saw the end of apartheid as an economic opportunity. After decades of economic sanctions against the country, South Africa was suddenly open to foreign investment. In turn, the Bank and IMF began to shape South Africa's future economic policy during "behind closed doors" negotiations between South Africa's white business community and Mandela's African National Congress (ANC). According to the Bank, "In 1991, the Bank resumed activities in South Africa through a comprehensive program of economic policy advice and capacity building."[17] South Africa's new economic ministers were regularly flown to Washington, D.C., to meet with heads of the World Bank and IMF, while the Mandela family was wooed with holidays at South Africa's lavish estates and in the Bahamas. "Corruption is a two-way street," economist Joseph Stiglitz once said. "If you want to avoid corruption, don't dangle big pots of money in people's faces."[18] In the end, Mandela's dream for South Africa was corrupted by pressure from the Bank and IMF. Kasrils, who was involved in the negotiations to end apartheid, explains in his autobiography:

> What I call our Faustian moment came when we took an IMF loan on the eve of our first democratic election. That loan, with strings attached that precluded a radical economic agenda, was considered a necessary evil, as were concessions to keep negotiations on track. . . . The ANC leadership needed to remain determined, united and free of corruption—and, above all, to hold on to its revolutionary will. Instead, we chickened out.[19]

During the negotiations, the South African team tried to amend IMF conditions that South African economist Vishnu Padayachee said had a distinct "similarity with the apartheid regime's thinking." The amendments proposed to the IMF "were proposed with a view to giving the democratic government greater flexibility and room to maneuver in respect of policies to address employment and meet basic social and infrastructural needs." But conflicts within the African National Congress and lack of transparency in the negotiation process undermined the strength of the South African position; the amendments "were not incorporated."[20] Padayachee feared that if the African National Congress could not find a way to outwit the IMF, its subsequent "failure to deliver on the RDP may threaten the very survival of Africa's newest democracy."[21]

South Africa's goal of maintaining the RDP had also not been helped by the weather. In 1992–93, South Africa had experienced the worst drought in living memory. Seventy thousand jobs were lost in agriculture and related sectors, wildfires spread, cattle died, rivers dried up, and desperate people moved to cities. Overall, 250,000 people were affected, and the nation's gross domestic product (GDP) shrank.[22] The IMF used this desperation to its advantage. It would not provide US$850 million for drought relief until it was assured that the ANC would follow the IMF's economic policies, which included not increasing wages, removing trade barriers, and reducing debt through cutting government services—the direct opposite of RDP policy.[23] As former Robben Island prisoner Dennis Brutus explained, "We've come out of apartheid into global apartheid. . . . This is the reverse of what we thought was going to happen under the African National Congress government."[24]

What happened in South Africa is not unusual. Time and again, the IMF has stepped in with "Faustian deals" for nations, promising that their only option for survival lies in their meeting the economic conditions of the IMF. What is unique about the case study of South Africa is that it demonstrates how supposedly neutral economic theory can in fact perpetuate racism. In South Africa, the IMF started the "ring of fire" with an austerity and privatization plan that ignored the very racism that the country desperately needed to overcome. Today, what the IMF is unprepared for is the fact that there is a well-oiled machine in South Africa for fighting apartheid, which has now turned against "global apartheid." According to Kasrils, "A descent into darkness must be curtailed. . . . The ANC's soul needs to be restored; its traditional values and culture of service reinstated. The pact with the devil [i.e., the IMF] needs to be broken."[25] The antiapartheid battle has seamlessly turned into an anti-IMF and antiprivatization battle, providing an example for other countries that are also fighting IMF-imposed austerity measures.

Postapartheid Water

In 1993, Mandela accepted the IMF loan for South Africa with a few conditions. First, South Africa had to sign the General Agreement on Tariffs and Trade (GATT), allowing foreign investors access to the country on an "equal" footing with local industry. Second, South Africa had to repay the debts of the defunct apartheid government. Both requirements would turn out to be important for future water policy, since they guaranteed that corporations like Suez could move in and force people in black townships to pay back apartheid-era debts for water services. The dream of redistricting cities to encompass black areas was also postponed until at least 2000, which meant that townships had to continue to operate with inadequate tax bases for upgrading their own water supplies. Because of this, the capital funds of the water corporations seemed to be the only answer in dire circumstances.[26]

By 1996, a new economic plan had replaced the Reconstruction and Development Program. It was called the Growth, Employment, and Redistribution program, or GEAR. It was created by fifteen economists, including two members of the World Bank. In the GEAR framework document, both race and apartheid are effectively erased from the economic history of the country. Unlike the RDP, the GEAR document never uses the words *racism, apartheid,* or even *inequity*. At the launch of GEAR, Deputy President Thabo Mbeki infamously said, "Just call me a Thatcherite," referring to British prime minister Margaret Thatcher's sweeping privatization policies, which included water.[27] South Africa's new plan for providing water was to accept foreign bids to run municipal water supplies and to operate on the World Bank's "cost recovery" model, meaning the public had to pay the full cost for water and sanitation infrastructure. Under this system, the infrastructure would be paid for not with beer but with higher monthly fees. In turn, rental payments in townships would see a dramatic increase.[28]

Biwater received the first contract for Nelspruit's water in 1999. Then Johannesburg went to Suez in 2000. One of the reasons Suez was able to acquire this contract was that it had the most experience in the country. During apartheid, Suez's subsidiary Degrémont had fulfilled more than two hundred contracts for water services or technology in white-only areas.[29] As expected, when Suez began running Johannesburg Water Company the first price hike was 55 percent. Price hikes were higher in the townships due to the impetus to attract industry downtown with bulk water rates. In 2003–4, for instance, poor communities faced a 30 percent rate increase versus a 10 percent increase for industry.[30]

Another problem with the "full cost recovery" model for Johannesburg was that residents were expected to pay back loans for the expensive World Bank–funded Lesotho Highlands Water Project, which supplied the city with water. Lesotho, a tiny water-rich country in the middle of water-stressed South Africa, had long ago been targeted for its water wealth. In 1986, the Bank funded a series of dams in Lesotho for the benefit of South Africa's apartheid government, even though U.N. sanctions were in place against South Africa. The Bank evaded these sanctions by claiming the project was not for South Africa but for the "development" of Lesotho, which the Bank stated was "virtually untouched by modern economic development" and "basically, a traditional subsistence peasant society." According to anthropologist James Ferguson, the Bank's description was "truly fantastical." Ferguson writes, "Lesotho was not 'untouched by modern economic development' but radically and completely transformed by it, and this not in 1966 or 1976 but in 1910."[31] By 1986, more than half the male population of Lesotho worked in mining and agriculture in South Africa. In reality, the Lesotho water project has had the inverse effect of further impoverishing the people of the country rather than "developing" it.

Ferguson rightly points out that the Bank's report should not be taken as "a sign of gross ignorance or incompetent scholarship"; rather, it had a specific agenda that it fulfilled, which was to justify a development project in Lesotho intended to illegally aid the apartheid government.[32] Even today, the Bank denies any involvement in South Africa under apartheid, claiming, "The Bank ceased lending operations to South Africa in 1966. . . . From the sixties until the dramatic political changes that ended the apartheid era, there were no Bank lending or other activities."[33] Technically, this is correct, since the money for the project was loaned to the Lesotho government. But the project was for South Africa, and South Africa laundered money through a London-based trust fund for loan repayments to the Bank.

The Lesotho Highlands Water Project, one of the world's largest water diversion projects, reroutes the Orange River to Johannesburg and Pretoria through five dams and 125 miles of tunnel, reversing the flow of the river. The dams displaced twenty thousand people who were strongly antiapartheid, though corrupt Lesotho officials were happy to cash in on the project. When the people of Lesotho fought against the project, the South African army took over the country, killing dozens of people, including seventeen who were protesting at the Katse Dam.[34] To this day, the plight of the displaced people from Lesotho remains unresolved and persistent child malnourishment is a problem. Lesotho resident Khethisa Leteka said, "The thing that bothers me most is hunger. It is the first thing I want to talk about. Indeed if we could be rescued from hunger by being given a small compensation, we would be very grateful."[35] The Bank admits that one-quarter to one-half Lesotho's population is "ultra poor," but the Bank's "poverty reduction strategy" still emphasizes "reforms to boost private investment and exports." It also recommends setting up a "Privatization Unit" to "improve the management and efficiency of public utilities."[36]

In Johannesburg, expenses associated with the $8 billion apartheid-era Lesotho Highlands Water Project had to be covered by the provincial government, necessitating higher water bills. Besides this expense, Suez's contract specifically required the city government to make a plan to deal with the expense of unpaid apartheid-era water bills. During apartheid, township residents had resisted apartheid through organized "rent boy-cotts" in which they refused to pay for housing, water, and electricity. One of the reasons for these boycotts, in addition to the residents' not wanting to support the apartheid government, was to protest the inadequate ser-vices supplied to townships. In retaliation for these apartheid-era boy-cotts, city councils would turn off the water and/or electricity to whole neighborhoods. In one instance, water was cut off to a township of fifty thousand in retaliation for protests against rising housing and water rates. Councils also responded to other antiapartheid organizing efforts with water cutoffs. In 1990, proapartheid city councils cut off water in dozens of townships in retaliation for attempts to repeal the law that kept public places segregated. The government's assault was called Operation Switch-Off, and politically active townships were specifically targeted.[37] As these examples show, water was repeatedly used as a weapon to force people to stop fighting apartheid.

Postapartheid, boycotts were suspended as people waited, hopeful that their apartheid-era debts would be erased. In 1995, Mandela ex-plained, "Non-payment of services had been aimed at fighting apartheid, but this was no longer necessary."[38] But the question remained as to what would be done with the arrears. In 1991, black townships owed more than $400 million to provincial administrations and utilities.[39] Ultimately, the IMF settled this question.

Gradually, it became clear that apartheid-era debts would not be for-given due to the agreement reached between Mandela and the IMF "be-hind closed doors." The new South African government would still owe foreign banks—mainly in Switzerland, France, and the United States—for money borrowed under apartheid, which meant that it would be difficult to forgive individual debts. In 2000, Suez thereby inherited the apartheid role of debt collector. Poor people were presented with bills of hundreds or even thousands of dollars, and again they either refused to pay or simply could not pay. The boundary between these two reasons for nonpayment remains slippery, as it was under apartheid. The fact is that many people could not even afford to have their water turned on due to a $7 connection fee. Township resident Solomon Mahlangu said, "If they want us to start paying, then they must scratch our arrears and let us start from the beginning."[40]

As more people became delinquent on their payments, the World Bank recommended that the city of Johannesburg advertise a "credible threat of cutting service."[41] Suez went further and simply shut off the taps without warning. In the first four months of 2002, more than ninety thousand households had their water or electricity turned off. City Councilman Mike Moriarty defended this action: "Council has to be ruthless and unforgiving against people who don't pay their bills."[42] In 2003, South Africa's Human Services Research Council estimated that up to ten million South Africans had had their water cut off since the end of apartheid due to "cost recovery policies." In Johannesburg, Suez advertised that it had installed millions of new connections while neglecting to mention that even more had been cut off, leading to an overall decline in the number of people served.[43]

Because township water bills remained folded into monthly housing payments, the city of Johannesburg then decided to evict residents who would not pay. To this end, the city contracted with the dreaded Red Ants, a private security force in red overalls known for swarming a neighborhood and violently removing residents. By 2007, more than two million people had been evicted from their homes as part of an effort to recover debt, including arrears from antiapartheid boycotts. Ironically, the residents of some townships even fought *against* having water connections installed in order to avoid losing their homes. It is important to note that this was not a strategy that occurred only in Johannesburg or was only thanks to Suez. In Cape Town, Richard Pithouse of the Centre for Civil Society described the same problem: "I've seen with my own eyes in Khayalitsa a woman with 200R (US$20) debt [for water] having her goods removed—she had no electrical goods so they took her bed and clothes—it's completely blindly, fanatically, fundamentalist ideology."[44]

Though Suez was perhaps more brutal and secretive in its methods, even public utilities were resorting to similar tactics due to requirements imposed by the IMF.

Over time, more and more people in South Africa were forced to turn to polluted rivers for drinking water. In 2001, in the Johannesburg township of Alexandra, four people died from cholera and hundreds more were sickened. High-density *E. coli* was also found in the Jukskei River running through the city, which led to panic even in the wealthy suburb of Sandton. Thousands of people from Alexandra were relocated in an attempt to stem the outbreak.[45] In 2008, another cholera outbreak followed, in a city where the disease was believed eradicated in the early 1980s. In the province of KwaZulu-Natal, the situation was even more dire. In the late 1990s, the water board had been pressured to practice "cost recovery" and so made people pay even for access to emergency communal taps. By 2000, thousands of cholera cases began being reported across the region. By the time the outbreak was contained, 120,000 people had been infected and 265 had died.[46]

In Johannesburg, Suez shared responsibility for the pollution of the rivers. Besides maintaining water services, Suez had been contracted to handle wastewater treatment, which was sorely lacking in parts of the city. To save money, Suez had provided residents in informal settlements with "ventilated improved pit latrines," or VIPs. Called "drop and store" systems, VIPs were essentially outhouses. Because they were set up above shallow water tables in porous soils, bacteria leached into the rivers. Besides the VIPs, Suez experimented with a "shallow sewage" system. Unlike the VIPs, this system had plumbing but required little water. Instead, people were expected to use "social capital" to unblock their own sewer pipes by reaching into the pipes at "inspection boxes" and pulling out waste by hand. The system was established in part for residents who could not pay for water to flush their toilets. The shallow sewage system came with a manual from Suez that read:

> Open all inspection chambers. Wear gloves. Remove all solids and waste from the inspection chambers. Do a mirror test for each chamber-to-chamber section. If waste material is found in a section, bring in the tube from the upstream inspection chamber until it comes into contact with the obstruction. . . . Wear gloves and remove waste material by hand.[47]

If this maintenance regime sounds less than palatable, Suez explained: "The population must take responsibility for these services to guarantee their operative sustainability . . . and to limit operating costs."[48] In short, removing feces from the toilet by hand was the only way to both keep the toilet working and keep costs down for Suez. Rather than constantly clean these toilets, some people let the inspection sites overflow and drain into the rivers.

Finally, when it became clear that a "culture of nonpayment" had set in, Suez began to introduce prepaid meters to people's homes. Called "self-disconnection systems," these meters required tokens to turn on the water. In Britain, similar meters had been declared illegal during the 1990s because health hazards were created when toilets could not be flushed. But Suez marketed the meters as environmentally friendly, naming the project to roll them out Operation Gcin'amanzi, or Operation Conserve Water. If people refused to allow the company to install the meters, their water was simply shut off. In Johannesburg, the city's website bragged, "With the amount of water already saved by Operation Gcin'amanzi, the project upgrading the water infrastructure in Soweto, the City could have filled almost 21,000 Olympic swimming pools."[49] The metaphor of filling swimming pools, which no one in Soweto would dream of owning, was not lost on residents. It hearkened back to the days when water to fill white swimming pools took priority over drinking water for black Africans. The new meters also kept homeowners from putting out fires in informal settlements where firefighting services did not reach. If owners did not have sufficient tokens, they had to watch their houses burn. Women, children, and individuals living with HIV/AIDS were more likely than able-bodied men to be at home when such fires broke out.

The general decline in water equity postapartheid could have been predicted given the external factors the country faced when it reentered the world economy. South Africa had had strong union leadership during apartheid, but South Africa's Congress of South African Trade Unions (COSATU) could not stop the postapartheid restructuring of the economy by the IMF and World Bank. Nor would demands for economic equity be heard, since the world seemed to mistake racial economic equity for communism. For instance, the 1986 U.S. Anti-Apartheid Act, which imposed sanctions on South Africa, also required the U.S. president to report to Congress about "the extent to which communists have infiltrated" antiapartheid politics.[50] As with many decolonization battles around the world, the United States interpreted a nationalist, prodemocracy battle against racism as a potential threat to its interests. Perhaps the relative isolation of South Africa during apartheid actually strengthened the solidarity of COSATU. When it was exposed to the pressures of a global economy hostile to unions and state management, even the apartheid government seemed easier to fight.

If the desire for desegregation and economic equity had not been mistaken for communism, perhaps South Africa would not be in the mess it is today. Instead, global economic orthodoxy made it impossible for the nation to escape apartheid-era racial inequality. Today, South Africa has the highest GDP of any African country, and mining is its main source of wealth. Yet a quarter of South Africans live on less than $1.25 per day, and unemployment is between 25 and 40 percent. It surpasses Brazil as one of the most unequal societies in the world. South Africa followed the IMF's cookie-cutter agenda of trade liberalization and cutting government spending—and the situation deteriorated to the point that the country's government began talking about default.[51]

"We'll Die Taking It"

Postapartheid water policy fell under the spell of global economic orthodoxy for various reasons, not the least of which was paranoia concerning communism. In part, global fears that the apartheid regime had been a bulwark against communism in Africa created a backlash against equity policies. As the apartheid regime departed, global economic institutions wanted guarantees that communist ideas would not gain a foothold in South Africa. In turn, it makes sense that the antiapartheid movement would shift into an antiprivatization movement, as participants sensed the similarities between global economic institutions and apartheid. In the case of water, the fight began early.

In 1999, Johannesburg councilman Trevor Ngwane fought against bringing in Suez to take over the city's water supply. For this, he was thrown out of the African National Congress. Ngwane then launched Operation Vulamanzi (Water for All), which encouraged people to pull out or bypass their prepaid water meters. Richard "Bricks" Mokolo from the Orange Farm township said, "Destroy the meters and enjoy the water.

The government promised us that water is a basic right. But now they are telling us our rights are for sale."[52] Other organizations quickly emerged with the same goal, like the Anti-Privatization Forum, which promoted the decommodification of all basic human needs, and the Concerned Citizens Forum in Durban, which trained "struggle plumbers" to reconnect water lines.[53]

At a 2005 protest in Durban, an angry township resident yelled, "At the end of the month, they come to cut off. They come with guns. But we have a right to life, and that's a right the government promised us and that's the right we're going to take. We'll die taking it. We'll die taking it."[54] Another woman wore a toilet seat around her neck to protest against inadequate sanitation. In apartheid days, South African police would arrest protesters and Intelligence Services would threaten and investigate them. Today, Intelligence Services is still involved in water politics. In Johannesburg, it placed newspaper advertisements that read: "It is a criminal offense to connect to a public supply without the Municipality's permission since this could harm other water users. . . . If you interfere with the restrictor system you can face a total cut-off because you may harm other people in the community."[55] Antiapartheid activists were once banned from attending political meetings. Today, antiprivatization activists are banned from participating in meetings against water privatization that support illegal reconnections. Trevor Ngwane complained, "When we fought for our rights under apartheid they imprisoned us. Now, when we fight for our rights, they still imprison us. . . . What has changed?"[56]

In 2004, the antiprivatization groups filed a class-action suit against the city of Johannesburg and Johannesburg Water (Suez), alleging discrimination in the installation of prepaid water meters. The plaintiffs alleged: "People in the wealthier, mostly white areas of Johannesburg don't have such meters. They obtain water on credit and can use as much as they like beyond the free allotment, and they don't have to pay until the end of the month or bill cycle. Moreover, there are many procedural protections prior to disconnection for failure to pay water bills, including months of warning letters."[57] Although the case won in the South Gauteng High Court and water meters stopped being installed temporarily, the Constitutional Court overturned that decision in 2009. The court claimed, "The right of access to sufficient water does not require the state to provide upon demand every person with sufficient water."[58]

Despite this legal setback, a small victory was won during the lawsuit. Due to lawsuits, protests, property destruction, and nonpayment, Suez was forced out of Johannesburg in 2006. (The company's contract was up for renewal and was instead canceled.) Ironically, Suez continues to describe its experience in Johannesburg as a success, claiming it was only hired to make sure "Johannesburg Water was sufficiently equipped to 'walk with its own feet'" in terms of billing and collecting arrears. Today, Johannesburg Water continues to maintain the policy of prepaid meters and full cost recovery inherited from Suez.[59] Suez ultimately concluded, "The 5-year management contract has been widely recognised as a success," claiming that it advanced the "social well-being" of Johannesburg. In 2010, Suez bragged, "When Suez signs a contract, our involvement goes far beyond the simple supply of services. . . . [We] make a contribution to the economic and social well-being of the community." When Suez does hint at a problem, it blames apartheid: "The legacy of Apartheid still showed itself in the sense that . . . the current service suffered from a lack of attention due to poor motivation of the personnel affected there, itself fuelled by a tradition of non-payment of utility bills which was a legacy of the years of civil resistance."[60]

In reality, the Johannesburg contract had referenced the very problems that would come to plague Suez. The contract required Suez to provide sufficient water to "maintain social stability among the populace."[61] In colonial countries, it was not uncommon for the government to state explicitly that food and water should be supplied in sufficient quantities to avoid social unrest. But this was unusual in a postcolonial context, where independence usually increased expectations for social welfare beyond minimal sustenance to guarantee order. Even in this limited sense, Suez failed to meet its obligations by cutting off people's water, then shifted the blame to apartheid. In suggesting that people had a "tradition" of nonpayment, Suez also deflected attention from the fact that people could not afford to pay their bills. In stating that personnel were "poorly motivated" while they "instilled new corporate values," Suez repeated the tired adage of the superior colonizer teaching the values of the work ethic. Postapartheid water politics sounded suspiciously like apartheid water politics—minus the words *black* and *white*.

Despite the Suez ouster, Johannesburg Water continues to be run on a corporate model, and strikes and riots continue in the country. But

South Africa is also exploring its options, as evidenced by its role in the new BRICS (Brazil, Russia, China, and South Africa) bank, the goal of which is to provide an alternative source of funding its members, without conditionalities like "austerity." Also, the Youth Party is now pushing to nationalize the mines, an idea that Nelson Mandela once promoted but later dropped. This does not have to mean the expropriation of mining corporations; rather, it could merely mean higher taxes so that the government would share in the profits. (Nigeria already does this with its oil, earning 50 percent of all profits.) There also does not have to be an across-the-board tax on foreign corporations, which could create capital flight; it could be a tax only on the mining industry. Since diamonds are located within national borders, it is impossible for De Beers to relocate these operations. If it did choose to leave, South Africa could take over the industry with a BRICS loan and implement the Reconstruction and Development Program, thus achieving "water security for all." It could also create an ecological plan for cleaning up its waterways and restoring health to a landscape decimated by mining wastes.

Clearly, investing in clean water for the people of South Africa still means having to "outwit" international financial institutions. According to presenters at a workshop on African water laws in Gauteng in 2005, "Whilst South Africa's new approach to WRM [water resource management] is considered progressive in terms of international trends and practices . . . incorporation of traditional systems of governance including the customary practices and laws have been largely overlooked."[62] Yet customary practices remain dominant in South African life, as a recent study in the Kat River Valley on the Eastern Cape revealed. Anthropologist Helen Fox discovered that "92% of the 44 respondents interviewed revealed that they are still practising traditional rituals which are linked to water."[63] Fox asked what would happen if certain sacred pools were destroyed and noted that replies fell into three main categories: (1) "It meant that the ancestors would be homeless." (2) "We could be mentally ill. People could be mad." (3) "It means that our culture is dead."[64]

South Africa is said to be full of river spirits, which are drawn only to certain kinds of rivers, "living rivers." In these rivers, *amagqirha* (diviners) have a baptism-like experience where they are able to see under the water and understand its health. South African diviners, usually women, are called to this role and receive intensive training through an apprenticeship program. Sacred waters are said to be full of mermaids, snakes, and spirits and cannot be approached without great care. Dam construction is believed to have upset the water spirits and caused aridity in the land. In northern South Africa, the waters of Lake Fundudzi are considered so sacred that outsiders must get permission to visit the lake and turn their backs to view the lake through their legs. Lake Fundudzi is believed to be the water that covered the earth before creation, but today the water flowing into Fundudzi is becoming polluted by sewage from the shantytowns on the edges of Johannesburg. According to anthropologist Penny S. Bernard, "[There is a] need to recognize the importance of in-digenous beliefs and practices in issues of riverine management. The re-pository of much of this knowledge comes from indigenous healers, who are regarded as the custodians of very ancient traditional wisdom and knowledge."[65]

Understanding the traditional practices surrounding water can help South Africa to preserve and manage water more effectively. Trevor Ngwane has said that what South Africa needs is "ecosocialism" compati-ble with traditional beliefs.[66] Ecosocialism is an international movement, based loosely on the ideas of Joel Kovel and John Bellamy Foster, that fosters a "green" version of socialism. Kovel writes, "Our obligation . . . is to find a way of society whose productive logic does not impose accumu-lation on the world."[67] Critical of the ecological damage done by capital-ism's demands for constant growth, proponents of the movement also ac-knowledge the damage done by communist societies to their ecosystems. Regardless of the means used to get there, South Africa's ecosocialists are uniquely poised with a group of well-educated antiapartheid organizers ready to take on what they call global economic apartheid.

Life in a Shantytown

East of Cape Town, Imizamo Yethu was built on empty land in an ex-clusive part of the coastal region that is arguably one of the most beau-tiful places in South Africa.[68] The rare and extremely biodiverse fynbos shrubland covers mountains sloping down to the sea, looking like blan-kets of bright green dotted with surprisingly exotic and colorful flowers. The region is a study in failure and contrasts. When Imizamo Yethu began to emerge spontaneously in the 1990s, the all-white Hout Bay neighbors hotly protested the "land invasion."[69] This is understandable when you see the thousands of tin-and-plywood shacks built up the side of a gorgeous, previously pristine green mountain. What was once "the view" for these wealthy residents had now become quite the opposite. Imizamo Yethu houses are built almost on top of each other and look like they may slide down the hill in the next heavy rain. Sewage runs between houses in rivers out to the sea. People started moving there when apartheid was ending, squatting in any open spaces they could find. Twenty years later, they are still there. Across the valley within walking distance are some of the most expensive mansions in all of South Africa.

In 2007, I visited Imizamo Yethu and met Mavis Tozama Ndoni, who said she had moved there with her children ten years before from Port Elizabeth, five hundred miles away. A few years afterward, her niece Ethel had also moved out to live with her and worked at a restaurant in Hout Bay. Near their house, a single shop advertised "Beads, sewing, and clothes repair" and sold vegetables. Mavis and Ethel both had loud laughs and friendly smiles and were proud that only five people lived in their two-room residence, compared to the ten people who lived in the attached house next door. "Too many people in the house next door," Ethel complained, but then laughed at her own relative good fortune.[70] Inside, newspapers covered the floor where the roof was leaking; about a third of the floor was covered in wet, crumpled paper. Ethel said there were plans to relocate all the residents eventually, but no one had told them when. She explained, "The city says we must clear out but don't say when or where we will go." Within these claustrophobic living conditions, the rates of rape and other crimes are particularly high. Tuberculosis is epidemic. Nevertheless, the main concern of the Ndoni family was that they would have to leave. Though they bragged about being better off than their neighbors, their smiles belied a tragic reality.

When I asked about the water supply, Ethel took me up the hill to a public tap next to four outhouses. "Most people get water here," she explained. "We have to carry it home in buckets."[71] Ethel was happy that her house was close to the public tap, an enviable position. Ethel and Mavis had even somehow illegally routed what looked like a garden hose from the public tap to their front yard. "People have to ask *us* for water," Ethel proudly stated, which clearly gave them power in the neighborhood. Then

Imizamo Yethu, one of Cape Town's poorest informal settlements, is in its most beautiful waterfront valley. Residents have waited more than a decade for the better homes promised to them.

she pointed at the toilets. "These are for all of us," she said simply. I had heard that about twenty thousand people lived in this settlement, though the number is constantly changing as more people move in. I could not imagine there were only four toilets. "Who are the toilets for?" I asked her again, and she replied that they were for "everyone here," sweeping her hand to indicate shacks as far as we could see.

In Imizamo Yethu, people have resorted to the "bucket system," throwing their waste into storm drains, the street, or bushes at night. There is also a problem with residents cutting through the chain-link fence at the reservoir and using it for both drinking water and toilet use, which affects the drinking water at Hout Bay. Still, Imizamo Yethu resident Priscilla Moloke said, "This is probably the only place in the world where I can literally sit with my feet in human shit and my back against my 2,000 Rand [$190] shack and look up to the mountains and across the valley on to a three million Rand [$380,000] house and think: I live in a lovely place."[72] Due to these unsanitary conditions, the river running through Imizamo Yethu has the highest *E. coli* load of all the rivers in South Africa.[73]

At a rally in Imizamo Yethu, union leader Tony Ehrenreich said he supported the land invasion. "It's time for people to take land from the wealthy and re-distribute it to the poor," he shouted to a cheering crowd. In response, the head of the Hout Bay homeowners' association called Ehrenreich "a lunatic [who is] breaking the law. This man is inciting race-hatred and inciting people to occupy land illegally." Another person complained that South Africa would "go the way of Zimbabwe" if people kept talking like that, a popular idiom when someone wants to imply the country is falling apart.[74] In many ways, Hout Bay and Imizamo Yethu seem to be a microcosm of a country on the brink as anger escalates on both sides—one side is angry about inadequate housing, water, and electricity; the other about "land invasion." Relations between the two parties in Hout Bay have at points deteriorated so much that the Institute for Justice and Reconciliation has had to be called in to resolve disputes. That said, Priscilla Moloke insists that she will stay: "I'm going nowhere. Here I can walk to the beach and it's a beautiful place. If there are too many of us, ask some whites to leave."[75]

In a graffiti-covered building with metal grates that was Ehrenreich's office in Cape Town, I stopped by to ask him what he thought of the criticism he had received. Ehrenreich at the time was monitoring a large strike in town, but he was still cheerful, smart, and enthusiastic. A tall, middle-aged man with dark hair, he was the only person I had met who seemed hopeful for the country's future, perhaps because he was caught daily in the fray. He replied, "As soon as you criticize anything, as soon as you criticize the inequalities, the obscene wealth. . . . I mean, I'm sure you've seen it. Some of the houses out there are better than any houses in the world. So as soon as you criticize *that,* then of course those people that are acting in defense of their interests will say, 'Yes, it's Zimbabwe.'" He paused for a moment, then whispered conspiratorially, "But I did say we should take their land." And he burst into an infectious laugh.

Tony believed the current riots and protests in South Africa had emerged because promises made when apartheid ended had never been realized, such as housing and water for all. "But why now?" I asked, "It's seventeen years after the fact." He replied seriously, "You know, there's a honeymoon period when people are hopeful and optimistic. But people, in a real sense, start to see and feel the problems, so there are a lot more uprisings now, a lot more demonstrations. People are a lot more radical. . . . Unless you change fundamentally social and economic relations, I think the vote means nothing."

Ehrenreich's statement confirmed my sense that dissatisfaction and frustration were sweeping the country. I had asked everyone I met so far, "Do you think the country is better or worse off since apartheid ended?" I had received a variety of responses, but surprisingly, more people—both black and white—thought the situation was worse. The more racist people claimed that the country was falling apart as evidence that apartheid should not have been ended. It was almost as if they wanted it to fall apart to prove they had been right. The more liberal white people were happy that the evils of apartheid had ended and that now South Africans had more freedom to socialize with people of all colors, but still worried a great deal about the future. On the other hand, black people were happy they did not have to carry passes and could move around freely, but complained that their economic situation had deteriorated. Those few who had been lucky enough to rise in the ranks to the middle classes could not believe their good fortune but saw the enormity of the problem. Ehrenreich put things succinctly when I asked him the same question: "Economic apartheid has just taken its place. We have a vote, but we can't eat that."

Suddenly, Ehrenreich was interrupted with an urgent phone call; people were being arrested somewhere in town. "I have to go," he apologized, "things are getting bad." At that time, what would become the longest public-sector strike in South Africa's postapartheid history had just started; it lasted a full month. It was a bad time to visit, though strikes and protests like this were getting harder to miss. Schools and hospitals shut down. The U.S. embassy advised tourists not to enter the country, since millions of people had walked off their jobs and taken to the streets, with unpredictable results. Students who were angry about exams being canceled blocked the freeway to the airport with burning tires. The antiprivatization groups came out in solidarity with the strikers. "Strike Talks Postponed while SA Burns," the headline in the *Sowetan* read: "The residents were protesting over the lack of service delivery."[76] Police and young people engaged in running battles in the streets, and downtown

Cape Town was all but shut down by marchers chanting slogans. Hospitals were blockaded, and a doctor told me that protestors were smashing hospital equipment even during operations. Stories like this abound in the country, sometimes true and sometimes nothing more than paranoid exaggeration.

Ultimately, the strike was pivotal in ending the presidency of Thabo Mbeki, who submitted his resignation in 2008. But South Africa continues to be overwhelmed by community protests that are often indistinguishable from riots. In 2012, protests erupted in a Pretoria township after the people there had gone without clean or reliable water for two months. "No water comes out when the taps are opened," a resident complained. In 2013, the South African Human Rights Commission announced that it had received 144 complaints about human rights violations relating to lack of water in the past year. On March 3, 2013, thirty-four-year-old David Makele died of thirst and exhaustion while walking to a neighboring village to find clean water for himself and his neighbors, who had gone without water for days. His death occurred on the eve of National Water Week. A writer for the *Daily Maverick* described the growing atmosphere of discontent stemming from water unavailability:

> After being deprived of their basic human right—access to water—
> communities erupt into rage. And as the mismanagement of this
> country's water resources intensifies and more communities face life
> with an uncertain water supply, or water that's not fit for consump-
> tion, this country increasingly begins to look like a dry tinderbox
> waiting for a match.[77]

Nelson Mandela's dream of "free water for all" to heal the community instead has become a nightmare of burning cities, or "rings of fire."

After leaving Ehrenreich's office, I headed over to Langa township to see the prepaid water meters. Andile Nzuzo described the township's meter system to me:

> We now have prepaid electricity. Same for the water. You will find
> in front of the houses a water meter. Each and every house has a
> water meter. . . . Currently, if you are using a water meter, you get
> six thousand liters of water free and then you pay for what is extra,
> which is why you always hear people in townships say, "Save water,
> drink beer."

Indeed, the conversion of worker housing into bars in the township seemed to support this philosophy. Beer was said to be cheaper than water because the industry received the cheapest water rates. Inside one tavern, six men sat around drinking beer; five of them said they lived there—these workers' rooms were still in the process of being converted to a tavern. Inside a bedroom, next to the prepaid electricity meter, was a single-size bed where apparently a whole family lived, based on the laundry hanging around the bed. Two other men shared the closet-sized room; both were planning to move, but they did not know where they would go. The entire dormitory shared one water source; a single faucet, which was used for cooking, bathing, and washing. Outside, Nzuzo showed me a prepaid water meter.

Apartheid was once built into the very landscape of South Africa, and unfortunately that division of the land and water was never undone, but instead perpetuated under the directives of the World Bank and IMF. Yet just as Suez now describes its experience in South Africa as a success

An old workers' hostel in Langa, Cape Town, now converted into a bar. The only public sitting area in this apartment building is at the bar.

story, so does the World Bank. A 2007 World Bank report claimed: "Apartheid had created an economy which was highly isolated, protected, regulated and distorted. . . . At the time, few observers would have predicted that more than a decade later, the country's economy would be in the excellent shape it is in today." Claiming the country had more than a decade of "sound macroeconomic policy" behind it, the Bank praised privatization as a success.[78] Ignoring that South Africa has one of the highest income-inequity ratios in the world, the Bank seemed to suggest that apartheid was bad only because it was overregulated, while economic deregulation had solved the country's problems.

Meanwhile, Trevor Ngwane decided to submit to ejection from the ANC rather than give in to water privatization and the IMF orthodoxy. He still advocates the ecosocialist movement, which calls for "revitaliz[ing] ecologically sustainable traditions and giv[ing] voice to those whom the capitalist system cannot hear," as stated in the Ecosocialist Declaration. In 2007, an elected committee prepared this declaration, which was endorsed by representatives from thirty-five countries. It argues for greater social planning and an expansion of the public sphere in order to "avoid global warming and other dangers threatening human and ecological survival." Today, 84 percent of South Africa's rivers are threatened or endangered, literally strangled by toxic algae blooms and polluted with acid mining waste. And Trevor Ngwame, who once said that one million jobs were lost due to IMF requirements imposed on South Africa, is now an organizer for the One Million Climate Jobs campaign in South Africa, which seeks to create employment by promoting alternative energy sources and industry.

What is encouraging for South Africa are the sheer numbers of people involved in wide-ranging social and union movements, like Trevor Ngwane and Tony Ehrenreich, as well as the numbers of diviners and healers who still thrive in the country. Also, many people still refer to the constitution, which they know gives them "the right to access water," and they are again invoking the principles of the Reconstruction and Development Program.[79] What is particularly salient in the case of South Africa is that, because the country's economic inequities are really racial inequities, fundamental weaknesses in the supposedly abstract values of the IMF are laid bare. The IMF has in reality allowed, even encouraged, a racist distribution of wealth to continue. This gives South Africans moral weight in confronting this institution and allows the government greater leeway in demanding IMF reform. Exposing this racism is a crucial step in stopping further abuses. In the meantime, life for many in South Africa is still precarious. In 2010, I heard that a flood had hit Mavis and Ethel's house in Imizamo Yethu, caving in the walls of their precious home. I do not know if they survived.

FOUR

Mother Ganga Is Not for Sale

HIGH IN THE INDIAN HIMALAYAS, a battle played out between a seventy-nine-year-old man and the company that was going to flood his hometown, Tehri. A wiry, tall man at six feet, six inches, with a white beard and sparkling blue eyes, Sunderlal Bahuguna once fought against the British, inspired by Gandhi at age thirteen. But in the 1990s, his battle was against a dam and aqueduct that would divert the water of the Ganges River 121 miles south to Delhi, where it would end up in a treatment plant run by Suez. Bahuguna sat at the dam site and protested for years, once fasting for seventy-four days in a hand-built tin shack where he lived. Every morning, he would go down to the Bhagirathi River to pray and bathe, and thousands of supporters would come to visit him in the afternoon. But after ten years of struggle, Bahuguna lost the fight. In 2004, when the Tehri reservoir began to fill, Sunderlal and his wife, Vimla, refused to leave their ancestral home. Instead, they sat in their house waiting for the floodwaters to overtake them. Eventually, the police forced them out, and Sunderlal watched his hometown flood as he floated over it in a boat. Today, Sunderlal and Vimla still live on the edge of the reservoir, refusing to move to a resettlement camp as the other residents have done. They remain as witnesses to what has been lost.

A family cremates a loved one on the Ganges River, which is said to provide the "nectar of immortality" and transport the deceased to the next world.

Ecologist Vandana Shiva has described the immensity of the loss of a naturally flowing Ganges for Indians: "The tragedy of it is not just that the deep sacred waters will stop flowing, but that it's being done for the most base crude greed of one of the world's biggest water companies. With the life of the Ganges, what is threatened is the belief of a billion Indians."[1] Hindus believe that in order to reach the next life, a person has to be cremated on the banks of the Ganges, and holy pilgrimage sites line the river's banks. Approaching the Ganges from any direction, one can see pilgrims walking barefoot for miles, carrying Ganges water in elaborate shrines back to their hometowns. Shutting off the flow of the Ganges is like shutting off access to the afterlife, and instead diverting life to Suez.

On a map, the numerous tributaries of the watershed of the Ganges resemble the complexity and shape of the bottom half of a human brain. The rivers are like small blood vessels that lead to one main channel or artery where the Alaknanda and Bhagirathi Rivers meet and run down the neck. In Hindu tradition, the Himalayas are the head of the god Shiva;

the forests are his hair. The Bhagirathi tributary is named for a man who prayed to the goddess Ganges until, legend has it, he brought her down to earth in the form of a river. But when Ganges came to earth, the force the river created was so great that it would have killed everyone—if it had not been tamed by Shiva's hair. To many Hindus, this means that forests and water belong together and must remain together, or the world will be destroyed. The forests split the river into several holy channels, slowing its full force; the Bahugunas live along one of these, the Bhagirathi River.

I knew that in order to understand the mass protest movement that had been spawned by the diversion of the Ganges River, I would have to find the Bahugunas, following in the footsteps of thousands of pilgrims up the Ganges. In the end, I found that the story of Sunderlal Bahuguna offers a clear example of two conflicting languages vying to define water. One is the language of privatization and the state, which have become cojoined in an effort to push "modernization" and alignment with "the global market." The other is the spiritual and practical language of people who live close to water, which is excluded from both the secular state and the corporate boardroom. Sunderlal and Vimla stand as representatives of the latter.

Finding Bahuguna

Finding Sunderlal Bahuguna was not easy, mainly because a heavy monsoon had caused floods and landslides throughout the Himalayas that summer of 2008. Hukam Chand was my guide up the mountains, and his actions were to become near heroic in getting me to the Bahugunas. Hukam was a gentle, slender man in his late forties, with a quiet tolerance far beyond mine. Forced to work in Delhi in order to earn money for his family in the mountains, he rarely saw them. "Twice a year," he said, then laughed, "if I'm lucky." Sadly, this is the situation for many Himalayan villagers who have lost their farms or livelihoods as the countryside has been depopulated. In the past few years, more than one hundred women have committed suicide in the Tehri region because their husbands left and they had trouble surviving on their own. Hukam had mixed feelings when he discovered we would pass by his village on the road up the river. He clearly wanted to see his wife and children, but he nevertheless refused to stop, explaining that we must head up the mountains while the sun was shining. "We may not make it otherwise," he explained. "Monsoon seasons are dangerous."

To make matters worse, I had insisted on traveling up the Alaknanda River, which scientists say is the true source of the Ganges, rather than the Bhagirathi, before backtracking to Bahuguna's town. It would be a long journey. "We could get stuck there for weeks," Hukam explained, unimpressed with my plan. Indeed, despite the fair weather, one landslide after another blocked the tiny dirt road that clung to the side of a cliff. There are no guardrails in the Himalayas, and I had heard that at least one bus plunged over the edge of this road every year, which made me nervous. At each landslide, people dutifully hopped from their cars to begin to clear the rocks, gradually building new roads around boulders that were too big to move. One landslide barely missed us; the ground was still billowing with dust and falling rocks when we hit the brakes.

Finally, we reached the town of Joshimath, a famous pilgrimage site full of temples, along the raging Alaknanda River. In a temple that was twelve hundred years old, a small black stone statue of the god Vishnu stood; its wrist was said to be growing thinner by the year as it oxidized or was touched. According to legend, when the wrist breaks, the mountains will crumble and block the river, shutting down one of the two major tributaries of the Ganges. (Tehri Dam already blocks the other.) The wrist was already nearing its breaking point, and people tentatively waited for the outcome.[2]

Joshimath is also near the birthplace of the Chipko movement, a popular uprising against corporate deforestation. After a large flood in 1970, villagers began to see a direct link between clear-cutting and landslides and decided to "hug" the trees (the meaning of *chipko*) to stop further cutting. Local activist Chandi Prasad Bhatt said, "Folk sense was the only body that surveyed the grim scene and drew conclusions. The causal relationship between increasing erosivity and flooding on the one hand, and mass scale felling of trees on the other, was recognized."[3] In Reni, two miles from Joshimath, women ran to protect the trees after the Indian government tricked the village men into leaving town to collect compensation checks in another city. Hugging the trees and refusing to budge, the women ultimately drove the contractors away. According to leader Gaura Devi, "It was not a question of planned organization of the women for the movement, rather it happened spontaneously. Our men were out of the village so we had to come forward and protect the trees. We don't have a quarrel with anybody but only wanted to make the people understand that our existence is tied to the forests."[4] The Chipko movement spread throughout the region and successfully stopped logging for more than a decade.

Beyond Joshimath, pilgrims can walk either to Badrinath Temple, known as Vishnu's abode, or to the Valley of Flowers, where God is said to have showered flowers from heaven that still grow there. Taking the less traveled route, I headed up the Alaknanda River to the Pushpawati River in the Valley of Flowers. *Pushpawati* means "possessing flowers," and flowers can be found floating in the river, including the Himalayan blue poppy, a translucent flower with petals as fragile as butterfly wings. One mountaineer described its petals: "They seemed to shine as though capable of retaining the sunlight and blue skies of two days ago. . . . Its petals seem imbued with an unearthly, ethereal light."[5] Beyond the Pushpawati headwaters is the Tibetan Plateau, which is called the "third pole" because it contains some of the world's largest ice fields and glaciers. This ice feeds the Mekong, Yangtze, and Ganges Rivers, the water supply of two billion people. Glaciologist Lonnie Thompson has called it "Asia's freshwater bank account." It is from this plateau that China plans to start the western route of its $80 billion South–North Water Transfer Project, which will link the rivers of southern China to the shrinking rivers of the north. But water security experts have warned the project could result in "tens of millions of environmental refugees," by diverting India's water supplies, and turn the area into "the world's battleground."[6]

Of course, on this peaceful hike, it was hard to imagine that this place had been called a "global strategic epicenter," the struggle over which could lead to a nuclear war between India and China. With more than six hundred species of alpine flowers, many of them endemic or endangered, the valley is a striking field of flowers that ends at a glacier at eleven thousand feet. It is also a UNESCO biosphere reserve that is home to the rare Himalayan musk deer, Asiatic black bear, snow leopard, brown bear, red fox, and blue sheep, along with the iridescent monal pheasant, whose numbers tend to go into serious decline when dams are built in their habitat.[7] Finally, it is home to the mythical Yeti (aka Abominable Snowman)—which locals insist is real and a British scientist recently claimed may be the descendant of an ancient polar bear. Hairs recovered

from an alleged Yeti matched the DNA of a polar bear from at least forty thousand years ago. Oxford geneticist Bryan Sykes told BBC News, "I
think this bear, which nobody has seen alive, may still be there and may
have quite a lot of polar bear in it. It may be some sort of hybrid and if
its behaviour is different from normal bears, which is what eyewitnesses
report, then I think that may well be the source of the mystery and the
source of the legend."[8]

Today, the glacier feeding the Pushpawati is melting at twice the rate
of other glaciers around the world, as is the ice cap above it, primarily because of its high elevation. Only a week after my visit, a glacier collapsed
on pilgrims hiking the same trail, killing eighteen people. I read in the
news that people had rushed forward to clear the glacial ice by hand just
as they had the landslides. But on the day I was there, my head was filled
with legends of Yeti and the beauty of fantastical flowers. Only reluctantly
did I turn away from the Pushpawati River and headed down the hill to a
more sobering reality.

On the way to Tehri, I began to sense a quiet despair in the towns
and villages. While religious pilgrims happily trampled the land on family vacations, locals were fighting against alcoholism and unemployment.
Sunderlal and Vimla had long campaigned to make the province "dry,"
but liquor stores were still ample and cheap. At one point, Hukam drove
around a man lying in the road. Other cars sped by as well. The man's face
looked blue, his head twisted at an odd angle. "What happened to him?"
I asked, shocked, twisting in my seat to look behind me.

"Maybe he drank too much, maybe he died," Hukam shrugged and
kept going.

Following the descent of the Ganges down to Tehri Dam, I realized
there were parallel universes in this region. There was the majestic natural world in which every nook and cranny seemed filled with a religious
tale—whether Sikh, Hindu, Tibetan Buddhist, or pre-Hindu spiritual beliefs. Then there was the economic landscape of a depressed region that
nevertheless once had been an epicenter in the battle against both the
colonial British and the Indian state. Finally, there was the landscape of
the dams.

Stopping at Tehri Dam, I immediately started taking pictures. Hukam
panicked. "No, we will be arrested!" he exclaimed. Instead, we drove to the
visitor's center, where I was given the "official" tour. The guide described
the process of construction and said that the dam was an engineering

feat, explaining the amount of earth, rocks, and people that had been used. Then there was the obligatory stop at the monument for those who died during dam construction. The official number was twenty-nine people, who had died all at once in a tunnel collapse. "Other than that," the guide said, "just one or two died here and there." Dam tours are the same around the world, which should not be surprising given that dam builders are part of an international fraternity. The phrases used are always "engineering feat" along with "cubic meters of water supplied" and "gigawatts of electricity created"—and always the official memorial for "one or two dead here or there."

Taller than the Hoover Dam, Tehri Dam is literally made out of broken rocks. Scientists have long pointed out that such rock and earthen construction is not safe for a dam this size, particularly in a region that is prone to earthquakes and landslides. The reservoir is forty-seven miles long and captures 50 percent of the waters of the Ganges. According to the International Commission on Large Dams, the dam site is "extremely hazardous."[9] An earthquake could cause the dam to crumble, or one large landslide could cause its waters to overtop the dam. And if the dam collapses, according to Bahuguna, "it will wipe out everyone in the plains below." This includes the ancient pilgrimage city of Rishikesh (population 100,000), which would be underwater within an hour. Next, Haridwar (population 340,000) would be covered in another half hour. Finally, the flood would spread out on the Ganges Plain below, where millions live. Even the World Bank refused to fund the dam due to its structural problems. The Soviet Union stepped in with the necessary funding, and, after the Soviet Union collapsed, the Indian state covered the rest. Now the World Bank contributes to the "rehabilitation" of the region, and to allegedly making the dam safer.

On September 21, 2010, the downstream public panicked when the *Indian Express* reported, "Tehri Dam Overflows, 60 Killed So Far." Due to heavy rains, the reservoir levels were so high that water had to be released to prevent a dam collapse. A dozen villages were evacuated and alerts were sounded in Rishikesh and Haridwar. Though villages were destroyed and people died, collapse of the dam was prevented by these extreme measures.[10] This situation repeated itself in the years that followed, and Tehri Dam now seems regularly to teeter dangerously close to overtopping, a problem further exacerbated by climate change.

After my dam site visit, the last stop on this trip was the Bahugunas' home. But without a phone, computer, access to e-mail, or even a listed address, they were difficult to find. Luckily, a hotel manager in the small town where Sunderlal Bahuguna had a post office box kindly pointed me in the right direction, down a long dirt road above the dam construction site. "Mr. Bahuguna is world famous, you know," he said, smiling and waving as we drove away.

"Yes, I know," I shouted out the window. Bahuguna is indeed in demand. He has regularly presented at U.N. meetings, has conferred with Indian prime ministers, and is friends with the Dalai Lama. In Nairobi, he infamously arrived at a U.N. energy summit with a bundle of firewood on his back. "Here is the energy you are looking for, the fuel you are hunting," he said.[11] In 1987, he was presented with the Right Livelihood Award for his work with the Chipko movement. Following a dirt road along the reservoir, we drove through a settlement where men were crouched on the side of the road crushing rocks with hammers for the dam. Next, we passed government block housing with women outside concrete pink apartments hanging their laundry. Beside the reservoir, tarpaper shacks were scattered under enormous electricity poles. The pink dam houses were only for government employees; the people living in shacks were transient laborers, many from the poorer region of Bihar. Finally, we hit a dead end and were stumped. Hukam asked someone where Bahuguna lived and was directed toward a yellow house perched on the hill. "Behind the school," the man said, "there is a hiking trail. It will take you there."

So I set off alone on a sketchy trail through dense brush. I passed a pig eating trash along the trail, but nothing else. Eventually, I lost sight of the house and realized I was lost. Finally, some friendly women directed me down a smaller side path that led to Bahuguna's house. As I approached, I saw a small woman crouched on the ground potting plants. It was Vimla. Without knowing who I was or why I was there, she immediately stopped her work and invited me inside, smiling. She did not speak English and I did not speak Hindi, so she ran to get Sunderlal while I took in the view from their house. Their wide concrete front porch overlooked the sign of their defeat, the reservoir that flooded their hometown with the Bhagirathi River. In front of the house was a large ugly construction area full of earthmoving equipment and piles of rock.

Then Sunderlal came out dressed in a traditional dhoti with an irrepressible look of mischievous happiness on his face. I could immediately tell why so many people looked up to him. I could not believe my good fortune that I had found them. Sunderlal and Vimla had previously lived in an ashram eighteen miles from Tehri, which was accessible only by foot. But they came back to Tehri, where his father once lived and worked for the forest companies, to fight against the dam, and had recently moved into this house. After the dam was finished, people scattered, moved to resettlement camps in Haridwar or to New Tehri. But they had stayed. Sunderlal once said he had to watch over the Bhagirathi River as he would a sick relative. He could not leave it.

Gandhian Ecology

Sunderlal Bahuguna still follows the teaching of Mahatma Gandhi, who once wrote, "God's air and water . . . should be freely available to all" and should "not be a made a vehicle of traffic for the exploitation of others."[12] Gandhi's vision for India was a nation filled with "self-sufficient village[s]" with their "own waterworks, ensuring clean water supply." Nearly obsessed with water purity, Gandhi would ask about the water supply almost immediately upon entering a village and then give advice on maintaining its cleanliness. He once wrote: "The Ganges water is regarded by us as holy, capable of washing off our sins. The idea is symbolical. Just as water washed the body clean, a devotee prays and hopes for the cleansing of the heart by the water of life. But if we contaminate our holy rivers as we do, how can their water effect inner cleansing?"[13] He believed that clean water could be maintained through adequate sanitation, sufficient forests, the collection of rainwater, and keeping the entire village area clean. But Gandhi's ideas were overridden by those of Prime Minister Jawaharlal Nehru, who infamously declared, "Dams are the temples of modern India." Gandhi believed in "village uplift" and small water reservoirs; Nehru believed in large-scale urbanization and massive dams. Today, Sunderlal Bahuguna continues to fight for the villages.

While Gandhi may have failed in his battle for designing an independent India, his followers have continued in his name—including Mirabehn, J. C. Kumarappa, and Sunderlal Bahuguna. All three have opposed large-scale irrigation projects and chemical fertilizers, projects that formed the basis of India's "Green Revolution." J. C. Kumarappa, a London-trained economist who once worked closely with Nehru, believed in reviving the ancient irrigation system rather than building new dams and canals, as well as conserving forests for water purity. He wrote: "Water supply depends on an efficient forest policy. The Government is overanxious on the revenue production of forests rather than there being a conserving ground for water."[14] Kumarappa wanted to continue Gandhi's tradition of creating small village industries, but Nehru dismissed his ideas as fanciful, calling his All India Village Industries Association the "All India Village Idiots Association." Today, Sunderlal Bahuguna continues to promote the ideas in Kumarappa's book *The Economy of Permanence,* which in turn support and build on Gandhi's ideas.

Inviting me to sit on a blanket on their veranda for tea, Sunderlal and Vimla told me about how the two of them first met. In contrast to her looming husband, Vimla is only four feet, eleven inches tall. She looks dwarfed beside him, though their sense of togetherness is palpable. Their story is touching, as is their body language. After India achieved independence in 1947, Vimla left home to join an ashram rather than marry, as her parents had demanded, primarily because she wanted an education, which was available at the ashram. There, she became a Gandhian-style activist devoted to protecting village livelihood and the Himalayan forests.

Meanwhile, Sunderlal was in Delhi working for Congress, where he was trying to protect the Himalayas through political channels. He met Gandhi at a prayer meeting when he was twenty-one years old. He said that Gandhi listened intently to his stories about the Himalayas and then quietly said to him, "You have brought nonviolence down to earth. You have made the Himalayas higher." According to Sunderlal, this one meeting helped him to carry on for decades. Sadly, their meeting also occurred on the day before Gandhi was assassinated. When I asked what it was like when Gandhi was alive, Bahuguna said simply, "He was a storm." But there was a ferocity and intensity to Bahuguna's voice when he said these words, sudden change in this usually meek, smiling man.

Sunderlal met Vimla during one of her civil disobedience campaigns in the mountains and says he immediately fell in love with her. But she still did not want to get married, despite her parents' protestations, and so she said no when he proposed. "I asked for a year to think about it," she explained. Finally, she told Sunderlal she would marry him if he would quit his job in Congress and get involved in civil disobedience with her

Sunderlal and Vimla
Bahuguna on their
front porch in front of
the "dead water" of the
Ganges River.

in the Himalayas. He has described that experience: "When on the day of
my marriage I announced my decision to renounce party politics, I felt
a sense of peace."[15] Afterward, Sunderlal and Vimla moved to an ashram
eighteen miles from Tehri, where they began working together to protect
the forests from the logging that was sweeping the valley.

And so the Chipko movement began, though people had already
been fighting for the forests for decades. During colonialism, British "forest laws" prohibited villagers from gathering wood or using forest products, claiming the trees belonged to England and were needed for their
railroads and ships. Villagers began nonviolent civil disobedience campaigns in which they collected firewood and helped those who had been
arrested for doing the same. The inspiration for the Chipko movement

came from an incident in which British police surrounded protesters at a meeting on the Yamuna River on May 30, 1930, and opened fire, killing up to two hundred people.[16] Of the early forest lawbreakers, Bahuguna has written: "Though the movement was then suppressed, we got inspiration from them. We established a memorial to those martyrs. In 1969, we repeated a pledge in front of their memorial. This became the background of Chipko."[17]

Sunderlal is usually given credit for leading the movement, but he claims it was actually his wife who started it, saying, "It was on account of her that women mobilized for the Chipko movement." For the women, whose husbands were often away for long periods of time, the forests were their only means of subsistence. Bahuguna explained, "In our area, women are the backbone of our social and economic life; because of soil erosion, the menfolk had to come down (to the plains) for their livelihood and women were left behind. The whole burden of managing the family fell on their shoulders."[18] Though lauded as an ecofeminist movement, Chipko was in reality based in necessity. Women did not start protesting because they suddenly felt empowered, or closer to nature, or more prone to nonviolence than men—all common misperceptions about Chipko. They did it because they needed the forests to survive, not only for fuel but also for the fruits, nuts, and honey the forests provide.

In 1973, while Vimla was working in the Chipko campaign at home, Bahuguna began to walk, claiming he wanted to figure out why people were poor. He did not return for 120 days, and then he left again. He spent several years walking, following Gandhi's model of traveling and talking to villagers. He said, "I tried to find out what were the causes of poverty of these people. It was due to the soil erosion, drying up of water sources and this was due to deforestation."[19] Along the way, he said he learned the "science of the ancestors," which he now claims is the only alternative to the "cruel science" of modernization.

Back at home, women began to feel emboldened by their successes against logging. "Women began to see their powers," Vimla said. "Female shakti (power) is not just for farmwork." Women braved arrest and imprisonment, and once Vimla was jailed alongside her mother and six-year-old son. "The women started to protect [the trees] day and night for 8 years—all based on the strength of community," Vimla once wrote. "Chipko could never have happened without women. . . . they faced jail without fear. They faced the burning of their huts in the forest by the contractors."[20] Finally, in 1981 a fifteen-year ban was placed on the felling of trees above an altitude of three thousand feet.

Scholars have often failed to recognize how intertwined the Chipko and antidam protests actually were. Sunderlal explained this to me: "My first project was to green the area because I knew that water would be one of the biggest problems ahead. So I wanted the forests to be healthy if they took the water away. The trees provide us with food: honey, fruit, and firewood." By 1972, when plans for Tehri Dam were announced, Sunderlal continued to make forest protection a priority, waiting for the moratorium on logging to be declared before shifting focus to the dam. But he always saw the two issues as interconnected.

Like the Chipko movement, the antidam campaign had its precedent in protests against British water policy. In 1842, when the British began building the Upper Ganges Canal to divert water from the Ganges to farmers on the Ganges Plain, the *North American Review* heaped praise on the plan: "The idea of making the great sacred river the source of prosperity and civilization to the people who had so long regarded it with superstitious veneration, of making it pour benignant waters over the fields of those who so long ignorantly worshipped its unused stream, was one that possesses a fine element of poetry."[21] Clearly, capturing the Ganges for profit was equated with "civilization" and eliminating "superstitious" uses of the river. Magistrate Charles Raikes also applauded the British engineers of this project: "The work of conquest has been completed; the work of regeneration must begin. . . . To raise up a degraded race, to cure the plagues of past bad government and bad morals, to prepare—if you may be so blessed—the way for real virtue and true religion—, to this you are called."[22] With typical colonial hubris, the British viewed diverting the Ganges River as a way of destroying local superstitions, instilling Christianity, and generally improving the Indian "race."

A battle in ideologies ensued. The "general feeling among the natives was," according to the *North American Review,* "that the work was one of most unmitigated presumption, and that nothing could be more absurd than to suppose that the mighty Gunga would ever so far forget herself as to forsake her ancient channel and consent to flow in a new one made by sacrilegious hands."[23] In 1914, protesters tried to halt an extension to the project when the British announced a new diversion sluice would divert the entire Ganges River. At first the British ignored the protesters and kept building, but the protests only grew and in fact contributed to the rise of the independence movement. For many Indians, trying to divert the entire river had revealed the ignorance and hubris of the British. It was to be the British Achilles' heel. In 1921, villagers throughout Uttar Pradesh took an oath to withhold the fees demanded by the British for their water systems. According to historian Gyanendra Pandey, "The peasants would no longer . . . pay for the use of irrigation tanks or pasture lands; for water, like air, was a gift of God, and . . . had for long . . . been used in common."[24] In this story, there is much that is reminiscent of the antiprivatization struggles in India today, revealing a link between old colonial power and the new power of the multinational corporation.

After the British left India in 1947, the World Bank continued funding the same colonial projects and extolling the British water engineers. A recent Bank report reads, "With British rule came the systematic and large-scale development of water infrastructure in India . . . [which] emphasized hydraulic works that would 'make the deserts bloom.'" It concludes, "The results were spectacular." The report then claims, somewhat remarkably, that British engineer Arthur Cotton is considered a "saint whose image is revered" in India and concludes with a poem called "Ode to an Engineer" that describes British engineers as "the very symbol of attentive and effective government."[25]

Following independence, the Bank funded the so-called Green Revolution, which introduced new hybrid varieties of wheat and rice that could be planted two or three times a year rather than once a year in the Ganges Plain. Unfortunately, these new varieties also required five to ten times more water, as well as chemical fertilizers and pesticides. When the Upper Ganges Canal ran low, the Bank provided loans to buy pumps for groundwater. Though it initially produced more food, the Green Revolution came at an enormous price to small farmers. In order to buy fertilizers and pesticides, farmers had to accumulate debts, which then made them susceptible to crop price fluctuations. A surplus in rice and wheat led to a price drop. On top of this, overirrigation led to salinization and loss of productive farmland. These were the same problems that had occurred in California. A recent Punjabi University study found "widespread contamination of drinking water with pesticide chemicals and heavy metals, all of which are linked to cancer and other life-threatening ailments."[26] Since there are no water treatment facilities in most rural areas, cancer rates are high.

Rather than a food bonanza, the Green Revolution has created a suicide epidemic. According to a 2010 report in the *Hindu* newspaper, "Almost 200,000 farmers committed suicide between 1997 and 2009—a national tragedy (although it is rarely treated as such) brought on by rising debt and the resulting economic and existential despair."[27] The trend has been for farmers to commit suicide by drinking pesticides, mostly DDT.[28]

Vimla Bahuguna's good friend Vandana Shiva, a physicist turned ecologist, has long been involved in the struggle against the Green Revolution. She met Vimla during the Chipko campaign and later became an important spokesperson against the "privatization" of the Ganges. She has since started a model biodiversity farm and organic restaurant near Tehri. She also runs an organization called Navdanya, or Nine Seeds, in a small third-floor office in New Delhi. The organization is dedicated to creating food security, as well as "finding non-violent means to farming, especially through the protection of biodiversity and small farmers."[29] Through the joint efforts of these two women, one begins to see how deeply the ecologies of water, food, and forests are intertwined, as well as the protest movements supporting all three.

Not only do the Bahugunas want to stop the diversion of the Ganges, they also want to change the way agriculture is done. Sunderlal argues for agroforestry, or what he calls "tree farming." At their house, a man around forty years old climbed up a short fence on the veranda and pulled something from a tree. "This is my son," Sunderlal said. "He is an attorney." He brought berries over, which were shaped like olives, and gave me a few to eat. They were juicy but bland. Then Bahuguna began to tell me about all the trees in the valley, constructing an imaginary landscape. "It used to be full of rhododendron trees, deciduous trees, spruces, and firs," he said. There were also pomegranates, figs, apples, mulberries, walnuts, almonds, and a tasty fruit called *kafal*. "There was everything you could want to eat." Today, he still believes that planting calorie-rich nut trees with a diverse understory is an answer to global food security problems, an idea once promoted by Gandhi.[30] Bahuguna once wrote about this plan: "Trees can give more in less land. If you use one acre of land to grow meat . . . then you will get only 100 kg of beef in a year. If you grow cereals, you'll get 1 to 1.5 tons. Apples you get 7 tons. Walnuts 10–15 tons."[31]

It was hard for me to picture how diverse the forests once were, since the trees all looked the same in the region. Despite the hard work of Chipko, most of the region was deforested both before and after the moratorium. "What about the reforestation that's going on around here?" I asked, having noticed what looked like tree plantations in the valley. Bahuguna replied unhappily, "They are planting the wrong kinds of trees. These kinds of trees did not used to grow here. They are all pines, and they poison the earth so that undergrowth cannot grow here. We used to be able to live off our forests." It turned out they were planting trees just to keep the mountains from sliding into the reservoir.

Old and New Tehri

Sunderlal had turned his attention to trying to save the river only after securing a moratorium on clear-cutting the trees. Then, he began repeated hunger strikes at the dam site, a common protest strategy in India that is also tied to religion. He built a shack that became his home, off and on, for many years. Bahuguna said, "In 1989, I sat in protest in a hut near the dam site. There, I undertook two fasts, for forty-nine days in 1995 and seventy-four days in 1996." I asked him, "Did the police bother you?"

"No, because India is a very religious country," he replied. "They could not disturb someone taking a fast." But he did say someone set his shack on fire once while he was sleeping inside, though they never caught the culprit.

"Did people join you on your fast?"

"Oh yes, hundreds of thousands. They came from New Delhi." In 1978, when the diversion tunnels were constructed, thousands showed up to block construction. Over the years, more people kept coming to protest or to visit with Bahuguna.[32] At Vandana Shiva's office in New Delhi, activist Amit Kumar told me about Shiva's involvement in the fight against Tehri Dam, including protests that went on for seven or eight months and even shut down the city of New Dehli. "But India keeps building more and more dams," he said.

Given Sunderlal's thirty years of fighting against the dam, I could not imagine how he felt when his town flooded. "Did you watch Old Tehri flood?" I asked. He got a stricken look on his face, the way people look when asked about traumatic events. He said, "I took a boat around while it was flooding. I felt bad, very distressed for everything." He clutched his heart to show his pain. "It wasn't just Old Tehri. Twenty-two villages were buried." A city of twenty-five thousand people, Tehri was on the pilgrimage route of the Ganges River and was filled with ancient temples and even a princely palace. In total, the dam displaced more than one hundred thousand people.

Bahuguna continued, "The worst aspect of the displacement is that the memory of how the people were connected is lost. Women especially grieved this loss." He looked to his wife, and we sat for a moment in silence, staring at the denuded hills and ugly, impounded water. The sound of earthmovers digging a road around the dam filled the air. Sunderlal suddenly frowned, "Now they want to build five-star hotels instead." I had seen pictures of Old Tehri, once home of the provincial prince and the capital of the region. Set on a peninsula between two rivers and backed by the stunning Himalayas, it was a beautiful town. Around the town, people grew crops on terraces.

Then Sunderlal said suddenly, "Dead water." He pointed toward the reservoir.

"What do you mean?" I asked.

"The water flows in hill rivers this way," he explained, making a snakelike gesture with his hand. "It is living water. Our ancestors knew this, so they picked these rivers for burying the dead. But the idea of living water is not known to modern man. . . . Building dams is the folly of modern man." This talk of "dead water" gave me a sudden sense of déjà vu. I remembered that the Maori distinguish between dead and living water, and so do black South Africans and Mapuches. It occurred to me then that Bahuguna was right; perhaps only "modern man" is not familiar with this concept.

As I sat with Bahuguna that day, a question kept nagging at me. I finally asked, "Isn't it painful to look at all this?" It was frankly hard for me to understand why he had chosen to stay, forced to look at the top of his old town's clock tower when the reservoir was low. But Sunderlal simply stared at me, not saying a word in reply. His gaze was solid and certain. I quickly felt bad for asking, for my own intrusiveness. Of course it was painful.

So I changed the topic. "What are your memories of Old Tehri?"

Immediately he brightened up, disappearing into his memories: "It was a place where people would meet in the marketplace in the evening. The most enchanting thing about it was that the village was at the confluence of two rivers. It was the center of the whole district, so people came from all over." I asked why he had not moved to a resettlement camp like the other villagers. He said, "I am an old man. I cannot walk. I would not move there." But he also explained that he would not accept the government's compensation money for his family home. "My father was a forest officer in Old Tehri," he explained. "It was his home." So the "dam people" let him stay in this sparse house, squatting above his old city. In terms of publicity, it was clearly better than leaving him in the street, given his international celebrity.

Sunderlal and Vimla stayed to watch the river die, and now they were mourning its death. But they also carried hope even as they sat as witnesses to destruction. They at least had a plan for both restoring the valley and providing more food and water in the face of a stalled Green Revolution. People were turning to them for solutions. As with Sunderlal and Vimla, there has been a resurgence of interest in Kumarappa after the failures of the Green Revolution. For many, it seems that a wrong fork in the road was taken after independence and it is time to try the other path.

Leaving the Bahugunas that day, I decided to head up the hill to New Tehri, where the government had moved the residents of Old Tehri. Sunderlal told me his other son was living there and gave me his phone number. "So I heard New Tehri is a model resettlement community?" I asked, offhandedly, thinking of the billboards I had seen that praised it as such. Throughout the region, New Tehri is described as the "first planned mountain city of independent India," clearly modeled on the British colonial hill stations, which are now popular summer resorts. According to the provincial government, "New Tehri is considered to be Asia's most comprehensive and successful rehabilitation programme. The gleaming township has developed into a lovely hill resort."[33]

Sunderlal laughed out loud. "It is a bad model," he said. "We call 'new' Tehri *naatayi* [bad] Tehri. In our language they say bad Tehri."

In my first view of New Tehri as I headed up the hill, it resembled concrete Soviet-style block apartments spilling down the hillside, painted pink to match the dam housing below. But at the top of the hill, New Tehri looked deserted. A few taxi drivers were smoking at a roundabout in the town center, which had a couple hotels, both closed. The buildings were moldy and flaking paint. Besides the drivers, I could at first find only a bunch of cows milling around, one even inside the enclosed shopping mall. In the center of an abandoned square, a mounted bust commemorated a Tehri activist who had set himself on fire in 2004.

Even Sunderlal's son was missing that day. Though I reached him on his cell phone, he explained that he had to leave town unexpectedly. So instead I found an open tea shop and asked the owners how they liked living there. "Everyone has moved away," Pare Shever said, "we cannot live here." I asked if they had water. He replied, "Water comes every three days, but it is dirty, and we don't drink it." Indeed, the provincial government claims that 60 percent of the region suffers from water scarcity, which is remarkable in a place that holds Delhi's water supply.[34] There also appeared to be no garbage collection, since litter was piled in strange places. Another man, Gambhir Singh Kathait, told me that "30 percent of the population had already left. It is too expensive to live here. There is no land for farming." Sunderlal Bahuguna had described these problems to me earlier: "There is the scarcity of water, and having to walk up hills. It is three kilometers above the lake. The government was supposed to lift water from a small spring to the village, but they did not follow through on this." Since the residents of Tehri no longer had land suitable for farming, and the hotel business was not exactly thriving, they had become dependent on food ration cards for survival; food was brought in from another city.

In New Tehri, the government tried to replicate the drowned city's historic monuments, like the clock tower. Today, these monuments sit as cheap imitations of a once thriving culture, emptied of meaning. Similarly, the city has a lovely view of one of India's largest water bodies, but the people have no way to drink from it. Even if they were to walk miles to the reservoir, its loose-rock sides would be too steep for them to crawl down to get a drink. And the springs in the region, once used as water sources, mysteriously stopped flowing after the reservoir filled.[35] On the PBS program *Now with Bill Moyers,* Vandana Shiva described the impact of relocation on women in particular:

> One hundred thousand people were displaced. And the women
> started to talk about how many women are starting to commit
> suicide. Because they can't walk to the water and the government has

canceled every local water scheme saying, "Now all the money, all the public wealth has gone into these mega-projects." . . . So we have women jumping into the Ganges because now the Ganges instead of being their mother for life has become a graveyard.[36]

Indeed, New Tehri looked like *naatayi* Tehri to me, perched on a deforested hill waiting for the tourists and water that would never arrive. Many had already headed to the cities in search of employment. If Tehri Dam was the "temple" of modern India, one had to wonder what was being worshipped there. Clearly, the postcolonial vision of India's leaders was not one of self-sufficient Gandhian villages but one of expanding urban slums.

Where Tehri Water Goes

Suez's Sonia Vihar water treatment plant, the end point for Tehri reservoir water, is located in the slums of North East Delhi along the banks of the Yamuna River. On one side of Sonia Vihar is a no-man's-land along the river's edge where shantytowns have been bulldozed, allegedly to prevent them from being flooded. On the other side, slums stretch for miles and miles with very little access to water. Like many urban rivers, Delhi's Yamuna River gradually dried up as the city grew to fourteen million people. Today, it is not much more than a sewer, and residents complain there is not even enough water to wash the sewage away. Gradually, wealthier people moved away from the Yamuna River and the poor moved closer. Slums now encroach on the riverbanks all across Delhi in areas prone to flooding. Houses wash away and are rebuilt.

Ancient Delhi was a water-rich city, served by hundreds of water-harvesting dams around its edges and surrounded by hunting reserves and resorts. According to water expert Anupam Mishra, "When the British first came to India, Delhi had almost 800 water sources of its own. Now there are no more than 10, and even those are heavily degraded. Delhi's groundwater is being depleted very fast."[37] Recently, an ancient reservoir in Delhi was rediscovered after having been used as a trash dump for decades. Underneath the trash, a natural spring was found to still be flowing.[38]

India's vast system of small dams and rainwater-harvesting systems supplied the country for thousands of years, maintained through a system of self-repair and taxation. In the fourth century B.C., Kautilya's *Arthashastra* set out elaborate conditions for developing and maintaining water systems, such as requiring that new settlements be built near natural waterways in order to avoid the expense of canals. It set fines for building a dam on someone else's land. It mandated rainwater harvesting and explained how collection systems should be built on houses. Finally, it forbade the privatization of public water supplies, punishing it as a violent act: "If a person . . . puts to mortgage or sale a charitable water-work, continued since old times, the middle fine for violence is to be imposed."[39] Kautilya's management system was practiced between 321 B.C. and 1857 A.D.—more than a millennium.[40] But then the British arrived.

As the British gradually moved into India, they came with their own hydraulic vision for the world. Rather than maintaining the ancient water systems, the British demanded that taxes be paid for their own water development schemes. British engineer Arthur Cotton described Indians' anger at these changes:

> The contempt with which the natives firstly spoke to us on account of this neglect to material improvements was very striking; they used to say we were a kind of civilized savages, wonderfully expert about fighting, but so inferior to their great men, that we would not even keep in repair the works they have constructed, much less imitate them in extending the system.[41]

British engineers wanted large dams, not small ones. After the British moved in, according to Professor Sanjeev Khagram, "more than 200 big dams taller than 15 meters in height had been constructed in India by 1950."[42]

After independence, Prime Minister Nehru continued building dams, viewing them as symbols of modern nationhood. (In contrast, Sunderlal Bahuguna said, "Large dams will stand as monuments to twentieth century stupidity.")[43] Happy to provide funding, the World Bank got involved in dam building in India in the late 1950s. Calling rainwater-harvesting traditions "wishful thinking," the Bank claimed these old systems relied "on a plethora of imaginative and then-effective methods for harvesting rainwater." The implication was that these methods—though "imaginative" and "wishful"—were ineffective for the modern world.[44] Yet one of the best-known examples of rainwater harvesting in the country is still at Gandhi's home, where water is collected on the roof and then diverted to a 24,000-gallon storage tank in the house.[45]

Today, an ever-growing percentage of India's urban population consists of ecological refugees: people pushed off their land by dams, mines, and industrial development. Ongoing studies reported by the Indian parliament secretariat claim that around sixty million people were displaced between 1947 and 2000. At least one study notes, "The reality is four times the number." (Many estimates are unreliable because local governments and the World Bank want to downplay the impact of their projects.) Between twenty-one and fifty-five million have been displaced by dams alone.[46] These figures do not include the tens of millions more that either have been or will be displaced by climate change and crop failures.

These people usually head to the cities looking for employment. In Delhi, according to *The Hindu*, 52 percent of the city dwellers were living in slums in 2009. On the Yamuna River, life is bitter. Residents have installed hand pumps, but the water is not safe to drink.[47] Without local water sources, women will often collect water from the houses where they work as maids. They are used to being called "water beggars" and looked on with disdain. People live on a little more than 7 gallons of water a day per person, with the water brought in from other locations in gallon-size plastic jugs. In contrast, according to a 2010 *Time* magazine article, people in central Delhi receive 132 gallons of water per capita per day.[48] There are no toilet facilities along the river, so people use the river's edge. Because of this, there are regular outbreaks of disease in these slums. And there are no doctors.

Sonia Vihar has 150,000 residents. It is perhaps the worst slum area in the city, filled mainly with migrants from the Indian countryside—primarily from the Ganges watershed region. According to the mayor of East Delhi, Annapurna Mishra, Sonia Vihar has "no drainage facility, no health center, no piped running water" and is "on the verge of a humanitarian crisis." As the new mayor of this area, Mishra complained, "Sonia Vihar water treatment plant is supplying water to a large part of the city but the people of Sonia Vihar where that water treatment plant is actually located do not have access to water from the plant." Instead, she said, "street fights are common over water in this ward." One girl recently died while trying to stop a water tanker; it ran over her.[49] Mishra described the plight of a young man in Sonia Vihar:

> Kumar's eyes brim with tears as he shows a dark brown scar on his left leg. . . . The 19 year old boy is barely able to explain in a choked voice that he has been attacked more than once while trying to fill his bucket with water from a public tap. . . . Public taps at Sonia Vihar being much fewer than needed, people often are ready to kill for drinking water.

Kumar described his living conditions: "This place is a hell." While drinking water is not available, "large stretches of stagnant black-green water breeding mosquito larvae" cover the slum.[50] In 2011, Sonia Vihar had a major jaundice outbreak, most likely caused by hepatitis spread by dirty drinking water.[51]

Approved in 2000, Sonia Vihar treatment plant cost $68 million (50 million euros) to build and promised to supply water to a third of New Delhi. It was also part of a much larger privatization plan for the entire city. In 2001, the city of Delhi applied for a World Bank loan of $150 million for "water sector reforms," hiring PricewaterhouseCoopers (PwC) to write up a plan to hand over Delhi's water management to foreign companies by 2015.[52] But then anticorruption activist Arvind Kejriwal (now chief minister of Delhi) found evidence of bid rigging by the World Bank, which had forced the Delhi Water Board to hire PwC.[53] Discovering a revolving door between PwC and the World Bank, Kejriwal wrote a letter to the Bank complaining about what appeared to be corruption in the Bank procurement process. In response, a Bank representative then referred Kejriwal to the World Bank's Department of Institutional Integrity, stating that he should file a complaint and allow them to do "an independent determination of that case." The Bank gave him a Web link that did not work.[54]

The PwC report recommended that the city be broken up into zones managed by competing water corporations, beginning with a pilot project in South Delhi. It also recommended that the Delhi Water Board begin a "staff rationalization" process, claiming that it was "bottom heavy" with employees. (A report by the Asian Development Bank found that the number of workers per one thousand connections shrank from twenty to two after privatization.)[55] PwC also recommended raising water rates as well as *reducing* the average amount of water supplied to the poor, from fifty liters to forty liters per day. Finally, it recommended eliminating government subsidies for the poor, which PwC called "regressive."[56]

At the same time, both the Bank and the Delhi Water Board (DJB) vigorously denied they were privatizing Delhi's water. The Bank set up a "frequently asked questions" page about the Delhi project on its website, which included the question, "Will this amount to the privatization of DJB?" The Bank answered:

> This is *not* a "privatization" of DJB. Under the proposed scheme all
> the water and sanitation assets will remain in the public domain. . . .
> The Bank is not proposing privatization of any part of DJB nor
> is there is a timetable for any privatization. As a matter of fact, at
> this time, the World Bank would definitely not recommend
> privatization.[57]

Responding to a question about rising water rates, the Bank wrote: "The pace of tariff increase is expected to be gradual, corresponding to improvements in service efficiency and delivery." Finally, the last question was, "Will water reach the poor?" The Bank replied, "The proposed reform specifically covers the poor. . . . The operators will also be obliged to set up a Poverty Outreach Unit in both zones and will be contractually required to improve water supply in poor settlements." In fact, the Bank promised the new service would "provide Delhi's citizens, including the poor in resettlement colonies [and] slums . . . with continuous (24/7) water supply."[58]

Despite the Bank's protestations, public pressure mounted in Delhi against privatization after the contract with Suez was announced. The contract was shrouded in secrecy, as was the citywide privatization plan, which only added to suspicions. Antidam protests turned into antiprivatization protests. In 2002, a group of demonstrators walked from the headwaters of the Ganges to the plains carrying a three-hundred-foot banner of blue cloth representing the river. Along the way, 150,000 people signed the banner. When the last link between the Ganges and Delhi was about to be completed, a rally was launched from an ancient city on the banks of the Ganges, Haridwar. Five thousand farmers, priests, and regular citizens showed up with signs that read, "Ganga Is Not for Sale." The rally was held on August 9, 2002, on the evening of Quit India Day, commemorated as the day the British were asked to leave India. More than a million people signed a petition that was circulated, requesting that the Ganges not be privatized. Then in 2004, thousands of protesters shut down the streets of Delhi when the government announced a tenfold hike in water prices. The protesters tried to storm parliament, and water cannons were used to push them away. Faced with this mounting pressure, as well as corruption problems, the Delhi Water Board withdrew its application for a World Bank loan in 2005.[59] This did not mean, however, that the government ceased following the recommendations of PricewaterhouseCoopers. The head of the Delhi Water Board wrote to a concerned NGO, "There is no move to privatize water in Delhi."[60] By this time, nobody believed him.

Meanwhile, Sonia Vihar was proceeding on schedule, though it was plagued with problems from the start. A 2005 *Times of India* article explained, "This is one jinx that Delhi has been unable to break. Seen as the city's only hope for salvation, Sonia Vihar plant has been running into problems right from the word go."[61] First, a tunnel collapsed at Tehri Dam, killing dozens and delaying the release of water through the Upper Ganges Canal. Since the treatment plant had already been completed, it was forced to sit empty for several months. According to the terms of the Suez contract, the Indian government had to pay Suez around $3,000 per day for every day that the plant did not receive raw water. One of India's national newspapers, *The Hindu*, reported in 2005, "It is a classic case of public money going down the drain with no one being held accountable."[62] (Later, Suez agreed to waive part of this fee.)

In January 2005, water finally reached Sonia Vihar for a short time, but was quickly stopped because of contract disputes with the Tehri regional government. The plant's pipes dried out and began to rust. Politician Vijay Jolly said that the mayor "needs to answer to the people of Delhi why she constructed such a huge plant at public cost when there was no written agreement for raw water with any State. It seems the plant was built to oblige a multinational company and not to benefit the people of Delhi."[63] On May 23, 2006, water was released into the plant for flushing again. Delhi's chief minister, Sheila Dikshit, said, "The flushing of the plant will take about 35–40 days. This water will finally reach the people of Delhi in July. This is a historic moment for us. Now Ganga water, which is considered pure, has reached us."[64] Unfortunately, when the treated water was finally released to the public in August, it was brown, contaminated with rust. The chief engineer of the Delhi Water Board,

A. K. Jain, apologized: "The water is not very clear and we have advised the residents to store it after running it for nearly 10 minutes. We hope by Wednesday evening the water will be crystal clear."[65] Finally, the plant was "officially" opened on September 19, 2006, starting a ten-year contract with Suez for operation and management with the option to renew for another ten years.

The cost of the plant exceeded its contracted price by more than three times, leading to dramatic hikes in water rates in Delhi. At the same time, the situation in Delhi's slums only deteriorated. On June 4, 2005, the chief minister of Delhi announced that 25 percent of Sonia Vihar water would go to the Cantonment area, where the Indian army was stationed and which already received five hundred liters per person per day, Delhi's highest water allotment. The rest was divided between South Delhi and East Delhi, with the majority going to South Delhi. Though the Sonia Vihar slum is in East Delhi, it did not receive any water. In fact, the city set "standards" for the amount believed to be needed per person per day in different parts of the city: "planned" areas, 255 liters; "resettlement" areas, 115 liters; and slums, 50 liters.[66] This essentially institutionalized inequity, even as PwC pushed for the slum standard to be lowered even further.

Ironically, Delhi is by no means a water-poor city. On the contrary, it has more water than Copenhagen, a total of 280–300 liters per person per day. Yet unlike Copenhagen, Delhi is perpetually in a water shortage crisis, particularly in the summers. Around Sonia Vihar, the water table has dropped twenty to thirty feet in the past decade; other parts of the city are even worse. When the levels get too low, the Water Board declares the area a "dark zone" and forbids further pumping because shrinking groundwater supplies contain concentrated pollutants. In certain Delhi neighborhoods, the groundwater contains mercury 1,570 times higher than the safe limit. In other areas, bacteria, nitrates, and fluoride are found. In fact, the Indian government now admits that much of the country's population is suffering from fluoride poisoning. Even the water tankers, the main source of water for many poor, have large signs on their sides that read, "This water is not potable water." But people are nevertheless forced to drink it.[67] Delhi's water shortages stem not from a lack of water availability, but from inequitable distribution, crumbling infrastructure, and pollution.

In 2012, the Delhi Water Board finally admitted it was privatizing water. Sheila Dikshit, chair of the Delhi Water Board as well as chief minister of Delhi, said, "Privatisation is necessary in the water distribution sector. We want to replicate the same model for the water distribution that we adopted in the power sector."[68] The board also revealed it was taking bids to run the water system in South Delhi. Shortly after this announcement, angry protesters spontaneously headed to the streets, primarily from poor areas that were not receiving water.[69] Nevertheless, the South Delhi contract was awarded to Suez. Meanwhile, due to this history of controversy, the World Bank has removed all references to Delhi and PricewaterhouseCoopers from its India "country report." Instead, the Bank is now focused on the necessity for water "tariff reform" in India's other cities.

End of the Ganges?

Today, the Ganges River is shrinking at a remarkable rate, and there are stretches where it has disappeared altogether. The depth of the Ganges around the ancient city of Varanasi was once two hundred feet; it is now thirty-three feet.[70] The rare Gangetic dolphin is now confined to deep pools along the Ganges, since the river has become too shallow for swimming. This unique creature is born blind, an evolutionary change due to living in a muddy river where sight is unnecessary. It orients itself by swimming on its side and touching the ground with its fin while it searches for food. Now it is often forced to swim in circles when it cannot escape the shallow pools. Unable to forage for food, the Gangetic dolphins are starving.

Even as the Ganges River is shrinking, devastating floods often strike the region. On July 16–17, 2013, a catastrophic flood began in the Himalayas, killing around six thousand people and leaving seventy-five thousand stranded in the mountains. Called an "Indian tsunami" by CNN, the flood wiped out the area above Joshimath and all its pilgrims, most of whom were traveling to the Hindu temple of Kedarnath but some of whom were on their way to the Sikh temple of Hemkund and the Valley of Flowers. *India Today* reported, "Survivors say they witnessed tonnes of waterborne debris flattening almost anything that stood in the way. Screaming pilgrims, their voices drowned out, did not stand a chance in the face of the ferocious flood that unbelievably tossed around boulders, several metres across, like paper balls."[71]

The flood was caused by a dam collapse, though it was not Tehri Dam. In the Himalayas as in Patagonia, glaciers are melting so quickly that GLOFs are forming and then bursting. Unlike in Patagonia, there are no GLOF warning systems in the Himalayas. Scientists working at the lake Gandhi Sarovar actually heard the ice dam bursting but had no way of reporting it to the people below. Instead, they ran for their lives. Located four kilometers above Kedarnath, Gandhi Sarovar is so named because Mahatma Gandhi's ashes were dispersed there in 1948. But in July 2013, Gandhi came crashing down the mountains in an unexpected fit of violence. Surprisingly, the thin-wristed Vishnu statute survived, as did Sunderlal and Vimla Bahuguna. As I watched in awe and horror back in the United States, the Alaknanda River devoured the hotel where I had once stayed, collapsing it into the river like a house of cards. It also destroyed another dam near Joshimath, the Vishnuprayag Hydroelectric Project.

But Tehri Dam survived. In fact, immediately after the flood, both the Uttarakhand chief minister and Tehri Hydropower authorities claimed that Tehri Dam had "saved" the cities of Rishikesh and Haridwar located below the dam. What they failed to mention, which activists quickly pointed out, was that these areas were hardly "saved." Both Rishikesh and Haridwar were flooded a day later, when Tehri Dam was forced to release water to prevent collapse. Below the dam, hundreds died. In Delhi, ten thousand people had to be evacuated from the Yamuna River area and were then hit with an outbreak of hemorrhagic dengue fever.[72]

A week after the floods, a group of twenty professors, lawyers, politicians, and activists—including Vandana Shiva—called upon the Ministry of Environment and Forests to halt hydropower projects in Uttarakhand and start an independent inquiry into the role of dams in creating the disaster. They wrote, "It is now beyond doubt that existing and under construction hydropower projects in Uttarakhand have played a significant role in increasing the proportions of disaster in Uttarakhand this June 2013." They cited the fact that several dam operators failed to open their gates in time, leading to overtopping of dams and flash flooding of downstream communities.[73]

Meanwhile, Sunderlal Bahuguna blamed the flood on clear-cutting, with a big "I told you so" to the Indian government. Immediately after the flood, he told the press, "I have been emphasizing for years to stop this reckless cutting of forests in hilly areas. If you keep disturbing nature, disasters like this will continue to happen." He also mentioned another problem with pine trees: "Walnut trees have wider leaves and are capable of absorbing water while pine trees, which the British had planted, cannot do that and thus land has become vulnerable to erosion and heavy rain can lead to floods and landslides. We should replace them once things are settled in the state."[74] Shiva's hair certainly did not slow this vicious "tsunami."

A month after the floods, Tehri Dam continued to be precariously at risk of collapse. Rather than saving downstream communities, the dam merely extended the period of flooding and mandatory evacuations below. Exactly one month after the flood, Tehri Dam authorities announced that the reservoir was again nearing its maximum water level of 825 meters, despite continued releases of large amounts of water. People in Haridwar and fourteen villages were forced to evacuate as panicked residents had to read in the press, "Incessant Rains in Uttarakhand Pose Threat to Tehri Dam."[75] The irony of claiming the dam had "saved" Haridwar while at the same time announcing that it would flood Haridwar was not missed by the people. And 2013 was not a unique year, aside from the number dead. Since 2010, the reservoir has reached or exceeded the "danger" level every year, and people downstream brace for more floods.

The current Indian government appears to believe that large-scale water projects—dams and canals—are the solution to its water problems, even as Californians are paying to remove dams verging on failure. For instance, the San Clemente Dam, one of many silted-up California dams, is vulnerable to collapse, so the state is paying $84 million to have it taken down.[76] Yet India, China, and other countries keep building. In February 2012, India proceeded with the national Interlinking Rivers Project, which will tie together thirty major rivers through thousands of miles of canals, largely east to west. China has a similar river-interlinking project, its South-North Water Transfer Project. Journalist Dinesh C. Sharma has described India's plan: "The project starts with a map of India with rivers marked in blue, decides that all the rivers need to be linked, and then talks of modalities of joining all the blue lines with a red pen." It treats rivers as pipelines, creating a "national water grid" for India.[77] In the Himalayas, it will dam even more sources of the Ganges River. It will also tap into the Yamuna River, which feeds Delhi, and send it south into the desert province of Rajasthan. In order to replace the Yamuna River, it will move rivers feeding the Ganges and send them south to Delhi, moving rivers around like so many chess pieces. At a cost of $120 billion, the project was initially considered too expensive to build. But in February 2012, the Supreme Court actually *ordered* the state to begin construction on the project in response to recent droughts. The first link, the Ken-Betwa link, received funding from the World Bank and will submerge part of the Panna Tiger National Park.[78] If completed, the Interlinking Rivers Project will be the largest interbasin water transfer project in the world.

At a conference at Wes Jackson's Land Institute in Kansas, where we were discussing global food security, I asked renowned journalist Palagummi Sainath what he thought of the Indian project. He said simply, "It's completely crazy."

"So you don't think they'll build it?" I asked.

"Oh no, they might build it. But it's still completely crazy."

The environmental consequences of this project would be extreme. It could cut off the entire Brahmaputra River during dry season, altering the fragile mangrove ecosystem at the river's mouth at the Bay of Bengal. The Gangetic dolphin would become extinct, along with numerous other species that use this estuary environment. Saline waters would also intrude into the aquifer system in Bangladesh, upon which the country depends for survival. Agricultural lands would become saline. And these are only a few of the consequences of diverting one river, let alone thirty of India's largest rivers. The project would also create international tensions, since India plans to build dams in Nepal and divert water away from Bangladesh. A war with Bangladesh would be disastrous, particularly given the nation's military aid and support from Pakistan. Meanwhile, China is vying to divert one river before India does with its South–North Water Diversion Project. International tensions over water are high in the region, and between nuclear powers.

So what can be done other than diverting large rivers and building more dams? When I asked Sunderlal Bahuguna this question, his answer was immediate. "Small dams," he said with certainty—that is, returning to the country's ancient water expertise. At Vandana Shiva's office, Amit Kumar had said the same thing, explaining, "Small dams that serve areas nearby do not cause landslides, do not evict villagers, and do not affect poor people."[79] In fact, people throughout India are today heeding this advice, reviving the ancient systems of small dams and rainwater harvesting. They are building and funding these systems at the community level, despite laws against doing so. Jal Bhagirathi is one of a growing number of grassroots small dam organizations that are reaching back to India's ancient history while connecting people through the Internet and Twitter. Its leader, Rajendra Singh, has helped to build 7,600 water reservoirs around India. He has been harassed by the Indian government for his activities, as he explained: "When we started this water harvesting structure, they gave me legal notice. Under the Irrigation Drainage Act 54, they are saying, 'You are catching the rain here. This rain is not yours.'"[80] Nevertheless, his organization continues to build, and rainwater harvesting is rising in popularity across the country. Jal Bhagirathi is now part of a national organization called Jal Biradari, or Water Community, the goal of which is simply to help poor people get water. The organization's brochure explains the problem: "Water costs nothing for those with everything and everything for those with nothing."[81]

By the end of my visit to India, I realized that Sunderlal Bahuguna is only one in a vast network that is creating a new water vision for the country. In 1988, Sunderlal Bahuguna, Medha Patkar, and Babe Amte, leaders of the antidam movement, met in the middle of India and drafted their "Appeal to the Nation." It read, in part, "We came from different parts of the country, all united by a common resolve—to ensure that people were no longer denied their basic rights over natural resources. . . . We appeal to the Nation to halt all big dams, here and now."[82] They argued that each village should be able to make decisions about its own development, taking its specific ecosystem into account. Mahatma Gandhi had once made the same argument, but he was outvoted by Prime Minister Nehru. Today, it seems like Gandhi's populist vision may be returning to rural India, though it is threatened by the World Bank and the Indian government.

On the day I sat with Sunderlal Bahuguna, I asked what he would do next now that the Tehri reservoir had filled—or what anyone could do. It was impossible to ignore the tragedy of the Tehri reservoir in front of us, his village underwater. It was hard not to feel a sense of futility. Rather than reply to my question, Bahuguna took out what looked like a diary and asked me to write my name and address down. Then he looked up and said, "Young people will revolt against the system, eventually. But for now, plant trees." Several months later, I ran across something he had written: "Whenever I feel that I might be losing in my crusade or have been left to fight it out all alone, I just go through this diary. . . . All these names are friends who lend me courage and support."[83] I felt honored to be one of those names.

III

WATER WARS IN THE MIDDLE EAST

FIVE

A Revolution of the Thirsty in Egypt

"WELCOME TO THE GREENER SIDE OF LIFE" beckoned the billboard on Cairo's Ring Road. The sign showed a man in a jaunty hat teeing off on a verdant golf course flowing into the horizon. I was stuck in traffic, breathing that mix of Saharan dust and pollution also known as "air," so I could see the appeal. Somewhere outside the city, in a gated community called Allegria—Italian for "cheerfulness"—a greener life awaited. "Over 80% of Allegria's land is dedicated to green and public spaces," boasts the developer's brochure, "meaning you'll never lose the peace and tranquility which goes hand in hand with outdoor living."

It was a scorching-hot summer, several months before the 2011 Egyptian Revolution. Beneath the expressway sprawled the informal settlements where an estimated 60 percent of metropolitan Cairo's eighteen million residents live.[1] Some were using billboard poles to keep the brick structures from collapsing. Many did not have running water, and those who did found the taps drying up as water was diverted to the lavishly landscaped suburban developments with names like Allegria, Dreamland, Beverly Hills, Swan Lake, Utopia—a diversion that was straining the capacity of state-run water distribution networks and waste treatment plants.[2]

When Tahrir Square erupted in the winter of 2011, the international news media proclaimed a "social media revolution" spurred by pro-democracy Egyptians seeking to overthrow the repressive regime of President Hosni Mubarak.[3] To a large extent unreported was the fact that the country was also in a *water* crisis, having dropped below the globally recognized "water poverty" line of one thousand cubic meters per person per year, down to seven hundred cubic meters per person.[4] It is no exaggeration to say that the January 25 Revolution was not just a revolution of the disenfranchised; it was also what some have called a "Revolution of the Thirsty."[5] In a land almost without rain, the Nile River supplies 97 percent of renewable water resources, and these days an increasing share of that water is being directed to the posh suburban compounds— where many of Egypt's political elite live—to support that "greener side of life." Meanwhile, in the years before the revolution, the state water utilities had dramatically hiked rates for residents in downtown Cairo, where some 40 percent of the population lives on less than $2 a day.[6]

Later that year, back home in the Midwest, as images of the uprising filled my television screen, I was surprised that commentators seemed unaware of the water crisis, and of the global geopolitical pressures that had made the crisis all but certain. The American media focused mainly on internal corruption and oppression. They did not report on the role of the international superpowers in influencing the Mubarak regime to privatize the country's public land and water; they did not report, for instance, that since the 1990s the World Bank has argued that privatization enhances "efficiency" and has mandated the policy as a condition for making loans, and that in 2004 this mandate led the Egyptian government to privatize its water utilities, transforming them into corporations that were required to operate at a profit, passing along the cost of new infrastructure through rate increases.[7]

Within months of privatization, the price of water doubled in some areas of the capital, and citizens started to protest. At one demonstration in northern Cairo in 2005, "angry residents chased bill collectors down the streets."[8] Those who could not afford the new rates had little choice but to go to the city's outskirts to collect water from the dirty Nile River canals.[9] In 2007, protesters in the Nile Delta blocked the main coastal road after the regional water company diverted water from farming and fishing towns to affluent resort communities. "The authorities sent riot police to put down these 'disturbances,'" wrote Philip Marfleet, a professor at the University of East London, even as "water flowed uninterrupted to the gated communities, and to country clubs and upmarket resorts of the Mediterranean and the Red Sea."[10] In the next few years such demonstrations only grew in intensity. As activist Abdel Mawla Ismail has noted, "Thirst protests or *intifadas,* as some people have called them, started to represent a new path for a social movement."[11] From this path the revolution that consumed the nation in 2011 seemed inevitable. People can live in poverty for a long time; they cannot live without water.

Golf City

To understand the growing inequity of water access in Egypt, let's return again to the "greener side of life." Established in 2007, Allegria is one of dozens of gated suburbs that have sprouted in the Sahara in the past decade. Created by the Sixth of October Development and Investment Company (SODIC)—the name recalls a victorious battle in the Yom Kippur War—Allegria is a cosmopolitan community organized around golf and swimming. It boasts a "happier and healthier lifestyle" and proudly advertises a Greg Norman Signature golf course with eighteen holes and "views of the Great Pyramids of Giza." Prospective buyers can choose among thirty villa plans, all designed by a renowned international architect. Each villa or apartment complex has its own private pool and gardens. Four corporations manage upkeep of the landscape alone.

Golf is not a new sport in Egypt—it was introduced in 1882, when the British colonial rulers built the Gezira Sporting Club—but it has gained wide popularity only in the past decade as developers have begun to promote the "golf holiday" to foreign tourists. It has now swept the Saharan suburbs, becoming a status symbol signifying the ability to conduct business anywhere in the world as long as there's a good fairway. In Egypt, learning to golf is now seen as a necessary step toward joining the global elite. Allegria capitalizes on the mystique, offering workshops and posting daily golf quizzes on its Facebook page. It hosts endless golf tournaments and themed parties, like "Allegria Basil Ladies Day," where, for around $150, women receive a welcoming basil drink, an "Italian

Basil Menu" lunch, and a round of golf enhanced with "basil-scented face towels." At the annual BMW tournament, new cars are displayed around the fairways and are available for test drives.

As in many far-flung exurbs, life in Allegria is necessarily self-contained. Women are encouraged to walk to the upscale shops and restaurants in the private city of Westown (also owned by SODIC) or take the free shuttle to Designopolis (ditto) to buy home furnishings. On weekends, families can visit one of the nearby amusement parks; DreamPark—designed by the company that created both the Mall of America in Bloomington, Minnesota, and Universal Studios in Los Angeles—provides relief from the desert heat with water-themed entertainments, including a dolphin show, jungle cruise, and log-chute rides. When the children are old enough, they can enroll in the prestigious British International School, which recently moved to Allegria from downtown Cairo.

Egypt's boom in luxury suburbs began in the 1990s with the first wave of privatization of government agencies and public land. Vast swaths of desert were sold at bargain prices to friends and relatives of President Mubarak, who also received guarantees of infrastructure like roads, electricity, and water lines.[12] These insider deals led to outrageous claims of water rights, like the assurance of unlimited fossil groundwater to a Saudi prince who wanted to grow food in the Sahara. International companies vied for contracts to build water treatment facilities. To be sure, life in the Saharan suburbia was not always as idyllic as advertised; developers of gated communities typically promised reverse osmosis filtration, but many found it cheaper to hook up to municipal water lines— and notoriously unreliable state-run water treatment plants—than to build dedicated facilities.[13] Still, residents paying up to $350 monthly in maintenance and utility fees expected clean water to flow freely when they turned on the tap, and more often than not it did. A recent study of two Cairo suburbs found that 69 percent of residents in Sixth of October City and 42 percent in New Cairo had tap water available at all times.[14]

All the while, as water was flowing and taxpayer money was shifting to the exurban oases, millions of residents of old Cairo struggled with little access to sanitary facilities. The ostentatious water wealth that made possible the "greener side of life" was becoming a symbol of government corruption. The Revolution of the Thirsty was gathering strength.

Old Cairo

Cairo is an extraordinarily congested metropolis, with twice the density of Manhattan, mainly because of its growing informal districts. Unlike some of the tin-and-plywood squatter settlements in some African cities, informal Cairo is a visually coherent environment of four- and five-story red-brick buildings, many with reinforcing bars jutting from the roof, awaiting the next floor. The planned and unplanned areas of the city are both crowded with markets and cafés, but in informal areas the under-the-table economy is dominant, and infrastructure must be bartered for and self-built because it is usually not provided by municipal authorities. In some neighborhoods, community-built roads are so narrow they can't accommodate emergency traffic, only *tuk-tuk* taxis. Plumbing services range from a trench in the road to a hole in the ground, both emptied by sewage trucks that sometimes discharge their waste into the Nile canals from which people draw their drinking water when the tap runs dry.[15]

The narrow alleyways of Cairo's informal areas, which lack city services such as trash collection and water.

In the informal area of Manshiyat Naser—known as "Garbage City" because its economy is based on garbage collection—an estimated one million people live in just four and a half square miles, making it one of the most densely populated districts in Africa.[16] Here less than 15 percent of clean water needs are met by the municipality; most residents depend on "hundreds of small private wells which draw from contaminated shallow aquifers" fed by the Nile.[17] Analyzing the area's water supply, an NGO found that 75 percent of the samples "did not meet the minimum acceptable standards for drinking water in Egypt." Yet because districts like Manshiyat Naser are extralegal, residents cannot demand better infrastructure. They collect water in jerricans, dig holes for toilets, and connect to electricity illegally.[18] One resident complained: "Can you tell me why those people over there [in the formal areas] get better streets, better water, and better everything than us? Are they worth more?"[19] And another: "If a pipe bursts in [an upscale neighborhood] it's fixed the same day. When pipes burst here, we go a week without water. Officials consider it a blessing—an opportunity to sell our water share to one of their cronies."[20]

Like many Manshiyat Naser residents, Umm Amr works as a *zabbaleen*, or trash collector, sorting during the day the trash that her husband brings home at night; the trash is then packaged and sold for recycling, providing the family's main source of income. As described in a poignant article by journalist Julia Gerlach, Umm, who is in her thirties, lives in a tiny room on the ground floor of an old house where she and her daughter sleep on the floor. Her husband sleeps on a bench; her two sons have the best accommodations—the one bed in the house. All the families in her three-story building share one bathroom, and Umm gets water from a neighbor across the street. Some days she simply goes without. "We wanted to build water pipes," she says, "but they said we shouldn't because the house is too old and the walls are rotten. The water would [cause] the house to collapse."[21]

In 2008, Umm Amr's problems became more pressing when rockslides killed at least 199 people and injured 55 others in Manshiyat Naser, due to untreated sewage soaking into the cliffs above her house. Afterward the national government designated certain areas as "unsafe" and required residents to relocate to a housing project twenty miles west of Cairo.[22] Once there, the lucky ones got jobs as housekeepers or landscapers at places like Allegria, but others had no employment or income in the suburbs and found that there was no public transportation back to the city. As a result some residents defied the relocation order, provoking a swift and ruthless official response; in an extreme case, a bulldozer was driven into a house in Manshiyat Naser with the family still inside.[23]

The story of the ongoing Egyptian Revolution is in many ways the story of Manshiyat Naser writ large. By the summer of 2010, in neighborhoods across Cairo, frustration with the lack of civic infrastructure, the scarce water and poor sanitation, had already begun to boil over. But revolutions do not happen unless people are capable of organizing, and by this point millions of Cairenes in extralegal communities had amassed decades of experience in self-organization. Urban planner Kareem Ibrahim has described the situation: "Basically, there is no urban planning aside from what people, primarily lower socioeconomic classes, have informally taken upon themselves to address. . . . It's as if people have accepted that they're not really citizens of a country that has responsibilities towards them."[24] During the "Friday of Anger" protests on January 28, 2011, Manshiyat Naser residents set the neighborhood authority office and local police stations on fire; both local authorities and police had been responsible for the mass evictions. Families then occupied the empty government buildings until they were evicted by riot police.[25] Minirevolutions like this occurred around the country but were rarely televised or even tweeted.

Yet even as revolutionary fervor was intensifying, and right up to the final days of the Mubarak regime, international investors and the World Bank were lauding the success of Egypt's privatization program. As a *Forbes* advertorial sponsored by major banks and developers had declared: "Despite the global economic crisis in 2009, Egypt managed to sustain a 4.7% growth in GDP—an enviable rate for most countries—largely due to strong growth fundamentals [and] effective market reforms." The market reforms—that is, the privatization programs—had indeed raised the country's GDP, but only by creating an enormous real estate and water speculation bubble for those with the right connections. In 2010, the World Bank praised Egypt as "among the world's ten most active reformers," citing "impressive poverty reduction" and "rapid economic growth." The Bank promised to continue supporting "Egypt's reforms in the water supply and sanitation sector," including its policy of cost recovery and privatization.[26] Then, in January 2011, the nation rose up, and many wondered how the World Bank could have gotten it so wrong.[27] As in South Africa, World Bank projects had actually increased inequity—and thirst.

Despite the Bank's protestations of success, Wikileaks cables reveal that the CIA knew that the situation in Egypt had been deteriorating for years due to IMF- and Bank-imposed "reforms." In 2007, U.S. Ambassador Francis Ricciardone Jr. wrote to the CIA, "The average Egyptian is not yet feeling the benefits of growth. The next round of reforms . . . have the potential to cause social upheaval. Implementation will require significant political will." In another letter, Ricciardone revealed what the next round of reforms would tackle: "the massive subsidization of food, water and energy." In other words, the Egyptian government would stop keeping prices for bread and water low enough that poor people could afford them. By 2008, Osama Al-Ghazali Harb told U.S. ambassador Margaret Scobey that the "current deterioration in Egyptian culture, education, health care and economic equality is the worst in the past 200 years." He reported that thirty to forty million people were living in "inconceivable" poverty in slums and that he was anxious about the "country's current instability."[28] Nevertheless, the IMF and World Bank continued to push the country to reform—all the way to revolution.

Postrevolution Water

After the early success of the revolution in the winter of 2011, in the heady days after Mubarak's resignation, former government officials and land developers were brought up before the interim authorities to answer for their corrupt privatization deals. Magdy Rasekh, the founder and former chair of SODIC—and the father-in-law of Hosni Mubarak's elder son—fled the country to avoid arrest. He was tried in absentia, convicted of illegally seizing public lands, and sentenced to five years of hard labor and a $330 million fine, along with Mohamed Ibrahim Suleiman, Mubarak's longtime housing minister. Another developer of a gated community was sentenced to ten years in prison. According to *The National*, "Thousands of corruption allegations have surfaced and some of the country's best-known businessmen have gone on trial."[29] Mubarak was accused of receiving direct kickbacks from developers as well as shares in the new suburban developments; his assets—by some estimates as much as $70 billion—were frozen as Egypt tried to track down the sources of his wealth.

After the revolution, the looming question was whether or not the land and water requisitioned to create projects like Allegria would be returned to the government and renationalized. Most foreign financial analysts remained certain that this would not happen. According to Dubai analyst Ankur Khetawat, "We don't think the government will take all the land back. They will prefer to settle because it's all about money at the end of the day."[30] The consulting firm Frost & Sullivan, headquartered in California, predicted that private water companies, which made $1.35 billion in Egypt in 2010, would earn double that figure by 2015; as the firm's report concluded: "The water scarcity in Egypt is one of the most critical in the region. . . . This has created a lot of opportunities for development."[31]

Meanwhile, the World Bank, along with the International Monetary Fund, maintained a largely business-as-usual attitude toward the interim government and then President Mohamed Morsi, offering $4.5 billion in loans over two years to aid in "recovery." According to the World Bank, "About two billion dollars in loans would be linked to progress in government reforms," including privatization.[32] Since one of the driving factors for the revolution was massive corruption in land privatization schemes, President Morsi initially halted and even reversed some land privatization decisions. Since the military remained in control, he never touched military assets or land, representing 25–30 percent of the national economy. Nevertheless, his renationalization of property proved to be his undoing.

One major reversal, postrevolution, was the water privatization deal with Saudi Prince Alwaleed bin Talal, who had invested $500 million to grow grapes, citrus, vegetables, and cotton in Egypt's desert for export to Saudi Arabia. The government of Egypt had promised to supply water by diverting about 9 percent of Egypt's Nile River allotment from Lake Nasser to "Toshka Lakes," new lakes that would be created in the Sahara. For Saudi Arabia, the Toshka project meant access to the vast Nubian aquifer, which was also being mined by Libya's Great Man-Made River, a vast network of aqueducts and pipes.[33] The Egyptian contract was a near giveaway of land that guaranteed "cost-free and unimpeded" access to groundwater on the property. The government of Egypt justified "the favorable terms and subsidies provided to the agricultural developers in

Toshka by the resettlement objectives of the project."[34] Ultimately, the government wanted to relieve population pressures along the Nile, where 96 percent of Egypt's population lives, and lower a 9.3 percent unemployment rate by creating a community of agricultural laborers around Toshka Lakes. Since Saudi Arabia was in its own water crisis, Toshka Lakes would allow it to import water through food, a "virtual water"—while Egypt remained thirsty.

Initially, the revolution tabled this ambitious plan and the contract was annulled due to allegations of corruption. But the cancellation of projects such as these may have ultimately led to President Morsi's downfall. Canceling Toshka and other corrupt privatization deals made foreign investors panicky; they began to pull out of Egypt. The economy spiraled out of control. In the end, Morsi was forced to renegotiate contracts in order to bring back investors, and the Saudi prince ultimately got his deal, though reduced in size. For Morsi, however, it was too late. In 2013, he was removed from office.

After Morsi was ousted, the attorney fighting the Saudi prince, Hamdy El-Fakharany, dropped the case in disgust, claiming, "I have been battling for two eras and nothing has changed. I won't keep battling alone for the rest of my life." He particularly decried the "free irrigation water Bin Talal is given, while many Egyptian farmers are denied [this privilege]."[35] Of course, the problem with Toshka involves much more than the terms of a contract; the diversion of the Nile into the Saharan desert has created a 540-square-foot lake and several smaller ones that are quickly evaporating. The lakes have shown evidence of rapid drying when viewed by satellite.[36] As the country goes thirsty, Toshka Lakes are becoming saline because they have no outlet. In 2012, Toshka was called a "mega-failure" by *Egypt Independent*.[37]

Morsi was ousted for a number of reasons, including some of his Islamic-based rulings. More cynically, an e-mail from Stratfor's senior global analyst, Reva Bhalla, claimed that the Egyptian military had always been in charge of the results of the revolution and would never let the Muslim Brotherhood rule. She claimed the military encouraged the revolution because the Mubarak regime had planned to go after their assets, including an enormous water bottling company. Even so, Bhalla said the military's goal in supporting the revolution was to "revamp [Murabek's] regime, but not dismantle it." Shortly after the revolution, Bhalla wrote,

"This is the negotiation process we are seeing play out right now—whose time is done and needs time to transfer their assets overseas, who is 'clean' enough to stay, who can snatch up the assets that are now up for grabs (esp within the military), etc."[38] Revolution, unfortunately, can provide new opportunities for corruption as the wealthy flee the country with money from privatization deals and the military "snatches up" what is left. Morsi's interim government provided such an opportunity: a period of relative chaos with a leader who was not schooled in such "negotiations." But when Morsi became a threat to these machinations, he was simply thrown out by the military and declared a "terrorist," along with the entire Muslim Brotherhood.

Changing Egypt's unequal distribution of water may be nearly impossible in the face of military and international financial forces greater than those of any president. Without internationally enforced laws that allow a nation to abandon contracts found to be corrupt, environmentally disastrous, or otherwise unethical, so-called hot money will instantly leave the country at the first sign of a government wavering on promises of an investment-friendly environment. Egypt was forced to choose long-term ecological disaster and thirst in order to avoid immediate financial disaster; but disaster was merely postponed.

Epypt is entirely dependent on the Nile for its wealth. In ancient times, Egyptians divided the year into three seasons: flood, planting, and harvest. For thousands of years, they successfully used "Nilometers," wells that measured the water level, to predict water availability downstream for the coming season. But those natural rhythms were disrupted when the nutrient-rich floodwaters of the Nile were blocked by the Aswan Dam in 1970. Afterward, Egypt became an agricultural export economy with cotton as its primary industry. Though agriculture uses 85 percent of Egypt's water, its benefits have been declining dramatically; it now accounts for only 7 percent of the GDP. At the same time, overirrigated and underreplenished land is becoming salinized and desertified as the dam blocks nutrients and soil behind its walls. Egypt now imports most of its food. "Bread riots" are common; water revolutions are inevitable. Poor people with shrinking food and water supplies, when confronted with flagrant displays of water wealth, will perpetually be ready for revolution.

British geographer James Duncan once described the colonial city as "a political tract written in space and carved in stone. The landscape was part of the practice of power."[39] Today the green and gated suburbs of Cairo have become a political tract for the neoliberalism that undergirds the growing power of a global elite (never mind the corruption involved in their development). These suburbs are products of the corporatized and privatized paradigm that has dominated Egypt for many years; there in the desert the market logic is made manifest in extravagant and thirsty communities of air-conditioned villas and velvety lawns—in the promise that money can buy all the water in the world.

After the revolution, downtown Cairo's water kept flowing to the suburbs, and along with it the life of the capital. At the new campus of the American University in Cairo, in the suburb of New Cairo, there are twenty-seven fountains and "water features"; meanwhile, at the old campus in Tahrir Square, the library was set on fire, revolutionary graffiti covers the walls, and weeklong skirmishes sometimes break out between rioters and police.[40] All the while Allegria's profits are climbing, seemingly unassailable, after taking a brief dive in response to the fall of the Mubarak government. On the first anniversary of the revolution, Allegria announced, "To commemorate 25th January, we will offer 50% green fees." That month SODIC signed new real estate development contracts worth $36 million, and share prices doubled within six weeks.

SIX

Targeting Iraq's Water

"THAT WAS WHERE THEY DUMPED THE BODIES," *Forbes* writer Melik Kaylan told me, referring to a concrete reservoir where Saddam Hussein's army hid people they had killed. I had just come from that remote reservoir and was surprised that Melik knew of it. By then, Saddam had been dead for four years, and the tank was being used as a storage system for Ifraz water treatment plant. "Yes, I was told there were lots of dead bodies down there," he nodded enthusiastically as if discussing lost treasure. As a war correspondent working out of Baghdad for more than five years, Kaylan would know where the bodies were hidden. Yet in his stylish leather jacket and German glasses, he looked like he was going out for a cappuccino in New York City rather than waiting with me for a plane in Iraq. Around us, Iraqis pushed and shoved their way en masse through the airport metal detector as if a prize went to whoever got through first. I wondered if this was a habit for people long used to fleeing war.

But calm prevailed in that Kurdish and American-loving region in 2010. Flying into Erbil, the only clue I had I was in a war zone was that the plane did a steep and terrifying corkscrew spiral dive until we reached the ground. I was told it was to avoid missile strikes. After leaving Iraq, all I could think about were the people who could not get away, millions of people stuck there without clean water to drink. When I visited the U.S. Fluor–owned reservoir, a nondescript concrete square building in the middle of a dirt field, a lieutenant let me climb up top and lifted the locked metal doors so I could look inside. I was lucky, since the place was fenced and heavily guarded. It turned out this officer, who did not want to be named, had an ulterior motive. Below me, on top of a vast and deadly quiet underground tank of water, was a surface of brown scum. "Bad water," the lieutenant said. "Can you fix it?" Later, this image would stay with me, symbolizing what water privatization had done for Iraq.

Ten years after the United States invaded Iraq in 2003, the United Nations reported that water quality and availability had only worsened throughout the country, despite the fact that USAID and the World Bank had spent billions on water system "reconstruction" and despite the fact that Baghdad had been divvied up like war spoils between Veolia and Suez. In 2003, the U.S. Congress had established the Iraq Relief and Reconstruction Fund with $18 billion, which was used to build 158 water treatment facilities—largely contracted to the U.S.-based construction giant Bechtel, Texas-based Fluor, and Suez.[1] This was only the beginning of the spending. In 2009, Baghdad's mayor, Saber al-Issawi, said Suez and Veolia received another $5 billion to build and run the city's water supply system. He promised it would be operational in two years.[2] In total, U.S. taxpayers have spent $63 billion on reconstruction and relief in Iraq; this amount does not include the cost of the war. Yet in 2013, the United Nations reported an "alarming increase in water pollution," with more than a million cases of waterborne illnesses countrywide in 2011. Another study by the consultant firm Dunia stated, "Iraq's existing water and sewage infrastructure, including treatment plants and pipe networks, is largely in disrepair." In Baghdad, the U.N. report noted "almost daily incidents of tension or verbal arguments related to water access."[3]

So why have conditions continued to deteriorate in Iraq? In a 2013 report, Special Inspector General Stuart Bowen euphemistically wrote that much of the money spent in Iraq had "underperformed." Earlier, Iraqi prime minister Nouri al-Maliki obliquely said, "There was misspending of money."[4] Part of the problem was continuing conflict. After the war "ended," the country threatened to deteriorate into three autonomous regions—Sunni, Shia, and Kurdish. In this unstable environment, Iraqi politicians could buy votes by promising clean water, signing large contracts as evidence of their commitment, then abandoning or ignoring the projects after winning the election. For U.S. and French corporations working in this war-torn and unregulated environment, accountability was virtually nonexistent. Money was funneled from U.S. taxpayers to corporations through loans that the United States is still paying back. "We ran that war on a credit card," said Senator Patrick Leahy.[5]

Even more frightening is the possibility that this war may have been *started* for corporate interests, an idea that has received much speculation in the press. In a 2002 *Time* magazine article titled "Inside the Secret War Council," journalist Mark Thompson questioned the membership of a group called the U.S. Defense Policy Board, which he described as a "private think tank" in which "helmets often trump thinking caps."[6] Formed to advise the U.S. secretary of defense, the Defense Policy Board included Bechtel's senior vice president John Sheehan and board of directors member George Shultz. Not surprisingly, these men strongly advised that the United States should invade Iraq, though Bechtel defended them: "Shultz spoke for himself, not for Bechtel, in advocating intervention against the regime of Saddam Hussein."[7] Also on the Defense Policy Board was hawkish CIA director James Woolsey, whose wife, Suzanne, was influential in claiming that Iraq had weapons of mass destruction and arguing for a preemptive strike. Less than a year after the war started, Suzanne was appointed director of one of the five major companies selected for reconstruction work in Iraq—Fluor. As part of her compensation, she was awarded stock in the company. Finally, army acquisitions officer Kenneth Oscar, who had pushed for no-bid contracts with better "incentives" for corporations, became a vice president at Fluor in 2002.[8] These are only a few of the people with conflicts of interests involved in the buildup to war. One would think if the government at least wanted to avoid the *appearance* of corruption, these people would have been asked to recuse themselves from decisions about going to war. Instead, Bechtel was offered the first major contract for reconstruction in April 2003 after what the *New York Times* called "a heated contest among some of the nation's most politically connected construction concerns."[9]

The case of Iraq reveals one of the bleaker ways in which water privatization can be achieved: through force. Before the Iraq War even began, the Heritage Foundation laid out a plan for the country's reconstruction.

In a report titled "The Road to Economic Prosperity for a Post-Saddam Iraq," the authors wrote:

> The new post-Saddam federal government should develop a modern legal system that recognizes property rights and is conducive to privatization; create a public information campaign that prepares the people for structural reforms and privatization; hire expatriates and Western-educated Arabic speakers with financial, legal, and business expertise for key economic positions; deregulate prices, including prices in the utility and energy sectors; prepare state assets in the utility, transportation, pipeline, energy, and other sectors for privatization . . . and launch an effort to join the World Trade Organization (WTO).[10]

This was precisely the path that reconstruction followed, with corporate-built water supply systems, allegedly funded through "cost recovery."

At the same time, the Iraqi government was confronted with an Islamic majority that viewed water as sacred and a "gift of God"—in some places, water commodification was considered tantamount to blasphemy. A clash of interests was bound to follow. Rather than ask Iraqis to pay for water, Iraqi politicians were more likely to take money from USAID to build water treatment plants but then indefinitely delay the accompanying "water reforms" that would pay back the costs. Instead, costs were covered by the U.S. government—that is, us.

The Deindustrialization of Iraq

Baghdad was once known as the Garden City, Baghdad al-Zawhaa, with marble steps leading down to the Tigris River that flowed through its center. In the early 1990s, 95 percent of Iraq's urban population and 75 percent of the rural population had access to clean water. Baghdad's water was pumped directly from the Tigris and then purified in water treatment plants. According to a report from the office of the U.S. special inspector general, the government of Iraq had long "invested a part of its oil revenues to provide fully subsidized social services, such as water, sanitation, health, and electricity without any discrimination." Its water services were comparable to those in Europe. "By the early 1990s," the report continues, "Iraq's water sector was well developed and modern, equipped with sophisticated western designed . . . state-of-the-art technologies" and "high levels of efficiency."[11]

The 1991 U.S.–Iraq "Gulf War" changed all that. In contravention to the principles of the Geneva Convention, the U.S. military targeted electrical stations needed to maintain water treatment plants. (The Geneva Convention article states, "It is prohibited to attack, destroy or render useless objects indispensable to the survival of the civilian population," including "drinking water supplies and irrigation works.") While CNN discussed the effectiveness of "smart bombs" and "precision bombing," there was no mention of the fact that "dumb bombs" were being dropped on civilian infrastructure. According to the Washington Institute, "Power stations . . . [were] used as bomb dumps for carrier-based aircraft returning to ship. . . . attacks on dual-use power facilities caused cascading damage throughout the water purification and sanitation systems, exacerbating a public health crisis."[12] While 87 percent of the nation had electricity prior to the war, a U.S. target planner said the nation was bombed until "not an electron was flowing."[13]

The fact that the United States intentionally destroyed Iraq's civilian infrastructure remains undisputed, but the question of why has never been adequately addressed. According to Washington Post reporter Barton Gellman, "Some targets, especially late in the war, were bombed primarily to create postwar leverage over Iraq, not to influence the course of the conflict itself. Planners now say their intent was to destroy or damage valuable facilities that Baghdad could not repair without foreign assistance."[14] According to a 2002 U.S. Air Force report, the goal was "to attack the will of Saddam Hussein's despotic regime and perhaps the will of the people of Iraq itself." The report stated that "attacking the enemy's electrical power production and distribution system was a key element of the plan itself," one that "might achieve the desired psychological effects."[15] In short, the air force thought turning off the power would cause the people to revolt. Clearly, the plan failed.

Instead the people of Iraq were simply left without lights and water. Besides having their electricity shut down, Iraqis were dealing with U.N.-imposed sanctions that included a ban on importing chlorine, which could be used to make chlorine gas. These sanctions began four days after Iraq's invasion of Kuwait. The U.S. Department of Defense was clearly aware of the dangers to the civilian population in combining these sanctions with an attack on the water supply system. On the second day of the Gulf War, the U.S. Defense Intelligence Agency sent a memo explaining these consequences: "Iraq will suffer increasing shortages of purified water because of the lack of required chemicals. . . . Incidences of disease, including possible epidemics, will become probable." The memo concluded, "Iraq probably is using untreated or partially treated water in some locations. Full degradation of the water treatment system will probably take at least another 6 months."[16]

The first U.N. mission to postwar Iraq documented "apocalyptic damage" to the infrastructure, saying the country had returned to the preindustrial age. The World Health Organization reported, "The quantity of potable water is less than 5 percent of the original supply, there are no operational water and sewage treatment plants, and the reported incidence of diarrhea is four times above normal levels. . . . Children particularly have been affected by these diseases."[17] There were epidemics of typhoid, meningitis, hepatitis, and cholera. The office of the U.S. special inspector general for Iraq reconstruction reported that, in the first eight months after the Gulf War, there was a threefold increase in deaths of children under age five.

This was to be only the start of Iraq's water quality problems.

By 1995, the British Medical Association estimated that more than five hundred thousand children had died due to U.N.-imposed sanctions, mainly from starvation and waterborne diseases. All the while, the United States blocked resolutions to lift sanctions at the United Nations.[18] The waterborne typhoid disease had increased eightfold.[19] During the long period of sanctions between the two Iraq–U.S. wars, water treatment plants functioned only when jerry-rigged and when chlorine could be smuggled in. By the start of the 2003 Iraq War, these plants were barely holding together and were particularly vulnerable to attack. UNICEF warned, "This conflict will have more people dying from water treatment plants going down than from war itself."[20] A month before the Iraq War started, USAID secured bids to reconstruct the water infrastructure throughout Iraq, stating, "All systems are currently operating at a highly degraded level of performance, and will likely suffer further degradation as a result of a conflict."[21] In the second Iraq War, electricity stations were again targeted, but this time only with carbon fiber bombs, which disperse carbon filaments to short-circuit rather than destroy infrastructure. Since bids had already been solicited for reconstruction, it was crucial to maintain prewar costs to ensure successful bids.

The Iraq War started on the fifth day of the World Water Forum in Kyoto—March 20, 2003—and Loïc Fauchon expressed concerns about damage to water facilities in his opening remarks at the Forum. Years later, he recalled this moment: "We tried to remind the audience that the bombing of water facilities should never be tolerated. Most journalists turned their back to me because they thought I was supporting Hussein. And if you remember, a few days later those facilities were bombed— which violates the international right to water."[22] By then, Basra's electrical grid had already been knocked out on the second day of attacks, disabling the water pumps to the city. Running water in this city of 1.5 million stopped flowing, and the Red Cross warned of a coming "humanitarian crisis."[23]

A month after the war started, Bechtel was already tasked with rebuilding in a contract worth up to $680 million. The contract stated, "The contractor will commence repairs of water infrastructure in 10 urban areas within the first month. Within the first 6 months the contractor will repair or rehabilitate critical water treatment, pumping and distribution systems in 15 urban areas. Within 12 months potable water supply will be restored in all urban centers."[24] Bechtel did not complete these projects, perhaps because President Bush's infamous "Mission Accomplished" speech of May 1, 2003—stating that the war had ended—turned out to be embarrassingly early. Perhaps George W. Bush had been following the contract timetable rather than the reality on the ground; in order for Bechtel to complete its contract obligations, the war needed to be over by May 1.

By 2006, Bechtel left Iraq, having received $2.3 billion in reconstruction funds and claiming it had completed its contracts—but a U.S. government audit found that the company had "successfully completed less than half of the reconstruction jobs that the government hired it to perform in Iraq."[25] Of course, this was partly due to continuing conflict in the region; but people still needed drinking water. In the city of Hilla, with a population of around four hundred thousand, Bechtel was supposed to rehabilitate the water treatment plant within six months, but the plant's chief engineer said Bechtel never even contacted him, though he did notice some people painting buildings. He complained, "Bechtel is painting buildings, but that doesn't give clean water to the people who have died from drinking contaminated water. We ask of them that instead of painting buildings, they give us one water pump and we'll use it to give water service to more people."[26] In its defense, Bechtel later argued, "No one assumed that $680 million, the cost of building a medium-sized power plant in the United States, represented more than a small down payment on Iraq's vast infrastructure needs."[27]

As Bechtel was pulling out of Iraq, other companies moved in. In 2004, U.S. Fluor was hired to rehabilitate Baghdad's Al-Wathba plant for $600 million, due for completion by 2006. (Best known for building the Trans-Alaska Pipeline System, Fluor has also built refineries and military bases around the world and nuclear power plants in the United States.)[28] Despite the large amounts of money spent on rehabilitating Baghdad's water supply, little seemed to show for it. By 2007, the Iraqi Environment Ministry said that 36 percent of Baghdad's drinking water was still unsafe "in a good month," and that figure jumped to 90 percent in a "bad month."[29] This was an optimistic estimate, compared to other studies completed the same year. According to the NGO Coordination Committee in Iraq, only 32 percent of the Iraqi population had access to clean water, and 60 percent of the population in Baghdad's suburbs were drinking from rivers. Baghdad resident Sahira Saleh said, "It is hard to say this but years ago I was praying for the death of Saddam Hussein, but today I wish he could come back to life and was in power again because at least in his time we used to have safe water, good sewage systems, had food to eat and our children never got diarrhea."[30]

In 2007, cholera spread across the city, as journalist Matthew Schofield reported: "Cholera has hit in the summers; it will come again.... The water is atrocious. And this is in Baghdad.... It gets much worse when you get outside. When you go down to Basra, you have stories of worms actually coming out of the tap."[31] More than two thousand people were infected and twenty-four died as cholera reached Baghdad.[32] Lacking running water, people drank from rivers or dug up the streets to tap into water pipes, which led to sewage leaking into the pipes that fed people's taps. Schofield wrote, "The stench of human waste is enough to tell Falah abu Hasan that his drinking water is bad. His infant daughter Fatma's continuous illnesses and his own constant nausea confirm it."[33]

At the same time, the World Bank was trying to figure out how to get people to pay for clean water. While billions were being spent by USAID on water treatment plants, the World Bank was funding "water sector reform" in Iraq. In 2003, the Bank established an office in Baghdad to support "its transition to a market economy." A Bank report claimed, "The future for a sustainable water sector requires good governance, market based and private-sector led growth, and diversification." The Bank also said Iraq needed "a new approach to water as an enterprise, with a more important role for the private sector." It was clear that Iraq had to meet these conditions in order to receive support from the Bank.[34] Of course, without meters or functioning treatment plants, "water pricing" was difficult to establish. For instance, when the U.S. special inspector general visited Nasiriya, he asked if water fees were being collected. A representative at the Provincial Council said that, because they did not have meters, they calculated water usage based on how often the reservoir had to be filled divided by the number of people in the area. But he then said they hardly ever collected the fees. On the other hand, Nasiriya residents complained they sometimes had to pay for water, but mostly in the form of "bribes."[35] Those who could not afford the bribes or bottled water simply got sick.

Baghdad had become not a preindustrial society but a deindustrialized society, where continuous access to running water and electricity was a remote memory of a once well-functioning city. In an attempt to avoid attacks on its contractors, Suez said it would supply clean water to Baghdad without ever entering the country, explaining, "The equipment will be delivered in Jordan and Iraqi employees will be trained in Degrémont plants based in neighbouring countries and in France."[36] Baghdad's mayor called Suez's project the "largest municipal water project in the Middle East" and said it would be completed by 2012.[37] To date, however, it has not been completed, and a 2012 study of Baghdad's other water treatment plants revealed they were still producing water with unacceptable levels of E. coli.[38] Outside Baghdad, conditions were worse.

A City of Fountains

There is one exception to the rule that "things are worse" outside Baghdad: Kurdistan. In the northern part of Iraq, Kurdistan is generally considered "safe." It is also where the water is. Filled with mountains and

cascading waterfalls, Kurdistan is home to people who were once per-
secuted by Saddam Hussein and so truly felt "liberated" by Americans.
For these reasons, I thought that water companies might have had better
success there.

The first thing I did upon my arrival in Erbil was check the tap in my
four-star hotel to see if the water was running. It was. The second thing
I did was run downstairs to ask the hotel staff if I could drink it. Three
people shouted at once, "NO!" Of course, I already suspected this would
be the case, but I also knew Ifraz water treatment plant had been supplying the city of Erbil since 2006. So where was the clean water? It turned
out I would spend the rest of my time in Iraq looking for this water as if
chasing a rainbow's end.

From the air, Erbil had looked like any Middle Eastern city, with
roads spread out in radials from the old city, giving it the appearance of
a dartboard. But on the ground, Erbil looked a bit more like Las Vegas
than like the dilapidated south of Iraq. In fact, it appeared to be a brand-
new city full of fountains. Following the second Iraq War, an enormous
amount of money flowed into this American-friendly region, creating a
bit of a gold rush feel in a city perpetually under construction. There were
car dealers everywhere, advertising Hummers, Cadillacs, or any luxury
car you wanted. There were giant spa complexes advertising "women
only." There were restaurants that looked more like amusement parks or
indoor malls. The city was expanding, clearly signified by the rising numbers on its concentric roads. "Roads are named for their distance from the
city. Now we are on 100 Meters Road," my taxi driver said. "The numbers
keep getting bigger."

But the main thing I noticed were the fountains. "This one shoots
waves of water," my driver bragged. "It's bigger than any fountain in all
of Europe." Below the old fortress city built on a mesa, called the Citadel, fountains, shallow pools, and walkways decorated the city's center.
One city park had cascading water pouring out of what looked like Greek
columns that traversed its entire length. Beneath the waterfalls, pools of
water cascaded down terraces through the park. Across the street, yet
another park had a house-sized plastic replica of the Citadel with water shooting out the top, creating elaborate waterfalls, pools, and rivers
around it.

In short, Kurdistan did not look like a war-torn or water-scarce

Water-rich and bustling downtown Erbil—but don't drink the water.

region. Only gradually did I realize that behind the thin veneer of apparent wealth was a "party-till-you-die" kind of fatalism. The region is surrounded by enemies: Iran, Turkey, and even Iraq, which the Kurdish seemed to view as a separate country. "This is Kurdistan," I was repeatedly corrected whenever I talked about "northern Iraq." Along the highway into Erbil, men gathered in groups from noon onward, sitting in the dirt and drinking. They seemed to be there every day, all day long. To me, it looked like a terrible place for a drink, but I was told that religion prevented them from drinking at home. Over time, I came to realize that the roller coasters and amusement parks were there because this was the only moment of peace the region had seen in decades. Everyone had suffered untold horrors. Men drank away their PTSD. Further south, the country was still fighting. But Erbil, which was relatively isolated, was the wealthiest—and the safest—city in the country. The city's residents had a moment of reprieve from violence, though still no clean water.

During my stay, Halwest Shekhani, who happened to be friends with the Kurdish president, Massoud Barzani, was my guide and translator. In another county, Halwest might have been a movie star or politician; he

The Citadel park in Erbil provides a Disney-like setting for family outings.

was a handsomely energetic young man with dark curly hair and a beautiful smile. But in Kurdistan, he was a guide and diplomat, showing American researchers, tourists, and politicians his country. At twenty-three,
Halwest seemed incredibly well educated, more knowledgeable about
American politics than most Americans. But he showed his age with his
obsession with Angelina Jolie and *Avatar,* a movie he had seen from a
bootleg copy from Thailand. He peppered me with questions about both
the 3-D version and Angelina, though his reasons for loving her seemed
more political than lascivious.

"She came here," he told me, "and said she did not want the Americans to leave. And she would not go to an Obama dinner." Indeed, I remembered Angelina Jolie had once said that Americans should not leave
Iraq until the refugee crisis had been solved. She had been a tireless advo-
cate for Iraqi refugees, which included two million externally displaced
and two million internally displaced people since 2003. But the Obama
comment surprised me. "Obama wants to pull out of Iraq," Halwest explained, "and then we will die. You can't just put all the chess pieces in

place and then knock the table over and say you're going home." Another time, Halwest shocked me by saying he missed Saddam Hussein. I gradually realized that he missed making fun of him, especially his laugh. "Heh . . . heh . . . heh"—he did a spot-on imitation. Halwest seemed to miss Hussein in the same way that some Americans missed Tina Fey as Sarah Palin, or Will Ferrell as George W. Bush. He was a joke.

Of course, the reality was that Hussein had destroyed Halwest's life. After the Gulf War, called the "Uprising" in Kurdistan, Halwest was forced to flee home on foot with his mother and six siblings. He was five years old. His family followed an enormous exodus of Kurds into the mountains, where they survived on wild onions mixed with yogurt and milk from their goat. Sometimes, he said, Iranians would throw bread to them from trucks on the border. The water made him sick, but he said, "The yogurt and herbs would calm my stomach. I can still taste that flavor in my mouth today." Halwest's father had gone to fight, and when the Uprising failed, he was taken to Saddam's Abu Ghraib prison and tortured for years. Today, he cannot walk properly and still suffers health effects from the water he drank while at Abu Ghraib, which Halwest said was untreated salty water from the Tigris River. Halwest said, "I could talk for ten years and still not tell you all the terrible things that happened under Saddam."

So we changed the subject. I asked Halwest about the water situation in Erbil, and he confirmed my suspicions. "Only poor people drink tap water," he answered, "because they have to. But they get sick." The rest drink bottled water from Turkey or the United States.

Historically, Erbil's inhabitants were supplied with water from a large underground reservoir, which once flowed up through artesian wells at the Citadel. Today, the Citadel is completely empty, its wells dry. It is a ghost town of residences ranging from gorgeous marble mansions with indoor courtyards to one-room mud-brick houses. The wells gradually started going dry only about thirty-five years ago as the water table sank, forcing residents to move away. In 2007, the last of the residents were forced to leave when the area was turned into a UNESCO World Heritage Site. Still, the Citadel is advertised as the "world's oldest continuously inhabited city." So I asked Halwest, "Does anyone live here?"

"No, no one," he replied.

"So it's no longer the world's oldest continuously inhabited city?" I pried.

"I suppose not," he said nonchalantly, implying there were more important things to worry about.

Ifraz water treatment plant was built by Fluor as an alternative to well water; the reported cost was $185 million, though this figure seems to vary quite a bit. It is one of the largest water projects funded by the U.S. government in Iraq, behind Fluor's Nasiriya water treatment plant in southern Iraq (which cost approximately $277 million) and Suez's Al-Rusafa water treatment plant in Baghdad (approximately $210 million). In 2006, Ifraz was opened with much fanfare and declared a success. At the opening ceremony, Kurdistan's prime minister, Nechirvan Barzani, said, "I am pleased and privileged to be here today to participate in the opening ceremony of the Ifraz water project. . . . This water project is one of the largest American projects that has been successfully completed in Iraq, and this fact carries much significance for us all. We thank the United States government for this valuable contribution to the reconstruction of our country."[39] Later that year, the United States awarded Fluor two more major contracts, one to rebuild Iraq's oil industry and the other to construct U.S. military bases in Iraq. During the Iraq War, Fluor saw a spectacular rise in profits. From 2010 through 2013, Fluor was ranked number one on the Fortune 500 list of construction companies. Annually, the corporation now makes about $12 billion in profits.

So of course I was shocked to be asked to fix "bad water" on a routine visit to Ifraz. Fluor had the billions of dollars, after all. I could barely pay my hotel bill. On the other hand, I knew that water projects had a history of being abandoned in the country, part of a larger reconstruction fiasco in Iraq. It turned out that Fluor had completed only 60 percent of Ifraz, which it called "Stage 1." It wanted more money to finish the rest. But by 2012, Iraq had still not been able to secure enough funding to complete Ifraz, though the government was in negotiations with a Japanese bank.[40] None of this should have surprised me. A 2013 report from the U.S. special inspector general concluded, "Because of . . . deficiencies in record keeping, the disposition of billions of dollars for projects remains unknown."[41] *Foreign Policy* magazine more succinctly described the problem in a recent front-page piece: "The Democracy Boondoggle in Iraq."[42]

Due to all the conflicting reports, I was anxious, of course, to finally see Ifraz. "Be sure with Fluor," the company's motto had promised.

According to the *Kurdistan Globe,* Erbil's clean water problem would be solved by the Ifraz water project, which would supply the city with water until 2035.[43] The *Kurdish Globe* explained, "The capital city shouldn't have to worry about another water shortage for the next 25 years. . . . The strategic Ifraz water project, funded by the United States, would treat and pump 10,000 cubic meters of water to Erbil every hour, supplying the whole city."[44] So what had gone wrong?

Ifraz was difficult to find, located on an unmarked dirt road leading to the Zab River. We got lost, and Halwest became quite worried that we might inadvertently end up in Mosul, a violence-ridden city full of insurgents. But then suddenly he brightened up and said, "Let's go there now. Why not? I'll do it!" Since he knew I wanted to see the Mosul Dam, I was afraid he was serious. I did not want to get killed.

"What, are you serious?" I replied, startled from the calm of endless wheat fields.

Luckily, the brown Zab River, the main tributary of the Tigris, appeared over the horizon before he could answer. We had found Ifraz. Driving up to the gate, we passed an armed guard in an elevated post. Next, the treatment tanks appeared, which did look state of the art. Ifraz pumps water from the Zab River, then treats it with a sand and charcoal filter after allowing the turbidity to settle in ponds. When we stopped so I could take some photographs, a man ran out and angrily yelled, "No photos!" Discovering he was the lead engineer on the project, I started asking about the plant. But he was already mad about the photos. "It works," he replied curtly, dismissing me.

"How does it work?" I asked. "Does it use charcoal or ozone filtration?"

He replied: "You know, it has motors and pumps. It works, it works."

I knew that the plant had been plagued with endless delays, but I could tell I would get no further information on this topic. So I asked instead if water was being pumped from the ground for treatment. He denied this quite vehemently, saying, "No, this will all be connected to Bekhme Dam. That is where the water will come from." I was shocked. Bekhme Dam had not been built, as far as I knew, and it had a very controversial history. It was called "Saddam's Dam" in the region, since it was once intended to flood out insurgent Kurds. Instantly, I decided we must go to Bekhme next to see if construction had started. Ifraz had been a bust, as it was still unclear to me whether or not the water was actually being pumped to Erbil.[45]

As we were leaving the area, the engineer shouted, "You can get pictures on the Internet."

Bekhme Dam and Bechtel

En route to Bekhme Dam, I was struck by the scenery, which was strangely unspoiled for a war-torn environment. The valleys were covered in lush forests, rolling green grassy hills, and stunning canyons with pristine rivers at the bottom. No one had told me Iraq would be this beautiful. When I commented on this to Halwest, he explained that this was Barzani territory: "Under Barzani rules, you cannot kill wildlife or cut down trees. . . . This is why Barzani areas are always the most green, like this. If it were up to people in Erbil, they would say, 'So there's only one deer left? It's mine!' But not the Barzani people."

Saddam Hussein had planned to build Bekhme Dam in part to drown out the Barzani who lived in the valley, since they were leaders in the resistance against him. (Hussein's adversary, Massoud Barzani, is now president of Kurdistan.) To implement his plan, Hussein hired Bechtel. If the dam had been finished, it would have been the seventh-largest dam in the world and the second time he had used water as a weapon against his enemies. In the south, he had already drained a vast wetlands and homeland to the Marsh Arabs in reprisal for a Shia uprising; half a million inhabitants had been forced to flee.[46]

"Saddam wanted to devastate the area by flooding out Barzani," Halwest said. Hussein had started burning down houses and forcing people out of the valley before he was stopped by the Gulf War. "But he also wanted the water and power."

Not surprisingly, the dam was initially a British idea. Archaeologist Ralph Solecki, who worked on artifacts in the valley, has described the history: "It had been identified as a good place for a high dam as early as 1937 when the area for the dam site was explored first by [British engineer] E. V. Richards." Solecki continued, "One of the low points in our own era was in 1975, when there was an evacuation of the valley and the inhabitants deported under threat that the dam was being built."[47] Dam construction was delayed by the onset of the Iran–Iraq war in 1980. But in 1987, San Francisco–based Bechtel was hired to build the dam, working for Saddam Hussein. (At the time, there were no international sanctions against him.) In an attempt to stop construction, Kurds attacked Bechtel employees, who had to be accompanied by military escort in the region. By 1990, the river had been successfully diverted, and equipment and materials were in place to fill in the dam—but then the Gulf War started.

Bechtel's role in Iraq at this time was not minor. Besides the dam, Bechtel had been in negotiations to build an oil pipeline across Iraq to a port in Jordan for $2 billion, which would supply the United States. For these negotiations, Secretary of State Donald Rumsfeld had visited Iraq in 1983, during which visit he was infamously captured in a photograph shaking hands with Hussein. In 1987, Saddam Hussein backed out of the deal and fell out of favor with the U.S. government.

Before the Gulf War began, Bechtel negotiated with the U.S. government to provide reconstruction services for Kuwait, including putting out oil fires for $2.3 billion. The United States also forced Saddam Hussein, as a precondition of his surrender, to pay for all failed U.S. contracts caused by the Gulf War. One of these contracts was for Bekhme Dam. After the U.S. attack on Iraq, Bechtel employees who had been working on various projects were stranded throughout the country. At Bekhme, Iraqi soldiers retreating south took four Bechtel employees hostage and allegedly used them as "human shields." At the same time, according to Ralph Solecki, the Kurds "dismantled the Bekhme dam works," since it was viewed as a symbol of Saddam's hatred. (Though when I asked Halwest who had torn down the dam, he said simply, "*Jach.* Traitors.") After the war, Bechtel claimed $1 billion in damages, to be paid by Saddam Hussein through the United Nations Compensation Commission.[48]

Whether or not Bekhme was now being rebuilt by Bechtel was, therefore, no small matter. Some have even suggested that, rather than weapons of mass destruction, Bechtel's investments in Iraq and Saddam's debts led to the U.S. invasion. Predicting the start of the second Iraq War, journalist Jim Vallette wrote: "Bechtel's long quest for a lucrative oil deal with Iraq may finally, after two decades of diplomatic efforts, be solved by brute force."[49]

On the way to Bekhme, Halwest and I stopped for lunch at a restaurant near the Little Zab River. I tried the fish from the river, which was full of bones but very tasty. Halwest apologized for not knowing its name:

"I know how different fish taste from each river," he said, "but I do not know their names. The Little Zab fish is very good, but the Greater Zab is even better." The restaurant owner then said the fish was called *capewi*, or fox's mouth.

"How do you feel about the dam?" I asked the owner.

He replied, "My life depends on this restaurant, so, no, I don't agree with the dam. It will flood this valley all the way to Turkey." If the dam is finished, estimates are that it will flood out twenty thousand people in scattered villages throughout the valley. But Halwest said this was a low estimate, since the refugee population had started returning post-Hussein.

Some people in the area, including Halwest, still wanted a dam, but a much smaller one. He explained, "The prime minister wants the original plan. I want a smaller one." Opinions on the dam vary, even in the region to be flooded. We stopped at a nomad camp along the way and asked a woman how she felt about the dam. She replied, "I want the dam to come. I want to have a sea to swim in." But then, she was able to move her house; others were not.

Besides the threat to people's homes, important Neanderthal artifacts in the valley, particularly at Shanidar Cave, are also at risk. This is what concerns archaeologist Ralph Solecki, who once hired Halwest as a research assistant. In 1978, Solecki discovered ten Neanderthal skeletons in Shanidar Cave, as well as ritual burial artifacts between ten thousand and forty-five thousand years old. It is the only site of its kind in the Middle East, and only 10 percent has been excavated.[50] As we passed the cave, Halwest called Solecki in the United States to tell him we were heading to the dam. "He always asks about the progress on the dam," Halwest explained. "He wants to know if it's going to happen."

In fact, Halwest was constantly talking on one cell phone while reading texts on another. He seemed to need only his knees to drive. I entertained myself with the view until a motorcade approached. Halwest said nonchalantly, "That's the president." Instinctively, I raised my camera for a picture.

"Don't do that!" Halwest suddenly yelled, grabbing my hand and pulling it down. "They will shoot." I could tell he was not kidding.

"Who, the *peshmurga*?" I asked, referring to the Kurdish military.

"No, the Americans," he said. "They don't know any better. They don't usually travel with the president, but I saw American soldiers. He must be traveling with a delegation of Americans today." Later, the chilling Wikileaks footage of American soldiers gunning down Iraqis holding cameras would remind me of this incident.

"How did you know it was the president?" I asked.

"I recognize his license plate."

Given that I had not seen one American soldier so far, I was surprised to suddenly encounter one who might shoot me. "These mistakes happen all the time," Halwest tried to explain. "The Kurds are not happy about it."

In fact, the Americans had hit a convoy that included President Barzani's brother with Maverick missiles in 2003. The missiles were intended for a nearby tank, but they inadvertently blew up the president's brother. Halwest explained, "Eighteen security people were killed and Barzani's brother is not the same. He was severely wounded."[51]

Suddenly distracted, Halwest pointed to a field on the left and laughed. "That's where the 'Invasion' started," he said, using the term Kurds use for the second Iraq War.

"Why is that funny?"

"Because when the Americans parachuted into this field, everyone was happy to see them," he explained. "But the soldiers lay on their stomachs in a circle with their guns pointing out." Halwest was laughing as he told me what happened next. An old man ran out to them with a tea tray, a standard Kurdish hospitality for visitors. He continued, "The Americans yelled at him to 'stay back,' or they would shoot. The old man did not understand what they were saying, so he kept coming. Luckily, someone stopped him, or he would have been shot." Then he turned serious, "That was when we thought, 'What kind of country are you from that your government will not even tell you that Kurdistan is friendly?' American soldiers thought an Iraqi was an Iraqi and that we were all the enemy. . . . Many Kurds have been killed because of this. No one told them that we wanted them there. What kind of government is that?" Halwest said he still felt sorry for the soldiers, who camped in the field for weeks, waiting for reinforcements. "It was so hot," he said. "But we all laughed at them, too. It was pretty funny."

"Now," he continued, "Americans only stay on their bases. They will not come into the city in their uniforms. They cannot carry guns in the city. We don't often see them."

Finally, we arrived at Bekhme Dam, which was nonexistent. There were cuts through the rocks and a spot where it looked like the dam should be, but only heavy rebar stuck out of the stone walls. The river was flowing calmly through the canyon. Nearby, a new housing complex with a mosque and minaret was apparently ready to house the dam construction workers. But the buildings were abandoned. After a four-hour drive in search of a dam that wasn't there, I was still left wondering where Erbil's water came from.

Leaving Bekhme Dam, our final stop was the reservoir where the treated water from Ifraz was being stored before being sent to Erbil about ten miles away.[52] In one tank, an enormous tomb of water looked fresh and clean. But in the other, there was the brown scum. Halwest, the lieutenant, and I peered down at it.

"Can I take a picture?" I asked and received a quick "No" from both Halwest and the lieutenant. After a long exchange between them, Halwest said, "His boss would be very mad if he let you take a picture, or even that you saw this. We're not actually supposed to be here." As we climbed back down, Halwest translated for the lieutenant: "He wants to know if that is normal, what's on the surface. Is it supposed to look that way?" I said it did not look good to me, to which he replied, "Do you know what causes it?" I said, unfortunately, no.

"An engineer came and looked at it and said we must throw all this out," the lieutenant said. "Here, I will show you where we dump the bad water."

Surprised, I followed him out to a grassy area in back of the building. Beneath a small ridge was a large concrete tunnel with a ditch below it that showed signs of recently dumped water. The ditch looked like it was being extended, which the lieutenant explained: "They are building an artificial river around all of Erbil." Continuing to translate, Halwest said that Erbil was only 7 percent green and should be 57 percent green like other cities. I wondered where he got these statistics.

Then Halwest suddenly exclaimed, "It's going to run right by my property! I knew I was right to buy it." He pointed excitedly across the ridge, where he had bought property for next to nothing, hoping the city would eventually reach out here. Realizing he would have riverfront land, he was delighted. I was only baffled. "Bad water" from Ifraz treatment plant was going to supply a whole new river around the city?

A Quest for Clean Water

In my quest for clean water for Erbil, I still had not found it. But neither did the Swedish NGO Qandil during a similar investigation in 2008. The problem, Qandil discovered, was not with the plant but with the distribution system. Ifraz was built with a "build-operate-transfer" (BOT) contract, which builds a new treatment plant but does "not extend water supply to new users and actually risk[s] diverting public funding away from improving distribution."[53] In short, there was a new water treatment plant but no clear plans for safely getting its water to the people. According to Qandil, "This problem is enhanced by the fact that *no proper map of the water network pipes exists*" and "no particular sewage system exists" in Erbil. Because of this, wastewater was contaminating the groundwater, which was feeding into the city water supply system. "The problems peaked, in particular, with the new water treatment plant coming into operation," due to the fact that Ifraz water overloaded the system and caused pipe breakages.[54] In 2008, Qandil concluded there was no clean water in Erbil; it then set a modest goal of providing clean water to one block of the city by 2010. By the time I arrived, residents in a small section of town had received notices that their tap water was now safe to drink. But, according to Halwest, "No one believes it."

It seemed like clean Erbil tap water was a mythological thing—some said it existed and others said it did not, and seemingly it could never be found. It was always in some *other* neighborhood, even as Ifraz was lauded as a near miracle by the Kurdish press and government. But this was the case in much of Iraq, where clean water was perpetually promised and promises were perpetually forgotten. It was hard to remember where it was supposed to be and when. It could be even harder to find the truth about it. Even the U.S. special inspector general, when he visited Erbil in 2010, concluded, "It is not possible to measure improvement in water and health outcomes." On one hand, a flash poll showed that 88 percent of Erbil residents were satisfied with water quantity and 85 percent with water quality.[55] On the other hand, a 2012 survey by Associates for International Research determined, "Tap water is not potable, even in housing compounds, so the use of large bottles of water is common for drinking and cooking."[56] That same year, a cholera outbreak hit the city.

Nevertheless, the U.S. inspector general's report on Ifraz sounds practically utopian compared to the report on Fluor's Nasiriya plant in the south. There, 76 percent of residents said they were "very dissatisfied" with their water quality, and zero were satisfied. One resident said that "tap water is not [even] good for laundry" and another said that the "water quality is very poor and it is unfit for drinking—it has a lot of impurities." In fact, 86 percent of residents thought that both purchased water and water from rivers and streams was better than that supplied by Fluor. The report also found significant failures in the water treatment plant, to the point that it was barely functioning. The computer system that monitored plant function was said to have "never worked."[57]

One possible reason for the vast discrepancy in how these two water plants are perceived is their location. Any U.S. government agency survey undertaken in Kurdistan might be likely to receive more positive results than a similar survey in the south. This can be surmised from the effusive pro-American responses on the Kurdish survey: "Thank the United States of America for having funded the project," or "[This] is one of the most important projects in the city that was established with American aid." Even someone who did not get water said, "[Though] I do not benefit from the water from this project, I think we should thank America for constructing and financing the Ifraz project." In contrast, attitudes about Americans are strikingly different in the south. When the survey asked what people thought about the United States funding a water treatment plant in the area, one woman replied, "I do not have love or favor towards the U.S. government."

Another major difference between the two regions is that Erbil already had a vast underground water aquifer before Ifraz was built. Unfortunately, as more people tap into the aquifer, it is quickly dropping and may soon be inaccessible. But in the south, water is available only from brackish and polluted rivers that are beginning to run dry. So the quality *and* quantity of water would have been much better in the north before the treatment plant came online. For this reason, as the inspector general admitted, "It is not possible to measure improvement in water and health outcomes." It may well be that all the U.S. survey discovered was that Kurdish Iraqis like Americans better than do Arab Iraqis. If an American interviewer is told there is clean water, it may have more to do with the kind of relationship the respondent wants to establish with the interviewer than with the actual quality of the water. In either case, it is

In Halabja, a polluted water tank still supplies the city.

clear that there is still no clean water in Erbil. That said, it is still far better off than most places in southern Iraq, and even most places in Kurdistan.

Halabja's Poison Water

If clean water is not available in Erbil, the situation is much worse in Kurdistan's Halabja, where people are still drinking the poisons from a 1988 gas attack by Saddam Hussein that killed five thousand people. The United States had promised Halabja a water treatment plant, but instead it decided to shift $3.4 billion designated for water, electricity, and oil development to training Iraqi forces. The Halabja water project, which would have cost $10 million, was abandoned. According to the *New York Times,* when engineer Nuradeen Ghreeb heard the news, "He sat on one of his beloved water pipes . . . and wept." Ghreeb said, "If the Americans think that training the Iraqi Army comes before clean drinking water for the people of Halabja, then we can't expect anything from them."[58]

The reasons chemical weapons were dropped on Halabja are disputed, both as to whether the attack was meant to kill Kurds or Iranians and as to who precisely was complicit in the attack. According to Halwest, people from Halabja saw American helicopters on that day. Journalists from the *Los Angeles Times* and *Washington Post* confirmed that U.S. Bell helicopters had been sold to Iraq and converted for the attack against Halabja. According to *Foreign Policy*'s analysis of CIA documents, the United States was also aware of Saddam Hussein's use of these weapons—and even provided him with intelligence for targeting. The article explains, "U.S. intelligence officials conveyed the location of the Iranian troops to Iraq, fully aware that Hussein's military would attack with chemical weapons, including sarin, a lethal nerve agent" in 1988.[59]

One of those locations was Halabja, where intelligence claimed Iranian troops had entered a few days before the gas attack. The results are hard to forget. When chemical weapons fell on Halabja, people say it smelled like apples. Then people started to choke, and within hours five thousand were dead. "The chemical attack on Halabja," President Bush said in 2002, "provided a glimpse of the crimes Saddam Hussein is willing to commit, and the threat he now presents to the entire world."[60] Five days after this statement, the United States invaded Iraq.

Soon after the invasion, Secretary of State Colin Powell went to Halabja to attend the opening of a museum that would serve as a memorial for victims of the gas attack. In 2004 he visited again for a memorial event held on the anniversary of the attack. At this event he said:

> For 15 years we have stood witness on this day to the victims of
> Halabja, that their deaths not be forgotten. But this year is different.
> This year the dreams of the Iraqi people to be free from the terror of
> the Saddam Hussein regime have come true. This year our bereave-
> ment has finally been lightened. This year a new light shines on Iraq,
> a light of freedom, a light of hope, and a light of justice.[61]

He was greeted by cheering crowds. People were optimistic that their water problems would be solved and their illnesses cured. But by 2005, U.S. attention had shifted to the military "surge" in the south. Promises to clean up Halabja's water supply were forgotten.[62] The mood in Halabja turned from hope to rage in two short years. In 2006, demonstrators blocked the road to keep politicians out and burned down the new multimillion-dollar memorial building. They wanted clean water, they said, not fancy new buildings. Police opened fire, killing a fourteen-year-old boy and injuring eight others.[63] Since then, politicians have abandoned the city. Halwest said, "The U.S. won't help clean up Halabja because they don't want to draw attention to their involvement in the attack."

While the memorial was restored to look brand new, the people in Halabja are still drinking the groundwater soaked with the green-apple-smelling chemicals. They are still getting sick. New Halabja, on the outskirts of the city, is in even worse shape. Started as a shantytown for people fleeing the chemical attacks, it now holds nine thousand residents who say they are lucky to get running water every ten days or so.[64] Once a thriving agricultural community, Halabja also had to abandon farming after the chemical attack because of the poisoning of the soil.

In old Halabja, I was the only visitor at the memorial. A guide was there to lead me through exhibits that were mostly photographs of the victims. He was also obviously sick; his eyes were teary and red, and his skin was blotchy. Though I politely refrained from asking about his condition, he eventually pointed at his face and said, "This is from the gas." Today, Halabja residents are suing the French companies that supplied the chemicals for the attack against them. They have few other options. Like Bhopal, India, which Dow chemicals poisoned, the city has been forgotten.[65]

At the entrance to the city cemetery a sign reads, "Ba'ath party members are not allowed to enter." There, I met a man whose whole family had died in the chemical attack. Halwest knew him and explained his situation: "He cannot marry again, because his children would be sick, and his children's children would be sick. When women become pregnant here, they have to go to a hospital in Iran. Many of them die." Outside the cemetery, we stopped to talk to some people who had heard a rumor that Japan might provide funding for a drinking water treatment plant.[66] They wanted to know if it was true. By then, the only people I believed about the water were the three hotel clerks who, when I asked if I could drink from the tap, shouted "NO!" I similarly wanted to shout, "NO! No one is coming." Instead, I simply said, "I don't know."

How to Exit Iraq

In March 2003, when President George W. Bush declared "Mission accomplished" from the deck of the USS *Abraham Lincoln*, contractors rushed in to Iraq to start reconstruction. But the country was actually still at war, and hundreds of contractors were killed. Ten years later, in March 2013, the office of the special inspector general for Iraqi reconstruction released its final report on the reconstruction program's success. One of the main lessons was this: "Begin rebuilding only after establishing sufficient security." Perhaps more damning, the report stated that there was no clear accounting of what had happened to project money in cases like Ifraz, since even the term "project" was loosely defined. In some instances, the report read, "project" referred to "the cost of building just one component." In other instances, "project" meant "the cost of work that was unsatisfactory and had to be redone by another contractor."[67] In this fashion, more and more money was passed from both the Iraqi and the U.S. governments to U.S. corporations. Melik Kaylan, whom I had met on his last visit to Iraq, summed up his experience as a war correspondent there: "We wanted to plant democracy there, instead we have likely demonstrated that freedom equals turbulence equals bloodshed worse than tyranny."[68]

Clearly, war zones are known for their potential to corrupt; in this sense, Iraq is no different from other countries. But Iraq also suffered from a naive and unwarranted optimism on the part of U.S. politicians about what privatization could do for a country. In 2003, Paul Bremer said at the World Economic Forum: "Markets allocate resources much more efficiently than politicians. So our strategic goal in the months ahead is to set in motion policies which will have the effect of reallocating people and resources from state enterprises to more productive private firms."[69] In reality, Iraq became a black hole for U.S. funding. In 2008, the World Bank loaned more than $100 million to Iraq for water infrastructure, after already spending hundreds of millions on the exact same thing. The Bank report noted, "The quality of the current water supply [is] well below national and international standards . . . especially when it comes to the bacteriological content of drinking water." As usual, the Bank again listed one of its mandates as "full cost recovery, including operation and maintenance as well as investment costs." At least this time it acknowledged this would be "difficult to achieve in the near future" and might have to wait until "conditions on the ground permit."[70] In the loan outcomes, the Bank said of the "full cost recovery" objective, "Study was undertaken but not agreed to."[71] In short, the Bank was pushing full cost recovery against the will of Iraqis. In 2011, the last American soldiers allegedly left the country after a failed experiment in "democracy building."

As the World Bank, the IMF, and the United States pressure the world to turn water into a commodity, the situation becomes a disaster in a country like Iraq. Ignoring Islam, which cannot be accounted for in macroeconomic policy, the World Bank misunderstood local resistance to water privatization. In Islamic tradition, water is to be shared communally. According to Ibn Abbas, the Prophet Muhammad once said, "All Muslims are partners in three things—in water, herbage (animal pasture) and fire. . . . Its price is *Haram*"—forbidden.[72] Besides ignoring religious beliefs, the Bank ignored traditional Iraqi water systems. For instance, Kurdistan has ancient water supply systems that have worked for centuries. These *karez* systems, known as *qanats* elsewhere, involve elaborate underground canals that bring water down from the mountains while avoiding the problem of evaporation. The *karez* systems once supplied the Citadel of Erbil, as well as cities throughout the region. But the Bank and USAID ignored these unique natural water filtration systems and instead promoted diverting water from rivers, pumping groundwater, and building more dams—their blueprint for "international best practices." A UNESCO study found that in 2005–2009, 70 percent of the *karez* systems dried up; because of this, more than one hundred thousand people were forced to leave their homes and head to cities.[73] The *karez* systems are drying up at an unprecedented rate due to overpumping, water-intensive irrigation, drought, and neglect. Villages in northern Iraq have become dependent on water brought in by tanker trucks for survival.[74]

Unfortunately, the *karez* systems are disappearing when the country is also losing its only other sources of water, the Tigris and Euphrates. Across the border in Turkey, the World Bank–funded Greater Anatolia Project (GAP) is rapidly reaching completion. GAP consists of twenty-two megadams, the largest of which is Ataturk. Besides drowning Kurdish communities, these dams dramatically decrease water supplies to both Syria and Iraq, which has led to unrest in the former.[75] According to former Turkish president Suleyman Demirel, neither "Syria nor Iraq can lay claim to Turkey's rivers. . . . We have a right to do anything we like. The water resources are Turkey's; the oil resources are theirs. We don't say we share the oil resources, and they cannot say they share our water resources."[76] Turkey, already a water-rich nation compared to Iraq and

Syria, plans to use the water to grow cotton in the desert. Meanwhile, Syria has deteriorated into civil war.

As the water pressure of the Tigris and Euphrates decreases, saltwater from the ocean has started to push inland into the estuaries. Near Basra, people have complained about increasing water salinity, which is harming both agriculture and livestock. In 2009, Basra's agriculture director, Amer Suleiman, announced that his department would have to declare Basra a "disaster area" because of the high salinity level. "The future of agriculture in Basra is at risk and if things continue to deteriorate there is no hope for Basra to recover," he said. Residents noticed dying palm and henna trees and dying wildlife. The director of the water purification plant said the salinity level had increased fivefold.

As irrigated lands become desert, dust storms are also increasing throughout Iraq. At least twenty serious sandstorms have occurred in the past three years.[77] Iraq's water resources minister, Hassan Janabi, described the problem: "We've experienced salinity and desertification and villages are emigrating. And we are facing general emigration. They leave their land because they can't irrigate it. They go to the cities to find another job. Or they change from agriculture to small factories. Now Iraq is facing scarcity, really."[78]

The World Commission on Dams has pressed the World Bank to stop supporting dams on international waterways, including the Greater Anatolia Project, which the commission says fuels international tensions and causes water scarcity for downriver countries. The commission has recommended that the Bank support projects on international waterways only when "good faith negotiations" exist between the countries involved. This would mean ceasing funding for the Greater Anatolia Project. But the Bank has refused to comply, claiming the commission's recommendations are only "guidelines" and "not laws to be obeyed rigidly." The Bank's official response was: "The World Bank considers a blanket prohibition on work with an agency that has built a dam in contravention of good faith negotiations to be too broad and to foreclose many opportunities for productive collaboration."[79] Instead, the Bank promised to "notify" all nations along the international waterway, an action that clearly has not solved the problem for Iraq or Syria.

In response to complaints from Iraq, president of the Turkish Water Institute Ahmet Mete Saatçi has argued that Iraqis are being paranoid about how many dams Turkey is building. At a conference, he said, "I have been told by some Iraqi friends that we are even hiding reservoirs in Turkey. I told him that we have such a camouflage method that you can even see it in Google. So go to Google Maps, you can see what we have done." At this conference, I had the chance to talk to Saatçi about the Greater Anatolia Project, though he was quite defensive. When I asked about the impact of the dams on water quality, he said curtly, "The dams improve water quality." When I asked about flooding the rare and endemic species in the region, he said, "Do you know the area where we built the dams, have you been there? Have you seen any species? It's rock." I said that I had indeed been there and knew about its endemic flowers, which made him flustered. Again, he curtly insisted there was "nothing there."

"There's also the problem of cutting off water to Iraq and Syria," I finally stated the obvious. At this point, I was growing irritated with his condescending attitude.

"So what if water doesn't go to Syria and Iraq?" he shrugged. "What happens then?"

"Uh, people die?" I suggested, incredulously.

"Haha, no it is because of your bombs that they die!" he shouted. "Show me one person who has died of thirst in Iraq. No, it is because of your bombs they die."

Touché, I thought. There is no defending what the United States has done in Iraq; unfortunately, the U.S.–Iraq war is now being used as a justification for the bad behaviors of other countries around the world. Indeed, the U.S. invasion provided Turkey with the option of cutting off Iraq's water without fear of reprisal. Today, many Iraqis see their country as having devolved into a pawn in an even larger battle between Iran and Turkey. Americans are exiting an extremely fragile state, having set the stage for wars to come.

On my last day in Iraq, Halwest and I drove over Bastori River, which was almost dry. "They say it is global warming, but do you know what I think it is?" Halwest asked. "Turkey is cutting off our water supply." Indeed, as we headed back to the plains and Erbil, the sky grew black with dust. "It was not like this three or four years ago," Halwest said. "Sometimes it is so bad that you cannot breathe or drive."

With enemies on all sides, the future of Iraqi Kurdistan is precarious. "Turkey bombs the border every day, where they say the PKK is. But there are villages there," Halwest complained. "It is the same with Iran." In the south, there is al-Qaeda, which has only grown in strength since the U.S. invasion. Kurdistan has a good security force, but it does not have airplanes or missiles, and insurgents sometimes sneak in from the south. In 2007, a suicide bomber tried to blow up the parliament building in Erbil. Since blast walls surrounded the building, the bomber instead killed hundreds of people in the street. Halwest described trying to find his grandmother, who was trapped in the rubble. He said, "I was lifting bodies, and I can't remember crying, but I know I was crying. I just can't remember. 'Why did they do this?' I kept asking myself, over and over."

During my stay, an Iraqi journalist and friend of Halwest's was kidnapped, his body later found dumped in a river in Mosul. Halwest was afraid that when the Americans left, militant Islamists in the south would move north. "They call this the land of the infidels," Halwest explained, "because we are friends to Jews and Christians."

After leaving Iraq, feeling guilty about my own good fortune, I kept remembering a day when Halwest had surprised me with a visit to an amusement park at the top of the mountain, where we rode a roller coaster that swung out over a gorgeous green canyon. We dangled there, thousands of feet above anything, laughing in glee. Below us, women picnicked in their colorful sequined Kurdish dresses. Men preferred the Elvis Presley look, with slicked-back hair, thin ties, and tight jackets. It was a celebratory day, and everyone we met seemed in particularly good spirits. But on the way back to Erbil, Halwest suddenly veered the car toward a cliff's edge.

"Do you want to drive off?" he asked.

I hadn't heard what he said, so I nodded happily and said, "Okay." I assumed he wanted to park and show me something.

"You want me to?" he asked again.

Again I said, "Okay." Suddenly, we were inches from the edge.

"NO! NO! NO!" I shouted, and he slammed on the brakes, laughing. I thought he had gone insane.

"I was wondering. But I thought I should ask three times to be sure," he said. "I would have done it. Why not? Why shouldn't we? Then it will all be over." Then he shrugged his shoulders, in his nonchalant way, and headed the car back toward Erbil.

CONCLUSION

Imagining a Water-Secure World

AS I TRAVELED THE WORLD investigating its water problems, I saw unrest and heartbreak wherever I went, but the only place I suffered physical
harm was in the United States. It was at the 2009 G-20 Summit in Pittsburgh, where the heads of the Group of 20, the world's twenty wealthiest countries, were convening. At these annual meetings, presidents and
prime ministers meet with heads of the World Bank, IMF, WTO, and
United Nations to set financial policy for the world. A few months after
the G-20 meeting that year, the U.N. General Assembly would vote on a
resolution that would make water a "human right." At the U.N. meeting,
some suspected the United States would sign on to the U.N. resolution;
others did not. For this reason, I was curious about the agenda—both of
the policy makers and of the protesters—at the 2009 G-20. In the official
G-20 publication, Loïc Fauchon promoted the World Water Forum, ap-
plauding the heads of state who had attended the last Forum, claiming it
spoke "loudly" of a "change in emphasis from the hydro-technical to the
hydro-political."[1] I wasn't sure what this meant, but I knew what Loïc Fauchon wanted. He wanted more money to flow in the direction of water.

But 2009 was also a year of financial crises. The United States was
barely on the other side of a financial crisis caused by the collapse of the

housing market. Europe was heading into its own recession, from which it still has not emerged. It seemed that global financial crises had grown too large and frequent for the IMF to manage; some were even suggesting the IMF had *created* these crises, starting with the Asian financial crisis of 1997.[2] The World Bank's future was also precarious since alternative lending institutions were now competing with the Bank. For instance, China was providing loans without conditionalities, and the BRICS bank also looked like a formidable rival. In South America, countries were forming a South Bank. An economist at the G-20 explained the problem: "Over the next 10 to 20 years the World Bank faces three options: it can continue on its current path of gradual decline; it might be radically scaled back and eventually eliminated; or it can dramatically reinvent itself." The main reason for the Bank's troubles, he argued, was that "developing countries find it insufficiently responsive to their needs."[3] To me, it seemed that the world could be on the cusp of change.

At the same time, private water contracts were dramatically failing in nations not represented at the G-20. Studies had shown that corporate water management had actually reduced people's access to water in the past decade, thus pushing back the U.N. Millennium Development Goal (MDG) of halving the number of people without access to clean water by 2015. In 2006, a study from Public Services International concluded, "The net contribution of 15 years of privatisation has thus been to significantly reduce the finance available to developing countries for investment in water."[4] Even when corporate water contracts required the extension of water networks, these commitments were "invariably revised, abandoned or missed." In short, private finance had not helped supply more water to poor people. "Instead," the report claimed, "it is clear that the emphasis on the private sector over the past 15 years has had a negative impact on progress towards the water and sanitation MDG with major implications for communities of poor people around the world."[5]

Today, even the World Bank is admitting that its water privatization program is failing. In a 2010 report the Bank concluded, "Cost-recovery targets have been wildly ambitious and unrealistic because of inadequate social assessment"—that is to say, the Bank had misread local conditions. According to the Bank, "Only 15 percent of projects that attempted any cost recovery actually achieved what they set out to do, and only 9 percent of projects that attempted full cost recovery were successful." Some of the reasons the Bank listed for contract failures were "civil unrest, conflict, or coup," "natural disasters," "financial crisis," "loss of private operator interest," and "change from a government that promoted PSP [private-sector participation] to one that did not."[6] But the most common reason for contract collapse was the corporate failure to extend water networks, which the Bank blamed on customer nonpayment. Law professor James Salzman explained the problem for corporations: "The initial sunk costs can be massive, not to mention the continuing costs of maintenance and upgrade. . . . A return on investment also requires general economic, political, and social stability over that period; yet, in many developing countries, this is far from a given."[7] In order to make a profit, corporations required two things: social stability and paying customers. They had found neither.

The International Center for Dispute Resolution has had to deal with these contract failures, since corporations have sued for compensation for their losses. In Tanzania, the company Biwater sued the government for $20 million after its contract was canceled. Suez sued Argentina for $1.7 billion, blaming the government for being unwilling to raise water rates. Bechtel sued Bolivia for $50 million after its contract was canceled due to a coup. (Ultimately, Bechtel withdrew its lawsuit in exchange for the government officially stating that the contract had failed due to civil unrest.) One might think that these contract failures would be enough for the Bank and the IMF to stop pushing privatization. Instead, the World Bank claimed they must "keep their eyes peeled" for crises that will make countries more receptive to privatization, explaining, "The impetus for change typically comes from a crisis, sometimes (such as a water quality disaster or declining water tables) within the sector, but more often outside because of an overall fiscal crisis or process of political reform."[8] Following such a crisis, the Bank claims countries are more "receptive."[9] It turned out that the next crisis would be in Europe, where the cracks in Greece's government were beginning to show. In 2009, the G-20 Summit clearly had a crisis on its hands.

IMF-ing Europe

As Joseph Stiglitz once argued, IMF-imposed privatization tends to be accompanied by "the IMF riot." The IMF deals with people who are "down and out," he explained, then "takes advantage and squeezes the last pound of blood out of them. They turn up the heat until, finally, the whole cauldron blows up."[10] Then, clearly, it is hard to make money when people are rioting.

It was precisely the "IMF riot" that had led attendees to question the perceived "legitimacy" of the IMF at the 2009 G-20. At the same time, they were aware that some institution was going to have to keep bailing bankrupt countries out to avoid global financial contagion. So G-20 members chose to grant the IMF even greater powers of "surveillance" and oversight, especially in Europe and the United States. (Even when the IMF does not provide loans, it performs "surveillance" of every country's economic growth and offers "recommendations" that come with a hammer.) They also made plans to give the IMF more money. At the Alternative G-20, also called the People's Forum, Joseph Stiglitz complained, "The IMF pushed all the things—privatization, liberalization, deregulation—that are the cause of the current [financial] crisis. Why would you give them more power for dealing with the crisis?" Yet this is precisely what happened. Since that fateful G-20, we have seen the results in Greece and other European countries, where water privatization and other "austerity" measures began to be imposed by the IMF.

As the Eurozone crisis traveled from Greece to other countries, the IMF pushed austerity measures, including water privatization. By 2013, the IMF had provided money to ten European countries: Greece, Ireland, Portugal, Hungary, Latvia, Poland, Kosovo, Bosnia, Romania, and Cyprus. The money the IMF paid out amounted to hundreds of billions of dollars. As part of its bailout package, Greece was forced to sell its stake in water utilities in its two largest cities, including Athens. Portugal began preparing for the privatization of its state-owned water company by "blocking access to free public water supplies, such as drinking water fountains." (Corporations often push for the removal of "free" drinking fountains, which is also happening on U.S. college campuses.) In Bulgaria, also following IMF "reform" guidelines, "in the beginning of 2012 there were 370 families in Sofia that were evicted because they were unable to pay their utility bills. And communities living in informal settlements, primarily the Roma, are completely neglected by the water company." In Spain and Italy, protests erupted over proposed water privatization plans.[11]

So far, Italy has successfully resisted water privatization, passing a resolution against it with a 96 percent no vote in 2011. At the 2012 Alternative World Water Forum, Italians showed up in force, carrying blue antiprivatization flags and acting like they had just won the World Cup after successfully overturning a law introduced by Prime Minister Silvio Berlusconi that would have opened the country to water privatization. Yet while voter referenda, marches, and petitions have long been democratic solutions in Europe and the United States, the IMF is unfortunately outside democracy. After the Italian referendum against water privatization, the Italian government began to find ways around the referendum in order to appease the European Central Bank and the IMF. The antiprivatization Italian Water Forum complained: "The regulator still allows profits to be realised by water operators. The name is different but the substance is the same."[12]

In Paris, citizens recently voted to terminate the city's contracts with both Suez and Veolia. Deputy Mayor Anne le Strat explained, "We were run by a private company [Veolia] for 25 years but recently we voted to become public. Since then, we have lowered rates but still increased profits. And these profits have gone back into the utility. We also have more transparency so people are happier." Even so, Veolia took credit for these improvements, claiming it had set the stage for the city to "walk on its own two feet," as Suez had once claimed in Johannesburg. Le Strat complained, "All of a sudden, now that Veolia is no longer operator, it wants to take credit for the reduction [Paris Water] is going to implement while also having the brazenness to claim it would have gone even further in decreasing prices. The obvious question is, why didn't Veolia offer to lower prices during the term of the contract?" On the contrary, Veolia "imposed successive increases whose accumulated effect over the period worked out at a rise of 260%."[13] Though remunicipalizing Paris's water has been a success, the IMF is already pushing for more "productivity of the services sector" in Paris, including water and energy, claiming France should "instantaneously reduce its regulatory burden" to encourage the "entry and competition" of private industry.[14]

In order to stop water privatization from being imposed from outside, the European Citizens' Initiative program was started in 2012. Under this Europe-wide initiative, if one million members of the European Union sign a petition requesting that the European Commission (the legislative arm of the EU) propose or review legislation, it will "consider" doing so. The first petition to reach one million signatures was organized by the nonprofit Right2Water and demanded that water supplies be exempt-ed from a European Commission directive to open markets in municipal services. (A directive is an order from the commission for its member countries to create legislation, in this case to open markets.) The petition also demanded that water be declared a "human right" in the European Union. In a victory for antiprivatization activists, the European Com-mission complied with the former request. However, the research blog Governance across Borders called it a "Pyrrhic victory" because the Euro-pean Commission ignored the second half of the petition.[15] In Europe, it seems the only way to get people to pay the "full cost" of water is through extrademocratic channels such as IMF or EU intervention.

The European Citizens' Initiative was created precisely because people feared that the EU was taking away their democratic rights. But for water corporations, these "rights" are a threat, as is social unrest; for them, "pricing" thirst means literally weighing how much social unrest they can tolerate before profit turns to loss. Unfortunately, the cost of un-rest is never added to the IMF balance sheet on austerity measures; doing so would create a more realistic picture of what "austerity" costs.

If Europe's shaky national economies created openings for water privatization, the shaky economies of municipalities in the United States have done the same thing. In cities ranging from Indianapolis to Stockton, California, bankruptcy has forced public utilities to seek investors to re-pair or upgrade water infrastructure. But after selling utility management to water corporations, city residents have experienced many of the same problems as those in the global South, including water rate increases and "boil water" notices. In Chualar, California, rates went up as much as 2,000 percent in one month. American Water said the increased rates were intended to promote conservation.

Situations like this have led to citywide battles against corporate in-terests in the United States. "People are just kind of weird with water," complained American Water's Catherine Bowie.[16] Through voter refer-enda, the California cities of Felton, Stockton, Madera, and others were able to throw out American Water and keep or regain control of their utilities. But referenda face fierce opposition from corporate interests. For instance, in Monterey, California, American Water spent $250,000 on a publicity campaign to defeat a referendum. California is in a unique position in even allowing this type of populist referendum to occur, so other states fare far worse. Across the United States, American Water has filed lawsuits and supported political candidates who oppose public water supplies. In Chattanooga, Tennessee, and Peoria, Illinois, American Water launched a $5 million campaign to prevent public takeover of the cities' water systems when customers became dissatisfied with American Water's management.

Though the United States is not under the same kind of IMF pressure faced by many European countries, pressures to privatize still come in the form of inadequate tax bases and political maneuverings. After a city turns its water supply over to corporate interests, it can be very hard for the city to reacquire control before the contract runs out, up to thirty years. One problem is that the alleged sanctity of "private property" stands in the way of cities retaking their water supplies through eminent domain, as has happened in Chile. According to Food & Water Watch, "Reversing privatization is very difficult, particularly when going up against well-funded public relations campaigns, political candidates and legal maneuvers."[17] After thirty years, corporate control of water can start to seem like the "new normal" as people who once lived with public water supplies die off and children are born into the new system. Clearly, the World Bank, the IMF, and private water companies are using a long-term strategy to achieve their ultimate goals. But the delicate balance they are attempting to maintain between unrest and austerity is, to say the least, unnerving.

Water as Right?

One of the biggest problems with turning water over to corporate interests for decades is the loss of democratic decision-making ability about this life-sustaining force. Again, this problem turns on the issue of definition: Do people have a "right" to manage and monitor their own water supplies, or is water an "economic good" to be sold for profit? In order to understand the battle between those who would define water as a "human right" and those who see it as an "economic good," it is essential to review the history of how these terms came to be employed. Defining water internationally as an "economic good" or commodity started in the 1980s in World Bank and U.S. economist circles, culminating in 1992 in the so-called Dublin Principles. At the International Conference on Water and the Environment in Dublin, the following statement was proposed and approved: "Water has an economic value in all its competing uses and should be recognized as an economic good." This language was quickly picked up and hyped as new "international best practices" by the IMF and World Bank. According to James Salzman, "This strategy was adopted in policies of international financial institutions, particularly in the Structural Adjustment Programs pursued by the IMF and World Bank in debtor countries. In Bolivia and other countries, privatization of water supply systems was made a prominent lending condition."[18]

In contrast, South Africa constitutionally declared water a "human right" in 1994. These two events—in Dublin and South Africa—set the parameters for a debate that continues today. In South Africa, viewing water as a "right" was born out of a long struggle in which rights had been taken away for half the population due to race. In 2000, the Cochabamba Declaration in Bolivia followed the South African model, stating, "Water is a fundamental human right and a public trust to be guarded by all levels of government, therefore, it should not be commodified, privatized or traded for commercial purposes."[19] The antiapartheid and indigenous rights struggles in these two countries eventually led to water being defined internationally as a "human right." In both South Africa and Bolivia, the battle for water rights was accomplished in the context of long anticolonial struggles for "human rights." In anticolonial battles around the world, colonized peoples adopted European "human rights" discourse to argue that they too were human and had rights. In this way, colonized peoples unveiled the hypocrisy of Europeans, who had two-tiered systems of citizenship and rights in the colonies—one tier for Europeans and another for "natives."[20] Similarly, declaring that water is a "human right" today implies that everyone is equal and is entitled to the same access to water; it is a statement about dignity and equality.

It is important not to underestimate the power of either side in creating these competing visions of water. Opponents of privatization were powerful enough to have "rights" language ultimately voted on in the United Nations. Financial interests were powerful enough to have water defined as an "economic good." In 2010, a U.N. General Assembly resolution declared that "the right to safe and clean drinking water and sanitation" was "a human right that is essential for the full enjoyment of life and all human rights." It further mandated that "states and international organizations" must "provide financial resources, capacity-building and technology transfer, through international assistance and cooperation, in particular to developing countries, in order to scale up efforts to provide safe, clean, accessible and affordable drinking water and sanitation for all." But the meeting was heated, and the vote was far from the unanimous decision that had been sought. With 122 yes votes and 41 abstentions, the vote was clearly divided along North–South lines. On the yes side, there was consensus among African countries, as well as among most other postcolonial nations. But only six European countries—France, Germany, Italy, Norway, Switzerland, and Portugal—voted yes. The United States, Canada, and other European countries abstained. (In fact, the U.S. representative first ended discussion in an attempt to table the resolution.) The U.S. representative claimed there was not "sufficient legal basis for declaring or recognizing water or sanitation as freestanding human rights."

Most Europeans and North Americans allegedly abstained because they had been drafting their own resolution at the Geneva-based U.N. Human Rights Council. Though Germany argued that the "European Union-led 'Geneva process' on water and sanitation" did not conflict with the General Assembly resolution, others disagreed. So what was the difference between the two resolutions? One of the differences was over money, since the Geneva-based group linked water rights to a certain "standard of living." The Geneva resolution stated, "The human right to safe drinking water and sanitation is derived from the right to an adequate standard of living," rather than linking the right to water to "the full enjoyment of life." Another difference in the Geneva resolution was that it specifically protected privatization: "States, in accordance with their laws, regulations and public policies, may opt to involve non-State actors in the provision of safe drinking water and sanitation services."[21] The U.N. General Assembly resolution did not. On the contrary, the Venezuelan representative had argued, "Since water was a necessity for life, [we] emphatically rejected its transformation into a commodity."[22]

The U.N. General Assembly resolution had also been drafted by a group of countries from the global South and introduced by Bolivia, for which U.S. representative John Sammis scolded the Bolivian representative:

> We also look forward to a more inclusive, considered, and de-
> liberative approach to these vital issues in Geneva than we have
> unfortunately experienced on this resolution in New York. . . . This
> again is an imposition on all of us [and] diverts us from the serious
> international efforts underway to promote greater coordination and
> cooperation on water and sanitation issues.[23]

The battle was clearly over who would *control* the process: U.S.–European countries or the global South. In an NPR interview, Maude Barlow described the abstentions: "So it was all of the Anglophone, neoliberal . . . countries who are able to continue to supply clean water to their citizens, which makes it doubly appalling that they would deny the right to water to the billions of people who are suffering right now."[24]

A month later, the U.N. Human Rights Council unanimously passed its own resolution, making it legally binding. (In contrast, the United States claims the U.N. General Assembly resolution is not legally binding—though a United Nations representative disagrees). But the Human Rights Council resolution is binding only for countries that have previously ratified the Covenant on Economic, Social and Cultural Rights. Noticeably, the United States is one of only half a dozen countries that has never done so. According to attorney Ann Picard, "The United States is historically suspicious of even recognizing economic, social and cultural rights as 'rights' that might be amenable to any method of enforcement."[25] In fact, the only international human rights treaties that the United States has consistently ratified are those on "terrorism" (such as "Suppression of Terrorist Bombing"). The reason for this is that the U.S. Congress has to vote on ratification, and Republicans, in recent years, have consistently blocked these votes. According to *The Economist,* there is a fear that these treaties "would usurp American sovereignty, a long-standing fear about the UN among some conservative Republicans."[26] Therefore, while the Geneva resolution on water is in theory legally enforceable, the United States has automatically and strategically opted out while also refusing to accept the General Assembly resolution as legally binding. Ironically, the U.S. Department of State claims that "a central goal of U.S. foreign policy has been the promotion of respect for human rights" and that it will "hold governments accountable to their obligations under universal human rights norms and international human rights instruments."[27] The

United States appears to have a two-tiered strategy of holding other countries accountable for the protection of human rights, but not itself. For example, the United States is the only country besides Somalia and South Sudan not to ratify the U.N. Convention on the Rights of the Child, which makes the United States lose its credibility in promoting human rights around the world. It also refuses to protect women's rights.

In contrast to the U.S. position on rights, corporations like Suez and Veolia have jumped *on* the human rights bandwagon as part of their new public relations campaign, claiming they are poised and ready to implement water as a human right. Having followed the "rights" struggle for more than a decade, I became suspicious when the water corporations shifted from an anti-rights to a pro-rights position a few years back. Corporate websites began suggesting that they had *always* supported water as a human right. This is not true. Instead, it appeared that corporations had strategically decided to co-opt the language of the "rights" advocates in order to both neutralize and gain from it; this is similar to the corporate strategy of adopting a faux environmentalist position, known as "greenwashing." Farhana Sultana and Alex Loftus have explained the results: "The right to water risks becoming an empty signifier used by both political progressives and conservatives who are brought together with a shallow post-political consensus that actually does little to effect real change in water governance."[28]

Particularly telling was the pro-privatization magazine *Global Water Intelligence*'s statement that passing the U.N. resolution was a "massive defeat for the Global Water Justice Movement."[29] How could winning the decades-long battle to have water declared a human right be considered a "defeat"? The reason was that corporations had already successfully co-opted the language and now could *demand* international funding in order to implement this new right. "Rights" discourse is premised on how much water an individual needs per day, which is internationally defined as fifty liters, even though this is far below the one hundred liters recommended by the World Health Organization. Knowing this is the model, water corporations have been pushing to have this amount subsidized by governments, and some subsidization is already occurring in Chile and other countries. Now water corporations can actually sue based on the U.N. resolution to force national governments to make these payments.

That said, the impact of having water recognized as a human right by the United Nations should not be underestimated. In particular, the resolution is now part of a package of legal strategies for indigenous and other peoples who are treated inequitably to maintain their rights to water. As Maude Barlow has pointed out, the Bushmen of Botswana have already been able to maintain their access to water by citing the U.N. resolution.[30] A citizen in the Netherlands whose water had been cut off by a private company also won a court case to have his water turned back on, based on the U.N. resolution. Finally, a state in which the U.N. mandate may have some impact is Israel, where people in the Occupied Palestinian Territories are denied access to clean water through the destruction of wells and other water infrastructure. Palestinians have far less than fifty liters of water per capita per day for general use, and waterborne diseases affect as much as 64 percent of the population. In 2011, the U.N. permanent observer to Palestine, Riyad Mansour, told the United Nations that "Palestinian people's right to water and sanitation continued to be violated by Israel, which currently exploited 90 per cent of the shared water sources, while exerting control over the 10 per cent of that allowed for Palestinian use. The result was a further reduction in the already-meagre water supply available to Palestinians."[31] Palestine will be a test case for how successful the U.N. "right to water" might be, particularly since Israel did not sign on to the General Assembly resolution. The unconditional support the United States has given to Israeli water policies despite these human rights violations is a source of strife around the world.[32] Unfortunately, Israel has conflated water rights in the Occupied Territories with rights to territory and self-determination, arguing that the demand for water is a veiled demand for territory. At the same time, Israeli settlers in the Occupied Territories are clearly aware that there is no better way to drive people out of these territories than shutting off their water.[33]

Regardless of whether water is declared a "good" or a "right," and whether the public or the private sphere supplies it, there is also the problem that no one seems to have the money to pay for it. Over the past decade, even the World Bank started to admit that wealth was becoming concentrated among the very rich around the world, which means that the rich are having trouble finding new places to invest their money. The poor are simply too poor to buy more things, including water. A shrinking middle class means both that there is a shortage of consumers and that tax bases are insufficient for public utilities to build (or even repair) water infrastructure. Corporations try to invest in water infrastructure but have not always been able to extract profits from consumers. Even their funds are limited compared to the scope of global water poverty. The chief executive of Saur once said, "The scale of the need far outreaches the financial and risk taking capacities of the private sector."[34]

Water as Blood

The "price" of thirst—that is, thirsty people—is social unrest, disease, and environmental degradation. Thirsty people will kill for water; they will drink from dirty rivers and die. People who lack adequate sanitation will continue to use rivers as toilets. At the same time, as corporations and banks try to "price" thirst, or put a price tag on it, they are pricing life and death. The true price of thirst is death, and death is now stalking many around the world. As Arjun Appadurai has said, "Today the insecurities of states and the uncertainties of civilians and persons have become increasing intertwined."[35]

If suicide has dramatically increased in India in recent years, it is also on the rise in Greece. In spring of 2012, a seventy-seven-year-old retired Greek pharmacist shot himself in a square in central Athens, leaving a note that said he could no longer take "scavenging in dustbins for food and becoming a burden to my child."[36] Along with suicides, water cutoffs are increasing throughout Greece and elsewhere in Europe. In France, a Veolia worker was fired for refusing to cut off the water of poor families in Avignon. In a radio interview, he said:

> I saw people who had nothing, living with their children, who begged me not to cut off the water supply and to give them a little more time to pay up. It could happen to anyone. You have to make a choice—either feed the children or pay the bills. These big companies pocket the money and redistribute it to their shareholders, without looking after their clients or employees. It's scandalous.[37]

What water corporations and city councillors seem not to realize is that allowing this to happen is ultimately disadvantageous for *them*. If people in Europe start looking for alternative water sources, which is already happening with the Roma, rivers will become even more polluted and waterborne epidemics will emerge again in Europe. People who live by rivers shit in rivers.

Given the associations among water, life, and disease, a better metaphor for water than money might be blood. At the meeting of the U.N. General Assembly in 2010, Bolivian U.N. ambassador Pablo Solón introduced the "water rights" resolution with a reminder that humans are two-thirds water and that the blood is like a network of rivers in the body, supplying nutrients.[38] Professor Jason Hubbart has similarly written that water is "a little bit like our own circulatory system—the way we humans transport nutrients and other essential elements through our bodies. If you want to check on a person's general health, what's the first thing you do? Take a blood sample."[39] Like blood in the human body, water keeps the planet functioning, supplying food for life on Earth. It carries nutrients around the planet and around our own bodies. And, as with our blood, we cannot survive without it. Given that this is the case, let us imagine for a moment what a market for our own blood might look like. Such a "blood market" is actually not hard to imagine, since something like it is already occurring in parts of the world, both legally and illegally.

Illegally, the poorest of the poor are often forced to sell their own blood, organs, or bones to survive. Body-part buyers are known to swoop into devastated areas, such as post-tsunami Sri Lanka, to illegally acquire these products from live sellers. Legally, the English national blood bank recently tried selling "surplus" blood donations on the open market and was met with a firestorm of criticism. The public demanded to know who was buying the blood, but the government said that sharing this information would adversely affect "commercial interests." One journalist responded, "Aside from anything else, it raises the question of whether the public would be in a better position if it sold rather than donated blood . . . so that its own 'commercial interests' had to be considered alongside the company's."[40] People who had donated blood argued that they had given their blood for free, so why should others profit from it? Yet this is precisely the argument for marketing water. As Suez CEO Gerard Mestrallet explained, "Water is an efficient product. It is a product which normally would be free, and our job is to sell it."[41] Activists have long argued that "water is life," and so for many the idea of marketing water is like marketing blood, bones, or organs. Of course this analogy can be taken only so far, but it raises important questions. For instance, who can afford to buy and who is forced to sell? Should others be able to take these "free" products and sell them for profit?

If water is like our blood, it has also become anemic and toxic. The World Health Organization estimates that four thousand babies die every day from drinking dirty water and almost one billion people lack access to a clean water source. In June 2011, a study published in *Organization & Environment* found that "when a country is under a World Bank structural adjustment loan it tends to have higher levels of child mortality," even though U.N. Millennium Development Goal 4 is to "reduce child mortality" by two-thirds by 2015.[42] The study showed that austerity measures were making it impossible for governments to address health problems, including infant mortality from drinking dirty water. In Greece, IMF-imposed austerity measures caused infant mortality to rise by 40 percent. Professors David Stuckler and Sanjay Basu wrote in the *New York Times,* "As scholars of public health and political economy, we have watched aghast as politicians endlessly debate debts and deficits with little regard for the human costs of their decisions."[43] While the IMF claims that countries must accept the "painful medicine" of austerity and produces podcasts with titles such as "Managing the Pain of Fiscal Consolidation," the truth is that the IMF kills people. An article in *Global Water Intelligence* reported, "This blood is on the hands of those utilities who have failed to provide safe water and sanitation to their existing customers, or extend it to new ones."[44] Cynically, *Global Water Intelligence* attempted to blame public utilities for these failures in order to push further corporatization, even though evidence has shown that private utilities have been much more brutal about cutoffs than public utilities.

As rivers and streams become more polluted around the world, politicians and large corporations have a long history of seeking out clean rivers farther and farther away and moving them *to* the cities, rather than cleaning up pollution in the rivers flowing through the cities, which could be compared to surviving on blood transfusions after intentionally poisoning your own blood. As India's Interlinking Rivers and China's South–North water diversion projects demonstrate, governments are now attempting to tap into pure glacial water and divert this water around the entire ecosystem. Today, this solution is becoming prohibitively expensive, threatening to bankrupt states and even nations; it is a constant quest for fresh, clean blood (water) in an increasingly disease-ridden world.

Besides searching farther afield for clean water, states are now scanning the globe for sites of "virtual water," the term used for water used to produce food and other commodities for export. (For instance, the Sierra Club has calculated that one steak requires 1,850 gallons of water to produce, for irrigated forage and drinking water.) In China, farmland and water supplies are both so polluted that the government has been buying land in Africa for farming. "Already an area of land the size of London is being sold to foreign investors every six days in poor countries," Oxfam has written, stating that 30 percent of Liberia has been "swallowed up" in only five years.[45] Toshka Lakes in Egypt is another example. The World Bank is not only supporting these sales but also funding irrigation projects on these new lands, including the Saudi prince's Egyptian acquisition. Oxfam has asked the World Bank to stop supporting such sales, but the Bank has refused.

On the contrary, the Bank clearly supports such long-distance water transfers. At the 2012 G-20 Summit, Loïc Fauchon argued for such methods: "Deep-well pumping, water transfers over large distances, water desalination, [and] recycling of wastewaters . . . count among the key opportunities that leading-edge technologies offer for the near future. Promoting public policies that will raise awareness of the fact that the time of easy water has passed is an obligation for all."[46] Since all of these options are expensive, Fauchon was clearly arguing that the public would have to pay more for water. But besides the expense, there are environmental consequences to each of these proposals. Deep-well pumping drains already depleted aquifers, long-distance water transfers deplete distant ecosystems of water, and desalination is highly energy-intensive and polluting, both from leftover salts and from energy use. In short, these "solutions" all create more problems, which means more cost; they also create greater inequity, not only between rich and poor but also between city and country.

If "large scale," "energy-intensive," and "far away" have been the siren call in the quest for clean water, it should by now be clear that the solution is the opposite. Water needs to be managed with the biology of the planet in mind, not drained from some and granted to others; this only leads to social unrest. According to Susan Spronk, public utilities took over control of water supplies in Europe and the United States in the late nineteenth and early twentieth centuries largely to "quell social unrest" raised by the activities of private water companies.[47] One has to wonder if we have reached a similar turning point today. If unrest and suicide are growing around the world, it may be time to start investing in public utilities and water cleanup again. (Europe provides a hopeful example in its Drinking Water Directive, which sets mandatory quality requirements for surface water before it can be treated for drinking water, which forces countries to invest in cleaning up their watersheds.) Of course, how the public allocates water also needs to be reenvisioned; after all, most large-scale water systems built for the public domain have created expensive, long-term problems. Unraveling the water systems of the past half century may take another half century to accomplish, but this can begin to occur only if the systems remain in public hands.

Reinvesting in public utilities may work for Europe and the United States, but such a solution is not available for the rural poor in the global South, where more than 80 percent of the "unserved" population lives— who are also "underrepresented" in global governance institutions.[48] These people have no access to water treatment facilities, and governments often do not have enough money to build them. These people do not care if their water comes from public or private services; they just want water. According to David Hall and Emanuele Lobina, "For the poor, any promise of a connection in or near your home has to sound good when you are trekking miles for water or buying from expensive street vendors even if you instinctively baulk at the prospect of handing control of public services to foreign companies."[49] For them, the question remains: Who will pay for it?

Public, Private, or Else?

The price of a thirsty world has been an increase in vultures, or corporations that would steal the last pennies from dying people. In fact, "vulture capitalism" is the term for loan sharks who prey on national economies strapped for cash. According to geographer Erik Swyngedouw, water privatization has served to test the boundaries of what capitalism can and cannot get away with. He writes, "Over the last two decades, water has become one of the central testing grounds for the implementation of global and national neoliberal policies."[50] For corporate interests, it has signified a desperate quest in a halting global economy for new ways to make money.

Calling water privatization a form of "accumulation by dispossession," Swyngedouw argues that water corporations have attempted to make profits by removing water from the "commons," or public use. In so doing, they have also created a unique form of social unrest, the fight for control of the commons. Swyngedouw writes: "Those dispossessed do not necessarily passively accept the theft of what they consider to be rightfully theirs. . . . The state [has] to step in yet again to assure accumulation by dispossession keeps going notwithstanding the proliferation of social protests."[51] For this reason, privatization has been most successful in places where people either do not notice it is occurring or where authoritarian governments or dictatorships enable it, as in China and Chile.

Rather than funding more large-scale diversion projects and urban sprawl in these countries, it may be better to focus on cleaning up watersheds and providing inexpensive and low-tech solutions to rural users. For instance, the World Health Organization now promotes solar disinfection for those without clean water; this process involves filling plastic bottles or bags with water and placing them on a corrugated metal roof or other surface exposed to sunlight for six hours. Though this does not remove chemicals, it can kill parasites and bacteria in the water—thus immediately reducing infant mortality. Funding massive water infrastructure without first attempting small-scale solutions has been a form of public theft, and the debt keeps getting bigger. In conclusion, I present below some alternative solutions, which are not exhaustive.

1. *Stop climate change.* The number one threat to the world's water supplies today is climate change. As stated earlier, if glaciers disappear, so does the source of the world's water. Damming melting glacial water to "save" it before it flows to the sea, which has been proposed, is not a solution; these dams would be overtopped as melting increases. There is no dam big enough for climate change. Stopping climate change can only happen through government regulations and programs that promote conservation and switching to alternative energy sources like wind, wave, and solar—not dams, which create new problems—as soon as possible.

2. *Stop throwing people off their land.* The traditional pairing of large-scale urban water infrastructure with large-scale dams has thrown millions of people off their land who then end up in cities. People are also being pushed off their land by corporate acquisition of communally owned property, plundering of resources, lack of employment, ruined

fields, and ecological problems. This has led to an enormous backlog of people in cities without clean water or sanitation, yet solutions have focused on how to provide water to these people rather than on stopping the flow of landless people to the cities. The world's megacities are simply not sustainable, sometimes requiring water to be diverted across entire countries. Even then, urban unemployment contributes to social unrest. A simple solution is to support and sustain the livelihoods of rural populations around the world.

3. *Recognize indigenous knowledge.* Water is both the source of the world's creation myths and the first thing scientists look for when they look for life on other planets. In its drops we can see the beginning of Earth, quite literally. As Langston Hughes once wrote, "I've known rivers ancient as the world and older than the flow of human blood in human veins." Perhaps for this reason, water is central to the world's religions—from the Christian ritual of baptism to the Hindu ritual of *puja* and the Muslim ritual of *wudu.* And before religions came to be, indigenous peoples practiced what Sunderlal Bahuguna has called "the science of the ancestors." Indigenous peoples around the world have long been aware of the problems that emerge when humans do not respect their water sources. But rather than seeking their input, planners have generally discredited and undermined indigenous knowledge, a legacy of racist colonialism. As Bolivian water activist Oscar Olivera said:

> They think the villages of Bolivia, the indigenous and peasant people in all the world, that they are ignorant villagers, that they don't know how to use water, and that they must be taught how to use water, how to save water. I would say that it's totally the contrary: the people, going back hundreds, thousands of years, have a culture of water, they know how to use water, they have a very different conception of water, that it is a common good, that it has to serve not only humans but animals and plants as well.[52]

Clearly, indigenous peoples need to be—at the very least—included in conversations about water. Learning "the science of the ancestors" also means acknowledging the rights of the people who are its practitioners.

4. *Revive small-scale and local solutions.* Besides acknowledging and respecting indigenous water systems, we need to implement them. Specifically, we need small-scale solutions for our water supply problems, like

household rainwater harvesting, small dams, and watershed restoration. Rainwater harvesting can take several forms. Gandhi used his basement to collect all the rainwater that fell on or around his house. Others store water in large cisterns attached to gutters. Rainwater harvesting is already used around the world—including in China, India, Sri Lanka, Myanmar, the United States (Colorado, Texas, and New Mexico), Brazil, the United Kingdom, and Israel—and are mandated in Santa Fe, New Mexico, in parts of Australia, and in many Caribbean countries. Californians could redirect roof gutters into large storage tanks. (In Los Angeles, lawns should also be illegal or come with heavy fines.) Another method for conserving urban water is to redirect storm-water runoff into deep pits, where it can percolate back into the ground. This method is already used in Los Angeles, in Mexico City, and throughout India. Replacing urban concrete with permeable materials can help accelerate this percolation. In desert regions, the use of *karez* systems can help stop evaporative loss.

5. *Regulate the "virtual water" market.* Approximately 80 percent of the world's water is used for agriculture, much of it for the global grain market. In the United States, this water mostly ends up in corn that is used both in processed foods for human consumption and as feed for the cattle and poultry industry. It is also shipped overseas, along with wheat. Eating less meat actually saves more water than fixing a leaky faucet; fruits and nuts are the most water-efficient foods. Organic gardens and especially permaculture also use much less water than agribusiness, and eating locally grown foods shrinks export-oriented agribusiness and keeps water in the country. Ironically, the World Bank pushes countries to do just the opposite, encouraging Iraq, for instance, to stop thinking of agriculture as a "source of *food production*" and starting thinking about it as a "*source of growth*."[53] Eating locally also offers protection from the fluctuations of the global grain market, which is sensitive to climate change, unrest, and drought. In 2008, rising grain prices caused food rioting around the world. In 2012, the United States faced a level of drought never before seen in its history. Less food is now stored in the global grain reserve—including corn, wheat, and rice—threatening global food security. Americans can protect themselves from this problem by eating locally when possible, but ultimately the U.S. government needs to stop subsidizing corn and wheat products in order to make organic and local foods more

affordable. Political problems with Russia, a leader in what is a very volatile global grain market, make this shift more important. The United States needs to stop the grain addiction.

6. *Imagine alternative economies.* Most people are by now aware that Chicago school economics has not worked. Still, economists and development specialists repeat the same tired debate over Keynesian versus neoliberal economic practices (i.e., "stimulus" versus "austerity") as if there were no other alternatives. This debate has been around since the end of World War II and is clearly stagnant. There is much more interesting economic analysis being done in postcolonial studies and cultural geography, largely ignored by traditional (or "orthodox") economists. For instance, geographer Stephen Healy argues that even the U.S. economy includes "household economies, gift-giving, barter, alternative finance, [and] self-employment cooperatives," but these "alternative economies" have been marginalized or hidden from view.[54] Outside the United States, informal economies are becoming a large part of the world's economy, but because these transactions are extralegal, it is difficult to quantify them for macroeconomic analysis. Similarly, alternative water systems have long been marginalized in international governance institutions. For instance, the *karez* systems of the Middle East and tank systems of India seem to have been discovered only recently in these circles, but they have been in use for centuries. Geographer Colin C. Williams argues that we need to acknowledge that "even in the heartland of commodification— the advanced 'market' economies—survey after survey uncovers . . . that non-market work is not some minor remnant left over from pre-capitalist forms and rapidly dwindling."[55] Rather, he asserts, it is alive and well. Dipesh Chakravarty has similarly argued that capitalist and noncapitalist modes of production have always existed side by side. Today, there are subsistence economies, Islamic banks, cooperatives, citywide bartering, informal economies, and other means of providing and maintaining livelihoods. It is only because IMF economists cannot easily quantify these systems, and because the field of economics attempts to reduce everything to quantification, that these large and growing worlds are ignored. By viewing capitalism as a fait accompli, we pass over possible alternatives. Nevertheless, alternative economics is spreading across many academic disciplines, as seen in anthologies like *Postcolonial Economies.*[56] The IMF should pay attention.

7. Imagine an alternative water blueprint. During the European colonial period, because European settlers were not familiar with the lands they were occupying, they tended to follow a "blueprint" for settlement, usually establishing entrenched fortress-type colonial cities that drew water from the hinterlands. In the countryside, water irrigation systems were engineered only for producing cash crops for export, funneled through these cities. This colonial water blueprint was dependent on a strong military as water was diverted away from natives to settlers. But if remaking the landscape by force was the method used in colonial occupations, anticolonial resistance involved undermining these boundaries. Activists commonly pulled up surveyors' stakes, blocked roads under construction, stopped deforestation, tore down dams, and refused payments. They were attempting to stop the brutality of modernization.

After independence, most postcolonial countries were swallowed up in the Cold War battle between the United States and the Soviet Union; both sides tended to delegitimate local agendas. For instance, if Russia and the United States are viewed not as communist or capitalist but as large dam-building states, there is little difference between them. During the Cold War, the ideology of rapid industrialization was being imposed upon the planet. But today, anticolonial resistance methods are being revived, as seen in South Africa and India, and are representative of a global struggle for a safer planet. For instance, boycotts were a huge part of anticolonial resistance, from Gandhi's boycotts on British goods to black South African (and global) boycotts on apartheid products. Today, boycotts can be an even more effective strategy, as Coca-Cola discovered when it started draining the groundwater in Plachimada, India, for bottled water. As *Global Water Intelligence* has described: "Today every corporation is under 24-hour surveillance, and it takes just days to get a boycott movement going. Concerns about Coca-Cola's water use at its Plachimada site in India were first reported in 2003. The plant was closed in 2004."[57] POM Wonderful, the Franklin Mint, Teleflora, and Fiji Water could be suitable targets for boycotts until Stewart Resnick returns the Kern Water Bank to the public. Coca-Cola, Pepsi, and shares in water companies are also potential targets. As the world becomes united through social media, populist resistance becomes more powerful and global NGOs can have greater impact, but even more important is envisioning and promoting a new water blueprint for the world that is outside politically imposed binaries like Republican/Democrat or capitalist/communist.

8. *Reform the globalization regime.* The IMF has repeatedly created financial fiascoes around the world, and yet it has been allowed to keep doing so without accountability. By 2013, the IMF had to admit to "notable failures" in the Greek bailout. The *Guardian* reported, "The International Monetary Fund admitted it had failed to realise the damage austerity would do to Greece as the Washington-based organisation catalogued mistakes made during the bailout of the stricken eurozone country."[58] Still, the IMF did not change its game plan. As the *Los Angeles Times* reported, "Britain and the Eurozone are steadfastly sticking to austerity measures despite increasing evidence that such action alone isn't working to revive their economies and is dragging down global growth."[59] This game plan is actually resulting in Europe and the United States losing credibility and power globally, and thereby becoming more susceptible to pressures from authoritarian regimes like Russia and China. It is not only the IMF and World Bank, after all, who are losing credibility; it is also the world powers backing them.

Today, defections from the IMF, both personal and national, are spreading. At the personal level, IMF director Peter Doyle recently quit in disgust, leaving a letter that read, "After twenty years of service, I am ashamed to have had any association with the Fund at all." He accused the IMF of having a "fundamental illegitimacy."[60] At the state level, Ukraine recently rejected an IMF loan—because of the IMF's austerity measures—in favor of a surprising and controversial turn to Russia for funding. Then the Ukrainian government was overthrown, and we are still witnessing the fallout from a country pulled in two directions. Ironically, the IMF and World Bank seem to be increasing the international power of Russia and China—a frightening development given these nations' anti–human rights records. IMF and Bank reform is today crucial for reestablishing some legitimacy for Europe and the United States.

For instance, Joseph Stiglitz has long argued that we need global governance institutions that can protect countries from financial or environmental collapse, not create such collapse. This might include establishing a regulatory board for international trade that would impose export barriers on countries that violate labor, environmental, indigenous, or human rights regulations. (Today, we have the opposite in the WTO.) Short of this, both the IMF and the World Bank need oversight committees that could provide trust-busting services, whistle-blower protections, revolving-door prohibitions, and legal services for those who want to sue the Bank. Currently, there is no protection for whistle-blowers at the Bank, and the Bank has immunity from legal prosecution for its contracts. And though the Bank functions as a data collector for global indicators, it has a history of presenting data in a way that makes its projects look successful. For this reason, more than one professor who has double-checked World Bank data has called it notoriously unreliable.[61] Finally, David Stuckler and Sanjay Basu have argued, "Each nation should establish a nonpartisan, independent Office of Health Responsibility, staffed by epidemiologists and economists, to evaluate the health effects of fiscal and monetary policies."[62] In this way, austerity-caused deaths and illnesses could be tabulated and figured into the economic risks of austerity measures. Even better, stop austerity measures.

Privatization in a Police State

Of course, it is easy to talk about "resistance" and quite another thing to be attacked by the police for doing so. This is what happened to me at the G-20 in Pittsburgh, where I lost part of my hearing in a police attack against protesters. This incident gave me greater respect for people in New Delhi, Johannesburg, Cochabamba, and elsewhere—many who suffered far worse fates.

The G-20 Summit was of course not open to visitors; streets were closed off for several blocks around the convention center. But the People's Forum was open downtown; it had scheduled talks and marches that would occur over those few days. So I headed to the first march I saw advertised to talk to the protesters and find out what the protest was about. I quickly discovered that downtown Pittsburgh looked more like a police state than a place of mediation. There were armored vehicles, police motorcycles, National Guard troops, and riot gear everywhere. I turned a corner on my bicycle and ran into a line of police in riot gear who were blocking the park entrance where the protesters were convening. In fact, hundreds of police in straight lines appeared to be surrounding the entire park to keep the protesters blocked in. Perhaps I should have turned back

The National Guard takes over downtown Pittsburgh in 2009.

then, but there were not many protesters and they all looked peaceful. Some carried signs about climate change and bank bailouts, while others were just having fun. But I could not easily talk to anyone without risking getting trapped inside the police line, which I did not want to do. Still, I was not scared. I was not doing anything illegal.

When the march started, the police followed, sharing strange military-like flanking directions on their radios. I was careful to stay outside the police line until one officer told me that I should head back to avoid getting hit by tear gas, which they were about to use. It seemed the police had created a fence around a couple blocks of the city to contain the protesters, with the river on one side. The police officer directed me back the way I came, so I followed his directions even though this meant I had to step inside the police line to get back to my locked bicycle and home. The street was nearly empty so it looked safe.

As I was heading back, a few dozen protesters suddenly turned the corner in front of me with a tanklike machine behind them. A second later, it blasted me with an ear-piercing high-pitched siren sound. I tried to run but was blocked in. Police with tear gas were behind me. I felt sick, I sat down, and I ultimately sued the city of Pittsburgh. I had been hit

Police outnumber
protestors at the
G-20 Summit
in downtown
Pittsburgh.

by a "sonic cannon," or long-range acoustic device, the first time it had
been used against U.S. citizens. A forensic audiologist determined that
the range of hearing I lost was identical to the pitch of the machine. The
city admitted this and awarded me some money, but it refused to stop
using the machine in the future, which had been my goal. The city even
refused to set public guidelines for how the device would be used, despite
the fact that my attorney discovered the officer who used it had not followed company safety guidelines by gradually increasing the volume in
bursts of not more than thirty seconds. Instead, he had turned it on me
full blast for three full minutes.

The G-20 is a lot like the World Water Forum—it matters if you are
inside or *outside*. Inside the World Water Forum, I did not see the protesters or police, though someone told me they were there. But outside
the G-20, that was all I saw. My experience in Pittsburgh taught me a
lesson. It seems the gaps between *inside* and *outside* are growing around
the world, and not only at these meetings, or only in the United States.

Perhaps those on the inside know that those on the outside are growing stronger than them. Perhaps that is why they think they need sonic cannons and water cannons. They are afraid, too.[63] Though I learned nothing about water privatization at the G-20, I did learn what its opponents are up against.

Despite (or perhaps due to) this militarized opposition to protests around the world, water privatization has become a public relations fiasco from which corporations are still trying to disentangle themselves. Perhaps water resists commodification. Perhaps people do. In 1874, a U.S. state Supreme Court clearly understood the problems involved in privatizing water when it declared, "Water is a movable, wandering thing, and must of necessity continue common by the law of nature."[64] Today, scholars call water an "uncooperative commodity," and perhaps it has turned out to be just that for water corporations.

But like water, corporate interests find ways to retrench and shift pathways. It is yet to be seen if our leaders—and indeed we—will reregulate water in time to avoid further destruction and monopolization of this vital force. The security of us all lies in the balance.

NOTES

Introduction

1. Claudia A. Deutsch, "There's Money in Thirst," *New York Times*, August 10, 2006.

2. The data in this paragraph come largely from the fourteenth edition of the *Pinsent Masons Water Yearbook, 2011–2012*, a standard in the water industry. See http://www.pinsentmasons.com. See also PricewaterhouseCoopers, *Water: Challenges, Drivers and Solutions* (London: PricewaterhouseCoopers, March 2012).

3. World Water Council, *Water, a Global Priority* (Marseille, France: World Water Council, 2012).

4. Pierre-Frédéric Ténière-Buchot, "Voices of Water Professionals: Shedding Light on Socio-political Processes in the Water Sector," (Re)Sources, January 30, 2013, http://www.re-sources-network.com/en.

5. Quoted in Bronwen Morgan, *Water on Tap: Rights and Regulation in the Transnational Governance of Urban Water Services* (Cambridge: Cambridge University Press, 2012), 64.

6. Réseau Projection, *From Planet of Slums to Planet of Solutions* (Paris: Réseau Projection, 2012), 19.

7. See Suez Environnement Water for All Foundation, *2008–2010 Report* (Paris: Suez Environnement Water for All Foundation, 2011), 19.

8. Peepoople, *Start Thinking Peepoo* (Stockholm: Peepoople, 2012).

9. World Water Council, *Be Part of the Solution: Become a World Water Council Member* (Marseille, France: World Water Council, 2012).

10. *Forum Gazette,* March 13, 2012, 8.

11. *Forum Gazette,* March 12, 2012, 8.

12. "The Grassroots and Citizenship Process: Involving Citizens in the Forum," World Water Forum, accessed June 15, 2012, http://www.worldwater forum6.org/en.

13. See Attac France, "An Alternative World Water Forum against the Water Merchants Forum," press release, February 24, 2012.

14. This quotation and those that follow from Anne le Strat and Maude Barlow are all from my own transcription of remarks presented at the opening session of the Alternative World Water Forum, Marseille, France, March 14, 2012. Translations into English were provided via headsets at the conference.

15. See Karen Bakker, *An Uncooperative Commodity: Privatizing Water in England and Wales* (Oxford: Oxford University Press, 2003).

16. Karen Bakker, *Privatizing Water: Governance Failure and the World's Urban Water Crisis* (Ithaca, N.Y.: Cornell University Press, 2010), xv, 87.

17. Ibid., 1.

18. "Financing Adaptation to Climate Change," *Forum Gazette,* March 15, 2012, 6.

19. "Anti-private Activists Debate with Private Operators at the 6th World Water Forum," AquaFed: The International Federation of Private Water Operators, accessed July 1, 2012, http://www.aquafed.org.

20. I must also include Helen Ingram, Catarina de Albuquerque, Carl Bauer, Ken Conca, Wendy Nelson Espeland, Pamela M. Doughman, and Joachim Blatter—and this list is by no means exhaustive. As clean water sources shrink, authors addressing the issue proliferate.

21. David McCullough, *The Path between the Seas: The Creation of the Panama Canal, 1870–1914* (New York: Simon & Schuster, 2004), 236.

22. Peter Hulme, "Beyond the Straits: Postcolonial Allegories of the Globe," in *Postcolonial Studies and Beyond,* ed. Ania Loomba, Suvir Kaul, Matti Bunzl, Antoinette Burton, and Jed Esty (Durham, N.C.: Duke University Press, 2005), 47.

23. This is according to the author Mark Twain, who was part of a worldwide campaign against Leopold's reign of terror. Today, Congolese historian Ndaywel e Nziem estimates the death toll at thirteen million. See Adam Hochschild, *King Leopold's Ghost: A Story of Greed, Terror, and Heroism in Colonial Africa* (New York: Mariner Books, 1999), 3. See also Michela Wrong, "Belgium Confronts Its Heart of Darkness," *Independent,* February 23, 2005.

24. Hochschild, *King Leopold's Ghost,* 42, 46.

25. Quoted in Patrice de Meritens and Fabry Joelle, *La Lyonnaise des Eaux (1880–2000)* (Paris: Suez, 2001).

26. The quotations from Ténière-Buchot in this paragraph and the next are from Pierre-Frédéric Ténière-Buchot, "Europe, Afrique, vers de nouveaux pou-

voirs," *Espaces Stratégiques* 3, no. 55 (1992): 117–34, my translation, http://www .institut-strategie.fr/strat_055_TENIERE-BU.html.

27. Quoted in Bakker, *Privatizing Water,* 64.

28. Ivan Chéret, "L'Origine des agences de l'eau: Une Experience africaine," in *Les Ingénieurs des ponts au service de l'Afrique: Témoignages 1945–1975,* ed. Jacques Bourdillon (Paris: Editions L'Harmattan, 2010), 55, my translation.

29. Sara B. Pritchard, "From Hydroimperialism to Hydrocapitalism: 'French' Hydraulics in France, North Africa, and Beyond," *Social Studies of Science* 42 (2012): 591.

30. This is from CNNMoney's Global 500 list for 2011, http://money.cnn .com.

31. Suez Environnement Water for All Foundation, *2008–2010 Report,* 3.

32. Quoted in "Our History," Veolia Water, accessed June 12, 2012, http:// www.veoliawater.com.

33. Quoted in "Générale des Eaux Group—Company Profile," Reference for Business, accessed March 12, 2012, http://www.referenceforbusiness.com/ history2.

34. The complete list of investors is published in "Compagnie Générale des Eaux," *L'Industrie* 2, no. 81 (August 20, 1853), 615.

35. Charles Dickens, *Little Dorrit* (New York: Harper & Brothers, 1873), 176, 243.

36. Michael Wolff, "The Big Fix," *New York Magazine,* May 13, 2002. See also Institute of Media and Communications Policy, "Media Data Base," http:// mediadb.eu, accessed May 5, 2014; and Harry Bradford, "These Ten Companies Control Enormous Number of Consumer Brands," *Huffington Post,* April 17, 2012, http://iatp.org.

37. "China Wealth Fund Buys Nearly 9% of Thames Water," BBC News Business, January 20, 2012, http://www.bbc.co.uk.

38. See Michael Goldman, *Imperial Nature: The World Bank and Struggles for Social Justice in the Age of Globalization* (New Haven, Conn.: Yale University Press, 2005), 31.

39. The World Bank makes its money by selling bonds to the general public and making loans to governmental institutions. World Bank bonds historically have a good return on investment, better than U.S. Treasury bonds, mainly because the Bank is backed by nations that use taxpayer money to buy shares. As in a corporation, shares buy influence, and the country with the most shares gets the most votes. Throughout the Bank's history, the United States has held the most shares, and the U.S. president has chosen the World Bank president, who has always been a U.S. citizen. The IMF has a similar system, where the most votes go to the wealthiest country. But unlike the World Bank, the IMF has historically been headed by a Western European.

40. Jane E. Goodman and Paul A. Silverstein, *Bourdieu in Algeria: Colonial Politics, Ethnographic Practices, and Theoretical Developments* (Lincoln: University of Nebraska Press, 2009), 13.

41. K. Varvaressos and R. Zafiriou, "The Reports of the Bank's General Survey Missions: A Synthesis," Report No. E.C. 45-a, International Bank for Reconstruction and Development, March 5, 1956. For instance, the Bank's first loan was to India, $10 million for "railway rehabilitation," including "the purchase from the USA and Canada of 418 locomotives," in 1949. Another loan was for the purchase of tractors for "reclamation" projects, or "new farms created out of wilderness." In 1947, India gained its independence from Britain, but the earliest Bank loans were for the completion of colonial projects.

42. Quoted in Maude Barlow, *Blue Covenant: The Global Water Crisis and the Coming Battle for the Right to Water* (New York: New Press, 2009), 39. In a 2012 *Forbes* article, Richard Behar described the World Bank: "It is an endlessly expanding virtual nation-state with supranational powers, a 2011 aid portfolio of $57 billion and little oversight by the governments that fund it. . . . Funds go down a rabbit hole and are almost impossible to track." As evidence, he cited $2 billion that recently went missing, attributed to a "computer glitch." Richard Behar, "World Bank Mired in Dysfunction: Mess Awaits New Head," *Forbes*, July 27, 2012.

43. Mike Davis, "The Imperial Economy of Late-Imperial America," *New Left Review* 143 (January/February 1984): 9.

44. Bakker, *Privatizing Water*, 131.

45. The World Bank funded its first urban water supply systems in 1962 (in Nicaragua) and 1963 (in East Pakistan). This information is based on my review of Bank documents and reports from 1940–1975. "Documents and Reports," World Bank, accessed June 5–10, 2012, http://documents.worldbank.org/curated/en. See also Bakker, *Privatizing Water*, 66.

46. "The World Bank Position on the Report of the World Commission on Dams," United Nations Environment Programme, Dams and Development Projects, December 2001, http://unep.org/dams.

47. The document quoted here was accessed at http://web.worldbank.org/WBSITE/EXTERNAL in 2012. The same site now reads, "Only sites that, in the Bank's view, have research or historic value are archived. . . . If the site you are looking for is not available on the Internet, and is not in WebArchives, then it is likely no longer available." The World Bank now makes available only documents published from 1995 onward.

48. World Bank, *An Evaluation of World Bank Support, 1997–2007: Water and Development*, vol. 1 (Washington, D.C.: World Bank, 2010), 34.

49. Shiney Varghese, "Privatizing U.S. Water," Institute for Agriculture and Trade Policy, July 2007, 2, http://iatp.org.

50. David Hall and Emanuele Lobina, "Water Privatisation," Public Services International Research Unit, University of Greenwich, April 2008, 2, http://www.psiru.org.

51. "At a Glance: Water," World Bank, 2013, http://water.worldbank.org.

52. "IFC Diversifies Its Water Lending Strategies," *Global Water Intelligence* 13, no. 6 (June 2012). See also David Hall and Emanuele Lobina, "Water Companies and Trends in Europe 2012," Public Services International Research Unit, University of Greenwich, August 2012.

53. See "IFC to Ramp Up Watsan Commitment," *Global Water Intelligence* 10, no. 12 (December 2009). Rao-Monari is quoted in "Veolia AMI Brings in Development Agencies to Enhance PPP Strategy," *Global Water Intelligence* 9, no. 1 (January 2008).

54. According to Bai-Mass Taal, executive secretary for the African Ministers' Council on Water (AMCOW), meeting of AMCOW at the World Water Forum, March 17, 2012.

55. Bertrand Dardenne, *Financing Local Water Utilities: Review of Some Experiences*, background paper (Paris: Agence Français de Développement, March 2012), 26.

56. Quoted in *Forum Gazette*, March 14, 2012, 2.

57. Quoted in Goldman, *Imperial Nature*, 242–43.

58. Ibid., 240.

59. "Drinking Water Service," Veolia Water, accessed June 10, 2012, http://www.veoliawater.com/solutions/drinking-water.

60. Suez Environnement home page, accessed June 10, 2012, http://www.suez-environnement.com.

61. Alan Snitow, Deborah Kaufman, and Michael Fox, *Thirst: Fighting the Corporate Theft of Our Water* (San Francisco: John Wiley, 2007), 77.

62. Saijel Kishan and Madelene Pearson, "Water Outperforms Oil, Luring Pickens, GE's Immelt," Bloomberg News, June 26, 2006.

63. Meng Jing, "Water Future: Opportunities Galore for Foreign Companies as Demand for Strategic Resource Escalates in China," *China Daily/European Weekly*, March 9–15, 2012.

64. Quoted in Steven Halpern, "Investing in Water: A 'Sleeper' Sector," DailyFinance, February 8, 2008, http://www.bloggingstocks.com/2008/02/08/investing-in-water-a-sleeper-sector.

65. Quoted in "Go with the Flow: Top Water Stock Picks," CNBC Stock Blog, August 11, 2008, http://www.cnbc.com.

66. In Illinois, American Water requested an across-the-board rate increase of more than 30 percent. The state granted rate increases of 17 percent to 26 percent. See Amy Werrick, "Cash Flows in Water Deals," *Wall Street Journal*, August 12, 2010. In Pittsburgh, according to Pittsburgh Water and Sewer Authority

director Michael Kenney, state water "rates are 25 to 30 percent lower than those charged by private companies." See Adam Brandolph, "Pittsburgh Weighs Water Privatization," *Pittsburgh Tribune-Review*, July 20, 2010.

67. See Jon R. Luoma, "Water for Profit," *Mother Jones*, November/December 2002.

68. AquaFed, *Sustainable Economics for Water and Sanitation*, JMM_ V2_2012-03-13.doc (Paris: AquaFed, 2012), 2.

69. Quoted in Richard Lawrence, "A Water Solution in a Bag," *Journal of Commerce*, August 29, 1996, 1–4.

70. Statement by an audience member at the session "Fostering Good Governance in the Water Sector: Key Lessons and Recommendations," World Water Forum, Marseille, France, March 15, 2012.

71. Julio Godoy, "Water and Power: The French Connection," iWatchNews, Center for Public Integrity, August 11, 2011, http://www.iwatchnews.org.

72. This information, which is also available in court documents, is from the film *Dead in the Water*, broadcast on "the fifth estate" on March 31, 2004, on CBC-TV; transcript available at http://www.cbc.ca.

73. *Forum Gazette*, March 17, 2012, 8.

74. Arundhati Roy, *The Algebra of Infinite Justice* (London: Flamingo, 2002), 33.

75. Evo Morales, "Message on Behalf of the Indigenous Peoples at the Third World Water Forum," in *Water and Indigenous Peoples*, ed. Rutgerd Boelens, Moe Chiba, and Douglas Nakashima (Paris: UNESCO-LINKS, 2006), 22–23.

1. Water Hoarding in a California Drought

1. Quoted in Rebecca Clarren, "Pesticide Drift: Immigrants in California's Central Valley Are Sick of Breathing Poisoned Air," *Orion*, July/August 2008, 56.

2. See "Huron California Water Quality Report," Water-Delivery.org, accessed August 1, 2012, http://water-delivery.org.

3. The show was funded in part by the Coalition for a Sustainable Delta, an organization set up by the owner of Paramount Farms, Stewart Resnick. Another group involved in the production was the Latino Water Coalition, which was set up and run with taxpayer money by Governor Schwarzenegger. See Malcolm Maclachlan, "Governor Presided over Birth of Latino Water Coalition," *Capitol Weekly*, October 8, 2009. See also Yasha Levine, "The Looming Water Disaster That Could Destroy California, and Enrich Its Billionaire Farmers," AlterNet, March 22, 2010, http://www.alternet.org.

4. Quoted in Dan Bacher, "Sean Hannity Spreads Dangerous Misinformation about California Water," California Progress Report, September 21, 2009, http://www.californiaprogressreport.com.

5. Nunes said, "Nowhere in the world has a democracy ever starved its own people of water. You know what country does that? Zimbabwe does that."

6. Janice Arenofsky, "Valley Fever Blowin' on a Hotter Wind," The Daily Climate, April 15, 2009, http://www.dailyclimate.org.

7. John Muir, *The Mountains of California* (New York: Century, 1894), 339.

8. Quoted in Maureen Cavanaugh and Pat Finn, "The King of California's Central Valley," KPBS, June 25, 2009, http://www.kpbs.org.

9. Mark Arax and Rick Wartzman, *The King of California: J. G. Boswell and the Making of a Secret American Empire* (New York: Public Affairs, 2003), 126.

10. See California Department of Water Resources, *History of California's Water Development, 500–2000*. Sacramento: California Department of Water Resources, n.d.

11. Quoted in Arax and Wartzman, *The King of California*, 81.

12. For a history of the Reclamation Act's impact, see Richard W. Wahl, "Redividing the Waters: The Reclamation Act of 1902," *Natural Resources & Environment* 10, no. 1 (1995): 31–38.

13. According to economist Richard Wahl, taxpayers have actually paid for 85 percent of these projects, which largely benefit corporate farms. Ibid., 33.

14. Arax and Wartzman, *The King of California*, 78.

15. Quoted in ibid., 12.

16. Quoted in ibid., 11.

17. Robert Gottlieb, *A Life of Its Own: The Politics and Power of Water* (San Diego, Calif.: Harcourt Brace Jovanovich, 1988), 12–13.

18. Quoted in Mark Grossi, "Westlands District a Powerhouse for Valley Farmers," *Fresno Bee*, November 7, 2009.

19. See ibid.

20. Quoted in L. G. Carter, "The Destruction of the American West," *Penthouse*, January 1999.

21. Gottlieb, *A Life of Its Own*, 79–80.

22. See Public Citizen, California Office, *Water Heist: How Corporations Are Cashing in on California's Water* (Oakland, Calif.: Public Citizen, December 2003), 10, 15.

23. Quoted in John Gibler, "Lost in the Valley of Excess," *Earth Island Journal* 5, no. 4 (2011), http://www.earthisland.org.

24. Quoted in ibid.

25. All quotations from Lalo Franco are from an interview I conducted with him on December 26, 2011, at the Tachi-Yokut headquarters.

26. William L. Preston, *Vanishing Landscapes: Land and Life in the Tulare Lake Basin* (Berkeley: University of California Press, 1981), 49.

27. Ibid., 36.

28. Raymond Jeff, "Yokuts in the Valley," ABC News 30, Fresno, August 1, 2009.

29. Quoted in Arax and Wartzman, *The King of California*, 218.

30. Dennis Hevesi, "James G. Boswell II, 86, Owner of Cotton Empire, Dies at 86," *New York Times*, April 9, 2009.

31. Parker told me that John Sterling of Sterling Wildlife Biology has called Kern Water Bank one of the top five freshwater wetlands in the United States.

32. In 1995, the Kern County Water Agency made an emergency declaration that the Kern Water Bank must begin pumping water underground in order to prevent flooding. Gregory A. Thomas, *Designing Successful Groundwater Banking Programs in the Central Valley: Lessons from Experience* (Berkeley, Calif.: Natural Heritage Institute, 2001), 91, http://www.n-h-i-.org.

33. "Sinking on the West Side," *Fresno Bee*, April 22, 2007. See also B. E. Lofgren and R. L. Klausing, *Land Subsidence Due to Ground-Water Withdrawal: Tulare-Wasco Area, California*, Studies of Land Subsidence, Geological Survey Professional Paper 437-B (Washington, D.C.: U.S. Government Printing Office, 1969), B-7.

34. See Michael Hiltzik, "Something's Not Right about This California Water Deal," *Los Angeles Times*, August 18, 2010.

35. Parker said, "So they met with the contractors and came to an agreement about how they would deal with things and one of the pieces of that agreement was to transfer the Kern Water Bank to the Kern County Water Agency." The Kern County Water Agency gave up 40,000 acre-feet, and the Dudley Ridge Water District, which was a participant, gave up 5,000 acre-feet. According to Parker: "It's a contractual amount for 45,000 acre-feet in any year that it's available. At the time, it was worth about $1,000 an acre-foot as a commodity. Some people had sold Table A water for $1,000 an acre-foot. So that's $45 million of assets that was given to the state."

36. Another result of the Monterey agreement was that farmers are allowed to store unlimited amounts of water outside their irrigation districts, as well as sell 130,000 acre-feet of water per year to urban areas. The article removed from the original contracts was Article 18(b). See "Monterey Plus Environmental Impact Report: Monterey Plus Principles and Negotiations," California Department of Water Resources, accessed August 1, 2012, http://www.water.ca.gov.

37. This is California State Senate Bill 970.

38. Carter, "Destruction of the American West."

39. Levine, "Looming Water Disaster That Could Destroy California."

40. Mark Grossi, "'Chinatown II'? Water Bank Sued as Wells Go Dry," *Fresno Bee*, September 5, 2010.

41. Quoted in ibid.

42. See Mike Taugher, "Harvest of Cash: Kern County Agency Buys Public Water Low, Sells High," *Contra Costa Times*, August 9, 2008.

43. *Tulare Lake Basin Water Storage District et al. v. United States*, Case No. 98-101 L, 49 Fed. Cl. 313, April 30, 2001.

44. Quoted in Mike Taugher, "Gaming the Water System," *Contra Costa Times,* May 25, 2009.

45. Gottlieb, *A Life of Its Own,* 109.

46. Before 1997, the length of such a contract could be only five years; now thirty years is a permissible term. Alan Snitow, Deborah Kaufman, and Michael Fox, *Thirst: Fighting the Corporate Theft of Our Water* (San Francisco: John Wiley, 2007), 8, 69. See also National Research Council, Committee on Privatization of Water Services in the United States, *Privatization of Water Services in the United States: An Assessment of Issues and Experience* (Washington, D.C.: National Academies Press, 2002).

47. According to Alan Snitow and Deborah Kaufman: "In 1978, just before the Reagan-era starvation diet began, federal funding covered 78% of the cost for new water infrastructure. By 2007, it covered just 3%." Alan Snitow and Deborah Kaufman, "Drinking at the Public Fountain: The New Corporate Threat to Our Water Supplies," Global Policy Forum, September 29, 2008, http://www.globalpolicy.org. See also Shiney Varghese, "Privatizing U.S. Water," Institute for Agriculture and Trade Policy, July 2007, 4, http://www.iatp.org.

48. "Top 10 Ways the Obama Budget Displaces Private Entrepreneurship," FreedomWorks, March 31, 2009, http://www.freedomworks.org.

49. See Public Citizen, *Water Heist,* 3, 8.

50. "Gateway Village: Master Planned Community," Pearson Realty, accessed August 1, 2012, http://www.pearsonrealty.com/Gateway/overview.html.

51. Quoted in Mark Arax, "Massive Farm Owned by L.A. Man Uses Water Bank Conceived for State Needs," *Los Angeles Times,* December 19, 2003.

52. The bank authority includes the Kern County Water Agency, Dudley Ridge Water District, Semitropic Water Storage District, Tejon-Castaic Water District, Westside Mutual Water Co., and Wheeler Ridge-Maricopa Water Storage District. Though technically public entities, votes are divided according to landholdings—corporations with the most land get the most votes. Kelly Zito, "Suit to Get Kern Water Bank Returned to State," *San Francisco Chronicle,* July 12, 2010.

53. "Centennial, California: A New Civic-Minded Community," accessed September 15, 2013, http://centennialca.com. See also "Centennial News: The Economic Issue," July 2009, http://centennialca.com.

54. See Roger Phelps, "Water Availability Is Wild Card in Possible Boswell Project," *Porterville Recorder,* March 31, 2005.

55. Lois Henry, "Hint of New Housing Could Lead to Water Peace," *Bakersfield Californian,* March 4, 2013.

56. Quoted in Arax, "Massive Farm Owned by L.A. Man."

57. See Stewart & Jasper Orchards; Arroyo Farms, LLC; and King Pistachio Grove, Plaintiffs, v. United States Fish and Wildlife Service; United States Department of the Interior; Ken Salazar, Secretary of the Interior; Rowan W.

Gould, Acting Director of the Service; and Ren Lohoefener, Regional Director of the Service's Pacific Southwest Region, Defendants, United States District Court, Eastern District of California, Complaint for Declaratory and Injunctive Relief, May 21, 2009.

58. Pacific Legal Foundation, accessed May 11, 2011, http://www.pacific legal.org.

59. See Don Schrack, "Drop in Import Duty Spurs Paramount Farms Pistachio Sales to India," The Packer, June 1, 2011, http://www.thepacker.com.

60. Quoted in David Bacon, The Children of NAFTA: Labors Wars on the U.S./Mexico Border (Berkeley: University of California Press, 2004), 37–38.

61. According to the National Resources Defense Council, the bill would "preempt state environmental laws, prohibiting the State of California from protecting its rivers, the Bay-Delta estuary, and their wildlife and fisheries." Doug Obegi, "Oppose the 'State Water Rights Repeal Act' (H.R. 1837)," National Resources Defense Council, Switchboard blog, February 27, 2012, http://switch board.nrdc.org.

62. The total votes in the House were 246 to 176 on H.R. 1837 (2011). See "Rep. Napolitano Pushes Back against Radical Republican Water Bill at Hearing," office of Congresswoman Grace F. Napolitano, press release, June 2, 2011, http:// napolitano.house.gov.

63. "The Man-Made California Drought," U.S. House of Representatives, Natural Resources Committee, accessed June 30, 2012, http://naturalresources. house.gov.

64. Barack Obama, "Statement of Administration Policy: H.R. 1837— Sacramento–San Joaquin Valley Water Reliability Act," February 28, 2012, from American Presidency Project, http://www.presidency.ucsb.edu.

65. "California's Draft Bay Delta Conservation Plan Needs Better Integration to be Scientifically Credible, Report Finds," ScienceDaily, May 5, 2011, http://www.sciencedaily.com.

66. An organization called Restore the Delta has real science backing its solutions, which include the restoration of Delta floodplains for water storage rather than water banks. The problem is that the organization's solutions involve "the reduction of water exports" from Northern California, and on its website (http://restorethedelta.org), Restore the Delta claims that "water contractors from the Central Valley have been relentless" in their opposition to the plan.

67. M. Pia Chaparro, Brent Langellier, Kerry Birnbach, Matthew Sharp, and Gail Harrison, Nearly Four Million Californians Are Food Insecure, Health Policy Brief (Los Angeles: UCLA Center for Health Policy Research, June 2012), 1.

68. United Nations Conference on Trade and Development, Trade and Environment Review 2013 (Washington, D.C.: United Nations, 2013).

69. Brian Stoffel, "U.N.: These 7 Companies Impede Global Food Security," Motley Fool, September 24, 2013, http://www.fool.com.

70. Quoted in "Afghanistan: Low Almond Prices Hit Farmers," IRIN, August 26, 2009, http://www.irinnews.org.

71. Quoted in Bill Blum, "A Run on the Water Bank," California Lawyer, December 2011, http://www.callawyer.com.

2. How a Coup Opened Chile's Water Markets

1. Mothers still seek children who were "disappeared" during Pinochet's seventeen-year rule—thousands of Allende supporters were rounded up, brutally tortured, and murdered. In 2012, 255 people were arrested and one person was killed in vigils that became violent after police confrontation. Associated Press, "Chile's 9/11 Protest Marks Anniversary of Pinochet Coup, Leaves 1 Dead," Voxxi, September 12, 2012, http://www.voxxi.com.

2. Naomi Klein's *The Shock Doctrine: The Rise of Disaster Capitalism* (New York: Picador, 2007) is a good source of information on this history, as is Juan Gabriel Valdés's *Pinochet's Economists: The Chicago School in Chile* (Cambridge: Cambridge University Press, 2008).

3. Besides this, the Water Code ignores the fact that a large amount of the water stored behind dams is consumed by evaporation. (In Chile, dams are often called "evaporators.") Hans Achterhuis, Rutgerd Boelens, and Margreet Zwarteveen cite numerous reports on the problems with water privatization in Chile in "Water Property Relations and Modern Policy Regimes: Neoliberal Utopia and the Disempowerment of Collective Action," in *Out of the Mainstream: Water Rights, Politics and Identity,* ed. Rutgerd Boelens, David Getches, and Armando Guevara-Gil (London: Routledge, 2010), 47–48.

4. All quotes from Juan Pablo Orrego are from two interviews I conducted with him, one in-person interview on December 20, 2010, in Santiago and the other via Skype in March 2012. See also "Senator: Endesa Water Monopoly Prevents Investment—Chile," BNamericas, May 4, 2001, http://www.bnamericas.com.

5. Jaime Guzmán, *Derecho politico: Apuntes de las clases del professor Jaime Guzmán Errázuriz* (Santiago: Ediciones Universidad Católica de Chile, 1996), translation by Juan Pablo Orrego. According to Bauer, "The 1980 Constitution was eventually accepted . . . as an essential condition for the transfer of power, and it cannot be altered without the agreement of the military and their right-wing allies." Carl J. Bauer, *Against the Current: Privatization, Water Markets, and the State in Chile* (Boston: Kluwer Academic, 1998), 11.

6. For a detailed history of this acquisition process, see Francesc Trillas, "The Takeover of Enersis: The Control of Privatized Utilities," *Utilities Policy* 10 (2005): 25–45. See also Carl J. Bauer, "Dams and Markets: Rivers and Electric Power in Chile," *Natural Resources Journal* 49 (Summer/Fall 2009): 583–651.

7. This deal is called Caso Chispa, or the Sparks Case, in Chile. See Juan Sharpe, "El controvertido estilo de José Yuraszeck, el nuevo patrón del fútbol," *El*

Dinamo, February 1, 2013, my translation from "uno de los mayores negocios o estafas . . . de la historia financiera chilena." Orrego said Chileans call it the "theft of the century."

8. Quoted in Joseph Collins and John Lear, "Pinochet's Giveaway: Chile's Privatization Experience," *Multinational Monitor* 2, no. 5 (May 1991), http://www.multinationalmonitor.org.

9. See "Enel, Acciona Acquire Endesa with $60 Bn Bid," Financial Express, October 6, 2007, http://www.financialexpress.com/news.

10. Bronwen Morgan, *Water on Tap: Rights and Regulation in the Transnational Governance of Urban Water Services* (Cambridge: Cambridge University Press, 2012), 118.

11. According to Morgan, "This was done in response to a general public backlash against privatisation, including an unofficial plebiscite conducted in the southern city of Concepción where a huge majority of the city's population rejected (unsuccessfully) the purchase of its regional water company by UK-based Thames Water." Ibid., 123.

12. See Bauer, *Siren Song,* 25–26.

13. World Bank Group, "Country Partnership Strategy for the Republic of Chile for the Period FY11–FY16," Report No. 57989-CL, January 11, 2011, 2.

14. Morgan, *Water on Tap,* 119.

15. From my interview with Patricio Segura in Coyhaique, Chile, January 3, 2011. Segura works with the Coalition to Save Aysén/Coalición Ciudadana Aysén Reserva de Vida, which is fighting against the HydroAysén dams.

16. Jessica Budds, "Water Rights, Mining and Indigenous Groups in Chile's Atacama," in Boelens et al., *Out of the Mainstream,* 201.

17. According to Orrego: "Mining is responsible for the consumption of at least 36–37 percent of energy in Chile. So my thesis is that somehow the triple vector that orientates our constitutional and legal system is the capture of the water, energy, and mining nexus. And I really think that's the way it is." See Bauer, *Against the Current,* 86. At the 2012 World Water Forum, the panel "Americas' Water" claimed that the water market in Chile had "encouraged the hoarding of water rights, speculation and their use to exert market power in the hydropower sector." Regional Process for the Americas Group, *Americas' Water Agenda: Targets, Solutions and the Paths to Improving Water Resources Management* (n.p.: Regional Process for the Americas Group, March 2012), 54.

18. María Florencia Jensen Solivellas, "Inmigrantes en Chile: La exclusión vista desde la política migratoria chilena" (paper presented at the Third Congress of the Latin American Population, ALAP, Córdoba, Argentina, September 24–26, 2008), my translation.

19. Jaime Massardo, "Five Hundred Years of Expropriation and Resistance: The Plight of Chile's Mapuches," trans. Malcolm Greenwood, *Le Monde diplomatique,* November 1999.

20. "La inmigración tendría como uno de los resultados más directos el aumento de la población, el mejoramiento técnico y el perfeccionamiento de las condiciones biológicas de la raza." Quoted in Ximena Zavala San Martín and Claudia Rojas Venegas, "Globalización, procesos migratorios y Estado en Chile," in *Migraciones, globalización y género en Argentina y Chile* (Buenos Aires: Centro de Encuentros Cultura y Mujer, 2005), 175.

21. Quoted in Claudia Bucciferro, *For-Get: Identity, Media, and Democracy in Chile* (Lanham, Md.: University Press of America, 2012), 140.

22. Margreet Zwarteveen, "A Masculine Water World: The Politics of Gender and Identity in Irrigation Expert Thinking," in Boelens et al., *Out of the Mainstream*, 79.

23. Phil Davison, "Paul Schäfer: Nazi Colonel Who Established an Anti-Semitic Colony in Chile after the War," *Independent*, May 24, 2010, http://www .independent.co.uk.

24. Del Anaquod, Margaret Thomas, and Kenneth I Taylor, *Report on the Present Situation of the Mapuche in Chile* (Washington, D.C.: Working Group on Indigenous Populations of the United Nations, 1984), http://www .cwis.org.

25. "Undue Process: Terrorism Trials, Military Courts, and the Mapuche in Southern Chile," *Human Rights Watch* 16, no. 5(B) (October 2004): 1–2, 5. According to Human Rights Watch, "Several United Nations bodies, including the Human Rights Committee, the Committee Against Torture, and the Committee on the Elimination of Racial Discrimination, have expressed concern about using the anti-terrorism law to prosecute Mapuche members for common crimes." "Chile: Amend Anti-terrorism Law and Military Jurisdiction," Human Rights Watch, September 27, 2010, http://www.hrw.org.

26. Zwarteveen, "Masculine Water World," 90.

27. "Chile: The Struggle of the Pehuenche against the Ralco Dam," World Rainforest Movement Bulletin, no. 42 (January 2001), http://www.wrm.org.uy.

28. Bauer, *Against the Current*, 110.

29. Ibid.

30. Quoted in Sophie Arie, "The Mapuches' Last Stand," *World Press*, June 21, 2011, http://www.worldpress.org.

31. "Undue Process," 15.

32. "Chile: The Struggle of the Pehuenche."

33. John Ahniwanika Schertow, "Continued Aggression Leads to Mapuche Declaration of War," Intercontinental Cry, October 30, 2009, http://www.inter continentalcry.org.

34. "Liberty and Justice for Chief Juana Calfunao Paillalef," letter to President Richard Lagos, Mapuche International Link, January 20, 2006, http:// www.mapuche-nation.org/english/html/news/letter-05.htm.

35. Quoted in Nina Dean, "Death by Spin: Piñera Orchestrates Ultimate

'Pacification of Araucania,'" Mapuche International Link, September 25, 2010, http://www.mapuche-nation.org/english/html/articles/art-21.htm.

36. In 2005, a fee for nonuse of water rights was implemented in an attempt to eliminate water hoarding. But an unintended consequence may be that HydroAysén rushes to build dams rather than pay the hefty fees. María de la Luz Domper, "Chile: A Dynamic Water Market," *Libertad y Desarrollo*, March 2009, 7.

37. In 1990, Tompkins sold his share of the company to a partnership that included his wife. He walked away, eventually, with more than $150 million. See John Ryle, "Lord of All He Surveys," *Outside*, June 1998.

38. Quoted in ibid.

39. During the Spanish campaigns against the Mapuche in central Chile, many Mapuche also fled to Patagonia, where they learned to hunt cattle that had gone wild and intermarried with the Tehuelche. See A. F. Tschiffely, *This Way Southward: A Journey through Patagonia and Tierra de Fuego* (1945; repr., Geneva: Long Riders' Guild Press, 2001).

40. Ryle, "Lord of All He Surveys." Orrego explained: "The fact that they took the sheep away was very controversial because some people in Patagonia identify Patagonia with the sheep, which were actually brought by the British. And the British killed all the Indians to raise the sheep. But people get confused. People identify sheep with Patagonia."

41. "Cuando el pueblo despierte, y la Region despierte de los consecuencias de las represas, seria el momento de repensar el modelo de la economic. Sin un plan maestro pais que demuestras cuanto consume, cuanto pueblo, que tipo de technologia, un ordenamiento territorial, y un buen entendimiento ecologico todos nosotros estamos abordo un naive sin timón, rumbo al abismo." My translation.

42. Kris Tompkins, "Wild Transformations," Patagonia, Holiday 2006, http://www.patagonia.com.

43. Ryle, "Lord of All He Surveys."

44. See John C. Fyfe and Oleg A. Saenko, "Human-Induced Change in the Antarctic Circumpolar Current," *Journal of Climate* 18 (August 1, 2005): 3068–73.

45. Marcus Sobarzo Bustamante, "The Southern Chilean Fjord Region: Oceanographic Aspects," trans. Ben Machado, in *Marine Benthic Fauna of Chilean Patagonia*, ed. V. Häussermann and G. Försterra (Puerto Montt: Nature in Focus, 2009), 53.

46. Jose Luis Iriarte, Humberto E. González, and Laura Nahuelhual, "Patagonia Fjord Ecosystems in Southern Chile as Highly Vulnerable Region: Problems and Needs," *Ambio* 39, no. 7 (2010): 465–66.

47. As reported in the *Guardian*, "Trade winds that sweep around half the globe are weakening as global warming disrupts normal atmospheric circula-

tion." Ian Sample, "Trade Winds Weaken with Global Warming," *Guardian*, May 4, 2006. Scientists have also found that the Circumpolar Current is gradually moving south due to "human impact." The current has moved forty-five kilometers south, with about half of that occurring since the 1950s. See Fyfe and Saenko, "Human-Induced Change."

48. Bustamante, "Southern Chilean Fjord Region," 53.

49. See Thomas J. Verleye, "Late Quaternary Environmental Changes and Latitudinal Shifts of the Antarctic Circumpolar Current as Recorded by Dinoflagellate Cysts (41°S)," *Quaternary Science Reviews* 29, nos. 7–8 (April 2010): 1025–39.

50. According to geographer Axel Borsdorf, "Important records of climatic changes in the Holocene associated with the displacement of the Westerlies drift and the circumpolar Antarctic current make this zone highly vulnerable to global climate change scenarios coinciding with the local intensification of human activities." Axel Borsdorf, "The Hydroelectrical Potential of North-Western Patagonia: Balancing Economic Development and Ecological Protection," in *Challenges for Mountain Regions: Tackling Complexity*, ed. A. Borsdorf, G. Grabherr, K. Heinrich, B. Scott, and J. Stötter (Vienna: Böhlau, 2010), 158.

51. See "Ocean Less Effective at Absorbing Carbon Dioxide Emitted by Human Activity," ScienceDaily, February 23, 2009, http://www.sciencedaily.com.

52. Today, legislation to protect glaciers is pending while water demand and competition escalate. A. Rojas, B. Reyes, L. Magzul, H. L. Morales, R. Borquez, and E. Schwartz, *Analysis of the Role of Institutions in Water Conflicts: Final Report* (Ottawa: Social Sciences and Humanities Research Council of Canada, Institutional Adaptation to Climate Change Project, July 2008), 11. See also Julia Thompson, "Aguas Andinas to Study Glaciers," *Patagonia Times*, April 30, 2008.

53. Benjamin Witte, "Chile's 21st Century Gold Rush," *Patagonia Times*, September 12, 2007.

54. Budds, "Water Rights, Mining and Indigenous Groups," 208. Gallardo is quoted in "Chile's 21st Century Gold Rush," Santiago Times, September 13, 2007.

55. See Rojas et al., *Analysis of the Role of Institutions*, 11; Jimmy Langman, "Under a Deluge: Global Warming, Glaciers and Dams on the Baker River," *Patagon Journal*, summer 2012, http://www.patagonjournal.com; "Glaciers Melting Fast in South America," LiveScience, September 5, 2012, http://www.livescience.com.

56. Cited in Langman, "Under a Deluge." See also Regional Process for the Americas Group, *Americas' Water Agenda*, 32.

57. James Rickards, *Currency Wars: The Making of the Next Global Crisis* (New York: Penguin, 2012), 163.

58. "Chile Considers Constitutional Reform of Freshwater Rights," Circle of Blue Water News, January 28, 2010, http://www.circleofblue.org.

59. See Jonathan Franklin, "Pro-Pinochet Celebration Leads to Street Protests in Santiago," *Guardian*, June 10, 2012, http://www.guardian.co.uk. See also "La hermana del organizador de homenaje a Pinochet fue torturada en dictadura: 'Oírlo me hiere.' Francisca González relató como su hermano no hizo nada para ayudarla," *Cambio21*, July 6, 2012, http://www.cambio21.cl/cambio21.

60. Armando Guevara-Gil, Rutgerd Boelens, and David Getches, "Conclusions: Water Rights, Power and Identity," in Boelens et al., *Out of the Mainstream*, 331.

61. In 1997, race relations conciliator Rajen Prasad further defined New Zealand as "a multi-ethnic society with an indigenous culture and with a founding document that regulates the relationship between iwi [Maori] and Crown." Quoted in Augie Fleras and Paul Spoonley, *Recalling Aotearoa: Indigenous Politics and Ethnic Relations in New Zealand* (Auckland: Oxford University Press, 1999), 221.

62. Quoted in Kevin Funk, "'Today There Are No Indigenous People' in Chile? Connecting the Mapuche Struggle to Anti-neoliberal Mobilizations in South America," *Journal of Politics in Latin America* 4, no. 2 (2012): 125–40.

63. Eddie Durie, "The Rule of Law, Biculturalism and Multiculturalism" (paper presented at the conference of the Australasian Law Teachers Association, Hamilton, New Zealand, July 2005), 1.

64. See Will Kymlicka, *Multicultural Citizenship: A Liberal Theory of Minority Rights* (Oxford: Oxford University Press, 1995).

65. G. Raumati Hook and L. Parehaereone Raumati, "A Validation of Māori Social Principles and the Global Fresh Water Crisis," *MAI Review*, no. 1 (2011): 9, http://www.review.mai.ac.nz.

66. Quoted in "Key Pokes Stick in Wasps Nest over Water Rights," New Zealand First, September 14, 2012, http://nzfirst.org.nz/news.

67. Hook and Parehaereone, "A Validation of Māori Social Principles," 9–10.

3. South Africa's Water Apartheid

1. "White Paper on Water Policy," South Africa, April 30, 1997, http://www.africanwater.org/wp3.htm.

2. Billy Nair, interview by D. Shongwe, July 12, 2002, for the "Voices of Resistance" Oral History Project, Documentation Centre, University of KwaZulu-Natal, Durban, http://scnc.ukzn.ac.za.

3. This is from an interview I conducted at Robben Island in June 2007.

4. Quoted in Evelina Rioukhina and David Winch, "'Anything Is Possible': Interview with the UN High Commissioner for Human Rights, Ms. Navanethem (Navi) Pillay," *UN Special*, no. 679, December 2008, http://wwwunspecial.org.

Boreholes were eventually sunk on the island, which provided more drinking water and better water for showering, though it was still brackish. In his 2002 interview for the "Voices of Resistance" project, Billy Nair said, "So you had to, you know, make do. That water, the borehole, the water is the one that you drank also on the Island."

5. Townships maintained a separate tax base and "had virtually no resources to provide their residents with adequate infrastructure or social services." South African Cities Network, *State of the Cities Report 2004*, ed. Andrew Boraine (Johannesburg: South African Cities Network, 2004), 25.

6. "At its heart, the apartheid city was a political economy of space," the South African Cities Network writes. "This had two central features: racially based spatial planning and a political economy that meant development for some at the expense of the majority." Ibid., 24.

7. "White Paper on Water Policy."

8. For an excellent overview of the history of township administration, see Ivan Evans, "The 'Properly Planned Location,'" in *Bureaucracy and Race: Native Administration in South Africa* (Berkeley: University of California Press, 1997).

9. South African Cities Network, *State of the Cities Report 2004*, 14.

10. See Abhijit V. Banerjee, Sebastian Galiani, Jim Levinsohn, Zoë McLaren, and Ingrid Woolard, "Why Has Unemployment Risen in the New South Africa?," *Economics of Transition* 16, no. 4 (October 2008): 715–40.

11. Sean Jacobs, "After Mandela," *The Nation*, June 23, 2013, http://www.the nation.com. See also Statistics South Africa, *Mortality and Causes of Death in South Africa, 2006: Findings from Death Notification*, no. P0309.3 (Pretoria: Statistics South Africa, 2008).

12. Quoted in "Mozambicans Flee South Africa Riots," BBC News, May 26, 2008, http://news.bbc.co.uk.

13. Hirsh Jain, "Community Protests in South Africa: Trends, Analysis, and Explanations," Community Law Centre, University of Western Cape, Local Government Working Paper Series No. 1, August 2010.

14. Franz Wild, "South African Protesters Attack Police Houses during Riot," Bloomberg News, January 22, 2013, http://www.bloomberg.com/news.

15. Ebrahim-Khalil Hassen, "Unemployment in South Africa: Feel It, the Ticking Time Bomb Is Here," South African Civil Society Information Service, June 23, 2011, http://sacsis.org.za.

16. Ronnie Kasrils, "Introduction," in *Armed and Dangerous: From Undercover Struggle to Freedom*, 4th ed. (Johannesburg: Jacana Media, 2013), as extracted in Kasrils, "How the ANC's Faustian Pact Sold Out South Africa's Poorest," Guardian, June 23, 2013. In 2010, Winnie Mandela said of her ex-husband, "Mandela let us down. He agreed to a bad deal for the blacks. Economically we are still on the outside. The economy is very much 'white.' . . . Mandela is now like

a corporate foundation." Quoted in Colin Fernandez, "Winnie Mandela Accuses Nelson of 'Betraying' the Blacks of South Africa," *Daily Mail*, March 8, 2010.

17. "South Africa: Country Brief," World Bank, accessed October 15, 2009, http://www.worldbank.org.

18. Joseph Stiglitz, "Challenging the G2o's Agenda of Corporate Globalization" (speech presented at the People's Summit, Pittsburgh, Pennsylvania, September 23, 2009). The People's Summit at which Stiglitz spoke was an alternative and concurrent event to the G2o of 2009.

19. Kasrils, "Introduction."

20. Vishnu Padayachee, "Debt, Development and Democracy: The IMF in Post-apartheid South Africa," *Review of African Political Economy* 21, no. 62 (December 1994): 589. Published in 1994, this excellent article foresees early on what would happen in South Africa due to IMF pressures.

21. Vishnu Padayachee, "Can the RDP Survive the IMF?," *South Africa Report* 9, no. 5 (1995), http://www.africafiles.org.

22. See Food and Agriculture Organization of the United Nations, Subregional Office for Southern and East Africa, *Drought Impact Mitigation and Prevention in the Limpopo River Basin: A Situation Analysis*, Land and Water Discussion Paper 4 (Rome: Food and Agriculture Organization of the United Nations, 2004), http://www.fao.org.

23. Padayachee, "Debt, Development and Democracy."

24. Quoted in Amy Goodman, "The Poetic Justice of Dennis Brutus," *The Citizen*, January 4, 2010.

25. Kasrils, "Introduction."

26. William Mervin Gumede, *Thabo Mbeki and the Struggle for the Soul of the ANC* (Cape Town: Struik, 2007), 94–95.

27. Naomi Klein, *The Shock Doctrine: The Rise of Disaster Capitalism* (New York: Picador, 2007), 209.

28. In 1994–95, the World Trade Organization (WTO) forced South Africa to drop trade barriers, leading to the flight of assets offshore (De Beers went to Switzerland, for instance). Some economists blame this shift for South Africa's rising unemployment after 1994, along with cuts to the public sector. For discussion of unemployment, see Judith Christine Streak, "The Gear Legacy: Did Gear Fail or Move South Africa Forward in Development?" *Development Southern Africa* 21, no. 2 (June 2004): 271–88. On the WTO's impact on South Africa, see Nnarndi O. Madichie, "Better Off Out? The Costs and Benefits of Sub-Saharan Africa's Membership of the World Trade Organization," *Journal of African Business* 8, no. 1 (2007): 5–30. According to economist Joel Netshitenzhe, "GEAR was a structural adjustment policy, self-imposed, to stabilize the macroeconomic situation." Quoted in Philip Harrison, Alison Todes, and Vanessa Watson, *Learning from the Post-apartheid Experience* (New York: Routledge, 2008), 62.

29. In 1986, Suez formed Water and Sanitation Services Africa (WSSA), a joint venture with another company named Group Five, and began the operation of wastewater treatment in KwaZulu-Natal. In 1992, it won a twenty-five-year contract in Queenstown (Eastern Cape), in 1993 WSSA signed a ten-year lease contract with Stutterheim (Eastern Cape), and in 1996 the corporation won the operation and maintenance contract for Zandvliet Waste Water Treatment Works (Western Cape). Ultimately Suez received more than two hundred similar contracts throughout South Africa. See Patrick Bond, "Johannesburg's Water Wars: Suez vs. Soweto," *Le Passant Ordinaire*, January 3, 2004. See also Peter H. Gleick, *The World's Water, 1998–1999: Biennial Report on Freshwater Resources* (Washington, D.C.: Island Press, 1998), 130.

30. Dale McKinley, "Water Is Life: The Anti-privatisation Forum and the Struggle against Water Privatisation," South African Regional Poverty Network, accessed November 20, 2009, http://www.sarpn.org.za.

31. James Ferguson, *The Anti-politics Machine: "Development," Depoliticization, and Bureaucratic Power in Lesotho* (Minneapolis: University of Minnesota Press, 1994), 49, 27. In the 1960–70s, 60 percent of Lesotho's males worked in South African mining or agriculture. See Jacques Leslie, *Deep Water: The Epic Struggle over Dams, Displaced People, and the Environment* (New York: Farrar, Straus and Giroux, 2005), 148. See also "South Africa: Country Brief."

32. Ferguson, *Anti-politics Machine*, 27.

33. World Bank Group, "Country Partnership Strategy for the Republic of South Africa for the Period 2008–2012," Report No. 38156-ZA, December 12, 2007, 12.

34. According to Sanjeev Khagram, "In 1998, when local public protests against the Lesotho government occurred, the South African government sent in troops to restore order. Dozens of people were killed when the shooting was over, including 17 at the Katse Dam." Sanjeev Khagram, *Dams and Development: Transnational Struggles for Water and Power* (Ithaca, N.Y.: Cornell University Press, 2004), 169.

35. Quoted in Femi Akindele and Relebohile Senyane, eds., *The Irony of "White Gold"* (Morija, Lesotho: Transformation Resource Centre, 2004), 7.

36. World Bank, "Kingdom of Lesotho: Interim Poverty Reduction Strategy Paper," Report No. 21834, December 2000, 4, 21, 27. These recommendations, which began to be implemented more than a decade ago, have not improved the situation in Lesotho, yet this document is still listed on the World Bank's website as the current strategy for Lesotho.

37. "ANC Expresses 'Serious Concern' after Councils Cut Off Services," South African Press Association, October 19, 1990.

38. "Mandela Launches Campaign to End Rent Boycotts," Agence France Presse, February 25, 1995.

39. Christopher S. Wren, "Pretoria Shifting Attention to Local Apartheid," *New York Times*, May 2, 1991.

40. Quoted in "20,000 Residents in the Dark after Not Paying Bills," African Eye News Service (South Africa), May 20, 1997.

41. J. Roome, "Water Pricing and Management: World Bank Presentation to the SA Water Conservation Conference" (unpublished paper, South Africa, 1995).

42. Quoted in Bond, "Johannesburg's Water Wars."

43. This startling figure prompted some controversy in the South African government. For the full story, see Ginger Thompson, "Water Tap Often Shut to South African Poor," *New York Times*, May 29, 2003.

44. Quoted in Bronwen Morgan, *Water on Tap: Rights and Regulation in the Transnational Governance of Urban Water Services* (Cambridge: Cambridge University Press, 2012), 163.

45. See Chris McGreal, "Cholera Township Clear Out Stirs Apartheid Memories," *Guardian*, February 14, 2001.

46. See Chris Bateman, "Cholera Victims in Soweto," *Continuing Medical Education* 26, no. 6 (June 2008): 310–11. See also "South Africa: Struggling to Provide Safe Drinking Water to the Poor," CBC News, March 31, 2004, http://www.cbc.ca.

47. Quoted in Bond, "Johannesburg's Water Wars."

48. From Suez's "Water for All Programme" website, accessed June 20, 2008, http://www.suez-environnement.com.

49. "Closing the Tap on Water Resources," City of Johannesburg, October 24, 2007, http://www.joburg.org.za. See Willem Wegelin and Ronnie McKenzie, *Leakage Reduction through Pressure Management in South Africa: Concepts and Case Studies*, TT 186/02 (Pretoria: South African Water Research Commission, 2002).

50. Thomas Karis, "South African Liberation: The Communist Factor," *Foreign Affairs*, Winter 1986/1987, http://www.foreignaffairs.com.

51. For an excellent analysis of South Africa's transition period, see Klein, *Shock Doctrine*.

52. Quoted in Thompson, "Water Tap Often Shut."

53. Gumede, *Thabo Mbeki*, 362.

54. Quoted from the short documentary film *Inkani* (2006), by Shannon Walsh and Heinrich Bohmke.

55. R. Kasrils, "Concerned about Water Supply and Sanitation . . . Concerned about Free Basic Water and Water Cut-offs?," advertisement, *Sunday Independent*, December 8, 2002.

56. Quoted in "March Stopped outside Wits," South African Press Association, August 25, 2002.

57. Indeed, the Water Services Act stipulates in section 4(3): "Procedures for the limitation or discontinuation of water services must—(a) be fair and equitable; (b) provide for reasonable notice of intention to limit or discontinue water services and for an opportunity to make representations . . . ; and (c) not result in a person being denied access to basic water services for non-payment, where that person proves, to the satisfaction of the relevant water services authority that he or she is unable to pay for basic services."

58. Lindiwe Mazibuko from the Phiri township claimed in the lawsuit: "Before 17 March 2004, all the members of our household had access to a full-pressure, unmetered, unlimited water supply for which a flat-rate charge . . . was levied (a 'flat-rate water system'). [Then] Johannesburg Water workers started digging trenches in the pavement outside my residence. When I protested, the workers said that they were digging trenches in order to lay pipes for the installation of a prepayment water meter system. . . . At the end of March 2004, without any notice whatsoever, Johannesburg Water switched off the water supply to my residence. At or around the same time, many of my fellow Phiri residents were experiencing similar cut-offs. . . . By 8 July 2004 many of the residents, including the members of my household, were still without water. On that day, however, the City, alternatively Johannesburg Water, blocked all access to Chiawelo 1 Reservoir in Phiri. This left the residents of Phiri entirely without any access to water. Once again, persons employed by Johannesburg Water or acting on its instructions were responsible for this action. Between 8 July 2004 and 11 October 2004, I was forced to obtain water from Block A, 3 kilometres away, using only a wheelbarrow to transport water twice a day. The attempts of some residents, whose water supply was disconnected, to manually re-connect their water supply were dealt with harshly by Johannesburg Water, which unilaterally imposed fines of R1 500.00 on residents." See Lindiwe Mazibuko & Others v. City of Johannesburg & Others, Case CCT 39/09, [2009] ZACC 28.

59. Other private companies continue to operate in South Africa, including the French company Saur, which acquired a thirty-year operating contract for the Dolphin Coast. The British Biwater now operates in Nelspruit. See Roger Cohen, "Francis Bouygues, Building Mogul and Media Executive, Dies at 70," *New York Times*, July 25, 1993.

60. The first quote is from a document accessed on December 14, 2009, at http://www.suez.com, which is no longer available online. In 2010, Suez released a pamphlet titled *Johannesburg Management Contract* (Paris: Suez Environnement, June 2010). This is available online at http://www.suez-environnement .com.

61. The contract maintains that the company must "provide sufficient lifeline and subsidised tariffs."

62. Daniel Malzbender, Jaqui Goldin, Anthony Turton, and Anton Earle,

"traditional Water Governance and South Africa's 'National Water Act': Tension or Cooperation?" (paper presented at the international workshop African Water Laws: Plural Legislative Frameworks for Rural Water Management in Africa, Gauteng, South Africa, January 26–28, 2005), http://www.acwr.co.za/pdf_files/o8.pdf.

63. Farai Kapfudzaruwa and Merle Sowman, "Is There a Role for Traditional Governance Systems in South Africa's New Water Management Regime?," Water SA (Online) 35, no. 5 (October 2009), http://www.scielo.org.za.

64. Quoted in ibid.

65. Penny S. Bernard, "Ecological Implications of Water Spirit Beliefs in Southern Africa: The Need to Protect Knowledge, Nature, and Resource Rights," USDA Forest Service Proceedings, RMRS-P-27 (2003): 153.

66. Trevor Ngwane, "Socialists, the Environment and Ecosocialism" (paper presented at the Rosa Luxemburg Foundation conference, The Global Crisis and Africa: Struggles for Alternatives, Randburg, South Africa, November 19, 2009), http://climateandcapitalism.com.

67. Joel Kovel, "Ecosocialism as a Human Phenomenon," Ecosocialist Horizons, August 3, 2013, http://ecosocialisthorizons.com.

68. According to journalist Pearlie Joubert, "80% of high school kids in Imizamo Yethu have used methamphetamines, and 40% of all black and coloured people are unemployed." Pearlie Joubert, "Ask Some Whites to Leave," Mail and Guardian, February 23, 2007.

69. Yunus Kemp, "Racial Tensions Rise over Hout Bay Land Issue," Star, October 24, 2001.

70. Besides overcrowding, Yethu suffers from a high rate of crime, as residents fight over scarce resources. Mavis told me that the area was so dangerous that I should not be walking there by myself. Crime peaked in 2004 with 900 property-related offenses, 754 violent crimes, and 17 murders. See Joubert, "Ask Some Whites to Leave."

71. According to the city of Cape Town, out of an estimated 115,000 households in informal areas, about 30,000 do not have access to "basic" water and 73,000 do not have access to basic sanitation. (The "basic" level is defined as fewer than 5 households per toilet and fewer than 25 households per water tap.) See Sustainability Institute, "Water and Sanitation in the City of Cape Town Integrated Analysis Baseline Report," under the UNF-funded project Integrated Resources Management for Urban Development, UNDP Project No. 00038512, compiled by Sonja Pithey, 2007.

72. Quoted in Joubert, "Ask Some Whites to Leave."

73. The Hout Bay Residents and Ratepayers Association reported, "In 2006 Dr. Justin O'Riain, together with Stellenbosch University epidemiologist Dr. Jo Barnes, tested a sample of water from the river. The safe maximum E. coli count

per 100cc is 300; anything over this figure is considered dangerous. The analysis revealed a staggering 9 billion." HBRRA website, accessed January 22, 2009, http://www.houtbay.org.za.

74. Quoted in Joubert, "Ask Some Whites to Leave."

75. Ibid.

76. McKeed Kotlolo, "Strike Talks Postponed while SA Burns," *Sowetan*, June 21, 2007, 4–5.

77. Mandy de Waal, "SA's National Water Week and Dry Reality," *Daily Maverick*, March 20, 2013.

78. World Bank Group, "Country Partnership Strategy," 5.

79. Journalist Tafazal Hussain writes: "The decisions to set up a development bank and the CRA in all likelihood are major challenges to the US and Europe-dominated World Bank (WB) and International Monetary Fund (IMF). These are seen as confidence-boosting measures not only for the people of the BRICS nations, but also emerging economies and poor countries in general which have often been browbeaten in political, economic and financial matters by global giants." Tafazal Hussain, "BRICS Offers Chance to Escape West's Grip," *Global Times*, April 7, 2013, http://www.globaltimes.cn.

4. Mother Ganga Is Not for Sale

1. Transcribed from "Extra Features: Expanded Interviews," in *Flow: For Love of Water,* directed by Irena Salina (New York: Oscilloscope, 2008), DVD.

2. The World Bank supports the Vishnugad Pipalkoti Hydropower Project on the Alaknanda River in Uttarakhand, as well as the Tehri Dam. See "India Hydropower Development," World Bank, March 23, 2012, http://www.world bank.org.

3. Quoted in Ramachandra Guha, *The Unquiet Woods: Ecological Change and Peasant Resistance in the Himalayas* (Berkeley: University of California Press, 1989), 156.

4. Quoted in ibid., 159.

5. Frank S. Smythe, *The Valley of Flowers* (Dehra Dun: Natraj, 2001), 113.

6. Nina Nikovic and Jean-Pierre Lehmann, "Tibet and 21st Century Water Wars," *Globalist,* July 11, 2013, http://www.theglobalist.com.

7. See V. Jolli and M. K. Pandit, "Influence of Human Disturbance on the Abundance of Himalayan Pheasant (Aves, Galliformes) in the Temperate Forest of Western Himalaya, India," *Vestnik zoologii* 45, no. 6 (2011): 523–30.

8. "British Scientist 'Solves' Mystery of Himalayan Yetis," BBC News, October 17, 2003, http://www.bbc.co.uk.

9. A committee of fourteen scientists "gave a unanimous report that there should be no dam." Sunderlal Bahuguna, *Fire in the Heart, Fire Wood on the Back:*

Writings on and by Himalayan Crusader Sunderlal Bahuguna, edited by Tenzin Rigzin (Amritsar: All India Pingalawara Charitable Society, 2005), 64.

10. Ravish Tiwari and Gautam Dheer, "Tehri Dam Overflows, 60 Killed So Far," *Indian Express,* September 21, 2010, http://www.indianexpress.com.

11. Girija Rani Asthana, "Sunderlal Bahuguna," in *Our Leaders,* vol. 12, ed. Geeta Menon (New Delhi: Children's Book Trust, 2005), 111.

12. Quoted in A. Ranga Reddy, *Gandhi and Globalization* (New Delhi: Mittal, 2009), 52.

13. Mahatma Gandhi, *The Collected Works of Mahatma Gandhi* (New Delhi: Publications Division, Government of India, 1999), 83:91, 83:113, 93:36, http://www.gandhiserve.org.

14. Quoted in Ramachandra Guha, "The Green Gandhian: J. C. Kumarappa," in *An Anthropologist among the Marxists, and Other Essays* (New Delhi: Permanent Blac, 2001), 85.

15. Bahuguna, *Fire in the Heart,* 75.

16. Ajay S. Rawat, *Garhwal Himalayas: A Study in Historical Perspective* (Dehli: Indus, 2002), 142. The number of dead in this incident is disputed. The Information Department of Uttar Pradesh claims it was two hundred people, but Sunderlal Bahuguna says it was closer to seventeen. Most scholars have cited Bahuguna's number.

17. Bahuguna, *Fire in the Heart,* 36.

18. Ibid., 35.

19. Ibid., 16.

20. Quoted in Lakshmi Sarah Eassey, "Vimala Bahuguna: Life-Long Activist against Tehri Dam," December 3, 2010, http://lakisarah.com/2010/12.

21. "Canals of Irrigation in India," *North American Review* 77, no. 161 (October 1853): 452–53.

22. Charles Raikes, *Notes on the North-western Provinces of India* (London: Chapman and Hall, 1852), 270.

23. "Canals of Irrigation in India," 455.

24. Gyanendra Pandey, "Peasant Revolt and Indian Nationalism: The Peasant Movement in Awadh, 1919–22," in *Selected Subaltern Studies,* ed. Ranajit Guha and Gayatri Chakravorty Spivak (Oxford: Oxford University Press, 1988), 265.

25. John Briscoe and R. P. S. Malik, *India's Water Economy: Bracing for a Turbulent Future* (Washington, D.C.: World Bank, 2006), 1.

26. Daniel Pepper, "The Toxic Consequences of the Green Revolution," *U.S. News & World Report,* July 7, 2008, http://www.usnews.com.

27. According to Akash Kapur, "It's not clear that the Indian economy—new or old—is sustainable without a solution to the problems confronting agriculture. The farming crisis is really a national crisis." Akash Kapur, "Letter

from India: Agriculture Left to Die at India's Peril," *New York Times,* January 28, 2010.

28. Pradeep Gupta, "Farmer Commits Suicide by Consuming Pesticides," *Times of India,* July 6, 2012, http://articles.timesofindia.indiatimes.com.

29. Navdanya, accessed May 30, 2012, http://www.navdanya.org.

30. Bahuguna, *Fire in the Heart,* 176.

31. Ibid., 40.

32. Ibid., 90.

33. "Tehri District," eUttaranchal, accessed October 12, 2013, http://www.euttaranchal.comri.php.

34. "Drinking Water," Tehri Garwal—Uttarakhand, accessed November 10, 2013, http://tehri.nic.in.

35. Chaitanya Krishna, "Let's Wake Up Lest Ganga Go the Saraswati Way," *The Hindu,* August 19, 2012, http://www.thehindu.com.

36. When Moyers tried to argue that markets are the best way to allocate water, Shiva replied, "I'm enough of a scientist to know that water is created in nature and not in markets. Markets can only allocate water and take it uphill to where the money is." "Interview with Dr. Vandana Shiva," *Now with Bill Moyers,* PBS, September 5, 2003, http://www.pbs.org.

37. Quoted in Anna Da Costa, "India Must Revive Age-Old Water Harvesting Methods," AlterNet, July 23, 2012, http://www.trust.org/alertnet/news.

38. Neetu Chandra, "Delhi: Sullied Ridge Pond 'Springs' a Surprise," *India Today,* April 16, 2012, http://indiatoday.intoday.in.

39. R. P. Kangle, *The Kautilya Arthashastra* (Delhi: Motilal Banarsidass, 1997), 229, 346.

40. Arun Kumar Singh, *Delhi's Water Woes: A Cross-Sectoral Analysis of the Water Crisis in Delhi,* occasional paper (New Delhi: Centre for Trade and Development, 2006), 14.

41. Quoted in Vandana Shiva, *Water Wars: Privatization, Pollution, and Profit* (Cambridge, Mass.: South End Press, 2002), 122.

42. In contrast, Indians used reservoir water only sparsely for irrigation, primarily storing water for times of droughts. Around Delhi, a third of a farmer's land would be irrigated, a third unirrigated, and a third fallow. Sanjeev Khagram, *Dams and Development: Transnational Struggles for Water and Power* (Ithaca, N.Y.: Cornell University Press, 2004), 67, 34.

43. Bahuguna, *Fire in the Heart,* 119.

44. Ibid., xx.

45. See S. K. Gupta, *Modern Hydrology and Sustainable Water Development* (West Sussex: Blackwell, 2011), 322.

46. Lok Sabha Secretariat, Parliament Library and Reference, Research, Document and Information Service, "Displacement and Rehabilitation of People

Due to Development Projects," New Delhi, India, December 2013, Report. No. 30/RN/Ref./December/2013. Other estimates are much higher, up to 350 million displaced. See Jacques Leslie, *Deep Water: The Epic Struggle over Dams, Displaced People, and the Environment* (New York: Farrar, Straus and Giroux, 2005), 24.

47. Ravi Nitesh, "'Broken Wings': A Visit to a Slum Area in Delhi," Youth Ki Awaaz, May 15, 2012, http://www.youthkiawaaz.com.

48. Jyoti Thottam/Pipola, "How India's Success Is Killing Its Holy River," *Time*, July 19, 2010, http://www.time.com.

49. Annapurna Mishra, "Status Report on Sonia Vihar," accessed August 1, 2012, http://annapurnamishra.blogspot.com.

50. Annapurna Mishra, "Councillor Mishra Introduces Direct Democracy to the 'Hell' of an Unauthorized Colony," Public Cause Research Foundation, March 30, 2010, http://www.pcrf.

51. "Dainik Jagran Impact: Delhi Government Takes Action to Prevent Jaundice," *Jagran Post*, August 16, 2011, http://post.jagran.com.

52. The Bank provided $2.5 million up front to hire an accounting firm to write up a plan that would transfer the city water supply to private entities, establish a plan for achieving full cost recovery, and increase water rates and fire enough workers to achieve "efficiency." Singh, *Delhi's Water Woes*, 50–52.

53. Kejriwal discovered PwC was ranked tenth in the initial evaluation of bids, but the Bank requested that PwC be moved up in the rankings, arguing that PwC was an *Indian* corporation and an Indian corporation should be included in the qualifying bidders. (The American firm PwC has an office in India.) And so PwC was brought up to sixth place, barely qualifying. After a fresh request for bids from this short list, PwC again failed to qualify. This time, the Bank demanded that the Water Board specifically "provide a brief explanation of what exactly are PwC's shortcomings." The Bank also demanded that the subcriteria be changed. The Water Board refused to do so, writing back, "A deeper analysis of the suggestion of the Bank would reveal that their objective is to ensure qualification of some more firms by making the sub-criteria less stringent." Refusing to change the subcriteria, the Board passed a resolution asking the Bank to reconsider its position. Again, the Bank refused, demanding that the Delhi Water Board start all over again. When the new evaluations were released, the Bank demanded that one of PwC's low votes be deleted because it was "at considerable variance" with others. Finally, PricewaterhouseCoopers won the bid. Letter to Mr. Wolfowitz from Parivartan, August 20, 2005, and letter to Mr. Kejriwal from Michael Carter, Country Director, India, August 24, 2005; both letters are posted on the World Bank's website, http://www.worldbank.org.

54. When I went to the website for the Bank's own Independent Evaluation Group (http://ieg.worldbankgroup.org) on August 20, 2012, almost half of the links were broken. The link for "Methodology" led to a page that said, "Coming soon."

55. Singh, *Delhi's Water Woes*, 58.

56. Ibid., 60.

57. World Bank, "FAQs: Proposed Delhi Water Supply and Sewerage Project," accessed May 20, 2011, http://www.worldbank.org.

58. Ibid. The former link to this FAQ page now redirects the user to "World Bank: India."

59. Singh, *Delhi's Water Woes*, 64.

60. Ibid., 56.

61. "Sonia Vihar Plant a Tough Jinx to Crack," *Times of India*, June 17, 2005, http://articles.timesofindia.indiatimes.com.

62. Sujay Mehdudia, "Sonia Vihar Water Treatment Plant on the Verge of Getting Rusted," *The Hindu*, December 7, 2005. Estimates of daily penalties varied widely due to a secrecy clause in the contract but were reported to be between 50,000 and 230,000 rupees. See "Pact with MNC May Add to DJB Woes," *The Hindu*, April 6, 2005.

63. Quoted in ibid.

64. Quoted in "Finally Sonia Vihar Springs to Life," *Times of India*, June 17, 2005, http://articles.timesofindia.indiatimes.com.

65. Quoted in "Tehri Water, via Sonia Vihar, Flows through Delhi Taps," Indo-Asian News Service, August 8, 2006, http://www.ians.in.

66. Singh, *Delhi's Water Woes*, 36–39.

67. Ibid., 41–42.

68. Quoted in "Get Ready to Pay More: Work to Privatise South Delhi Water Supply Starts," *Tribune*, July 3, 2012, http://www.tribuneindia.com.

69. See Ghar Bachao Morcha, "Delhi Report on Protest against Unequal Water Distribution by City Authorities," Sanhati, July 15, 2012, http://sanhati.com.

70. Thottam/Pipola, "How India's Success Is Killing Its Holy River."

71. Asit Jolly, "How the Hills Can Kill Again: Kedarnath Calamity a Proof of Long Ignored Threat by Melting Himalayan Glaciers," *India Today*, July 5, 2013, http://indiatoday.intoday.in.

72. Biswajeet Banerjee, "India Monsoon Floods 2013: At Least 102 Dead, 12,000 Pilgrims Stranded," Huffington Post, June 19, 2013, http://www.huffingtonpost.com; Sidhartha Dutta, "Sudden Rise in Dengue Cases, Malaria Down," *Hindustan Times*, August 08, 2013, http://www.hindustantimes.com.

73. See "Uttarakhand Disaster: MoEF Should Suspend Clearances to Hydropower Projects and Institute Enquiry in the Role of HEPs," South Asian Network on Dams, Rivers and People, July 20, 2013, http://sandrp.wordpress.com/2013.

74. Quoted in "Uttarakhand Floods: Sunder Lal Bahuguna Warns of More Disasters," *Indian Express*, New Delhi, June 21, 2013, http://www.indianexpress.com.

75. Jagdish Bhatt, "Incessant Rains in Uttarakhand Pose Threat to Tehri Dam," *Hill Post,* August 7, 2013, http://hillpost.in.

76. Bettina Boxall, "$84-Million Removal of a Dam on Carmel River Set to Begin," *Los Angeles Times,* June 23, 2013.

77. Dinesh C. Sharma, "Inter-linking Rivers Recipe for Disaster," *India Today,* April 5, 2012, http://indiatoday.intoday.in.

78. Vandana Shiva, "Resisting Water Privatization, Building Water Democracy" (paper on the occasion of the World Water Forum, Mexico City, March 2006).

79. A *Times of India* article argued, "Every summer it's the same story. Swathes of the city go dry, Delhi fights with Haryana and UP for more supplies, but nothing really is done to see that the situation gets better the next year. For starters, we suggest that the Delhi government make rainwater harvesting compulsory for all buildings—commercial and residential. . . . It may not fully solve Delhi's water crisis, but will certainly mitigate the problem. If cities like Chennai and Hyderabad can make rainwater harvesting compulsory, why can't Delhi?" Neha Lalchandani and Jayashree Nandi, "Delhi Water Crisis Grows as Haryana Cuts Supply," *Times of India,* June 14, 2012, http://articles.timesofindia.india times.com.

80. From the documentary film *Flow: For Love of Water.*

81. Jal Bhagirathi Foundation, *Milestones: Jal Bhagirathi Foundation* (Jaipur, India: Jal Bhagirathi Foundation, 2012), 48.

82. Quoted in Khagram, *Dams and Development,* 61.

83. Bahuguna, *Fire in the Heart,* 19.

5. A Revolution of the Thirsty in Egypt

1. The settlements are known as *ashwai'yat,* an Arabic word that means "random" or "haphazard." According to urban planner David Sims, eleven million of the people in Cairo live in informal areas. See David Sims, *Understanding Cairo in Revolutionary Times* (Cairo: American University in Cairo Press, 2011). To understand the complexity of estimating population figures for informal areas, see Regina Kipper and Marion Fischer, eds., *Cairo's Informal Areas: Between Urban Challenges and Hidden Potentials* (Cairo: German Technical Cooperation, June 2009).

2. Reem Leila, "No Flow," *Al-Ahram Weekly,* September 11–17, 2008, http://weekly.ahram.org.eg.

3. See Nadia Idle and Alex Nunns, "Tahrir Square Tweet by Tweet," *Guardian,* April 14, 2011. See also Emad El-Din Shahin, "Why Egypt Needs a Second Revolution," CNN, November 23, 2011, http://www.cnn.com.

4. See Shahira Amin, "Egypt's Farmers Desperate for Clean Water," CNN, November 10, 2010, http://www.cnn.com.

5. Philip Marfleet and Rabab El-Mahdi, "Egyptians Have Removed a Dictator; Can They Remove a Dictatorship?" ZNet, February 22, 2011, https://zcomm.org.

6. Alya Kebiri, "Egypt Water Pricing: A Viable Solution for Egypt's Water Crisis?," *World Environment Magazine*, June 2009, 70–74.

7. The mandate for the newly privatized water utility reads: "Just like a private company, the Holding's aim is to create profits." The mission statement now reads: "The purpose of the Holding company is to purify, desalinate, transfer, distribute and sell potable water, collection, treatment and safe disposal of wastewater whether by itself or through any of its subsidiaries as well as formation and management of a securities portfolio which may include shares, bonds and any other financial tools." Arab Republic of Egypt Public–Private Partnership Program, *6th of October Wastewater Treatment Plant Project: Information Memorandum* (November 2009), 24. See also Kebiri, "Egypt Water Pricing."

8. Kebiri, "Egypt Water Pricing."

9. Cam McGrath, "Poor Thirst as Nile Taps Run Dry," IPS News, September 6, 2010. See also Maat for Peace, Development, and Human Rights, "Violating Rights of Local Civilian," report submitted to Mechanism of Universal Periodical Review, August 2009.

10. Marfleet and El-Mahdi, "Egyptians Have Removed a Dictator."

11. Abdel Mawla Ismail, "Drinking Water Protests and the Role of Civil Society," Water Justice: Resource Center on Alternatives to Privatisation, June 8, 2009, http://www.waterjustice.org.

12. In those years the government of Egypt sold land for the price it would take to supply infrastructure, such as waste and water treatment, free from customs and state taxes. Alternatively, a developer could build the infrastructure and get the land for free. See the website of the New Urban Communities Authority, the government agency responsible for the development of the "New Towns," http://www.nuca.gov.eg/en.

13. One Allegria homeowner complained on Facebook, "There is no Main Tank & pumping station for Allegria & it is directly connected to the municipality water line!?" The Allegria Homeowners' Facebook page, which I accessed on October 30, 2011, appears to have been shut down following legal negotiations with the owners.

14. In 2010, SODIC listed "amounts collected" for "operation and maintenance of Allegria project" as $9 million. Homeowners pay for "basic services," including "security, waste collection and pest control, as well as maintenance of streets, street lighting, electricity, water, sewage infrastructure, and public gardens and landscape." See "Allegria: Property Management," SODIC, 2007. On the issue of water availability, see Salwa Abdel Maksoud Abdullah Eissa, "Intra-urban Migration to the New Cities in the Greater Cairo Region: Cause and Consequences" (master's thesis, American University of Cairo, spring 2011). See also

Sixth of October Development and Investment Company, "Consolidated Financial Statements for the Financial Period Ended June 30, 2010," 32.

15. Susana Myllylä, "Cairo: A Mega-city and Its Water Resources" (paper presented at the Third Nordic Conference on Middle Eastern Studies: Ethnic Encounter and Culture Change, Joensuu, Finland, June 19–22, 1995).

16. Amnesty International, *"We Are Not Dirt": Forced Evictions in Egypt's Informal Settlements,* MDE 12/001/2001 (London: Amnesty International, 2011), 12.

17. Roy Steven Nakashima, Gamal Zekrie Bisada, Obeid Faheem Gergis, Antoin Gawigati, and Jeffrey H. Hendrich, *"Making Cities Work": The Greater Cairo Healthy Neighborhood Program, an Urban Environmental Health Initiative in Egypt,* Activity Report 142 (Arlington, Va.: Environmental Health Project, September 2004), xiv. In contrast, the Housing Study for Urban Egypt, conducted in 2008 for USAID, "showed that 96.7 percent of households in Greater Cairo had access to a water faucet inside the dwelling and that 98 percent had access to proper sewerage lines." Steven Viney, "Minimalist 'Urban Planning' Keeps Cairo Afloat, but Not without Drawbacks," *Egypt Independent,* September 11, 2011. See also Sarah Sabry, *Poverty Lines in Greater Cairo, Underestimating and Misrepresenting Poverty,* Poverty Reduction in Urban Areas Series, Working Paper 21 (London: Human International Institute for Environment and Development, May 2009), 31.

18. See Nakashima et al., *"Making Cities Work."*

19. Quoted in Julia Gerlach, "Me and My Neighborhood," in Kipper and Fischer, *Cairo's Informal Areas,* 55.

20. Quoted in McGrath, "Poor Thirst as Nile Taps Run Dry."

21. Quoted in Gerlach, "Me and My Neighborhood," 53–59.

22. Also in 2008, the Mubarak regime passed a law stating that if a building were found in violation of code, it would automatically be demolished. (Previously, a 1976 law allowed for the builder to reconcile with authorities by paying a fine, which led to corruption.) Mubarak's new law, which had the greatest impact in Cairo, appeared to be a plan for the de facto demolition of sections of the city.

23. Amnesty International, *"We Are Not Dirt,"* 42.

24. Quoted in Viney, "Minimalist 'Urban Planning' Keeps Cairo Afloat."

25. Amnesty International, *"We Are Not Dirt,"* 3.

26. See World Bank, *Most Improved Business Reformers in DB 2010* (Washington, D.C.: World Bank, 2010). See also Daniela Marotta, Ruslan Yemtsov, Heba El-Laithy, Hala Abou-Ali, and Sherine Al-Shawarby, *Was Growth in Egypt between 2005 and 2008 Pro-Poor? From Static to Dynamic Poverty Profile,* Policy Research Working Paper 5589 (Washington, D.C.: World Bank, March 1, 2011); and "The World Bank Supports Egypt's Reforms in the Water Supply and Sanitation Sector," World Bank, 2008, http://go.worldbank.org. The Bank has deleted

this document from its website, though it continues to actively support public–private water contracting in Egypt.

27. According to sociologist Sarah Sabry, the World Bank estimates have been politically motivated and used as evidence of the success of privatization policies. Just after the revolution, an online Al Jazeera article cited neoliberalism and privatization as among the chief causes of the revolution. Walter Armbrust wrote, "Egypt did not so much shrink its public sector, as neoliberal doctrine would have it, as it reallocated public resources for the benefit of a small and already affluent elite. Privatization provided windfalls for politically well-connected individuals." Walter Armbrust, "Egypt: A Revolution against Neoliberalism?" Al Jazeera, February 24, 2011, http://www.aljazeera.com. The pro-privatization magazine *Global Water Intelligence* immediately countered: "It is an absolute travesty to suggest that privatisation is the root of the problem . . . [and] incorrect to associate the privatisation programmes in North Africa with corruption and incompetence." Instead, the article claimed, privatization led only to "transparency" and "competitive bidding." See "Winning the War on Corruption and Incompetence," *Global Water Intelligence*, March 3, 2011, http://www.global waterintel.com. See also Sabry, *Poverty Lines in Greater Cairo*.

28. Letter from U.S. Ambassador to Egypt Francis Ricciardone Jr. to Central Intelligence Agency, Group Destinations Arab Israeli Collective, National Security Council, Secretary of State, on September 6, 2007, No. 07CAIRO2726_a; letter from U.S. Ambassador to Egypt Francis Ricciardone Jr. to "Blank" on January 3, 2006, 06CAIRO35_a; letter from U.S. Ambassador to Egypt Margaret Scobey to Group Destinations Arab Israeli Collective, National Security Council, Secretary of State on November 2, 2008, No. 08CAIRO2297_a, Wikileaks, http://www .wikileaks.org.

29. Bradley Hope, "Fraud Inquiry in Egypt Drags in Top UAE Firms Damac and Al-Futtaim," *The National*, April 4, 2011.

30. Quoted in Zainab Fattah and Mahmoud Kassem, "Egypt's Developers Pay the Price for Ties to Mubarak's Regime," Bloomberg News, June 7, 2011, http://www.bloomberg.com.

31. Frost & Sullivan, *Assessment of Water and Wastewater Sector in Egypt*, Report No. P541 (Mountain View, Calif.: Frost & Sullivan, May 2011).

32. "Investing in the Arab Spring," *Voice of America*, May 26, 2011.

33. Leslie-Ann Boctor, "Egypt: Desert Reclamation the Country's Best Hope—or a Mirage?" Inter Press Service, July 30, 2007, http://ipsnews.net.

34. Mark Svendsen, Robert Cardinalli, M. Lotfy, Y. Nasr, and Nayef A. A. Moukhtar, *Private Sector Participation in Egyptian Water Management*, Report No. 70, Egypt Water Policy Reform Contract No. LAG-I-00-99-00017-00, Task Order 815 (Cairo: United States Agency for International Development/Egypt, June 2003).

35. Quoted in Salma El-Wardani, "Egyptian Lawyer Drops Palm Hills and Saudi Kingdom Cases, Voices Dissatisfaction with 'Revolution' Govt," *Al-Ahram Daily*, June 27, 2011, http://english.ahram.org.eg.

36. See "Toshka Lakes in Egypt Show Rapid Signs of Drying," The Watchers, July 16, 2012, http://thewatchers.adorraeli.com.

37. Andre Fecteau, "On Toshka New Valley's Mega-failure," *Egypt Independent*, April 26, 2012, http://www.egyptindependent.com.

38. E-mail from Reva Bhalla to "Emre," February 7, 2011, Stratfor e-mails, Wikileaks: Global Intelligence Files, e-mail ID 1708668, released on February 26, 2013, http://www.wikileaks.org/gfiles.

39. James Duncan, "Re-presenting the Landscape: Problems of Reading the Intertextual," in *Paysage e crise de la lisibilite*, ed. L. Mondada, F. Panese, and O. Soderstrom (Lausanne: Universite de Lausanne, Institut de Geographie, 1992), 86.

40. See "Street Art and the Power to Mobilize," *Daily News Egypt*, April 10, 2012; Amany Aly Shawky, "Streets of Cairo: From AUC Crossing to Battlefield at Mohamed Mahmoud," *Egypt Independent*, November 23, 2011; "Ministry, American University Catch Fire in Fresh Cairo Clashes," Ahram Online, January 26, 2013, http://english.ahram.org.eg.

6. Targeting Iraq's Water

1. Rick Emert, "Iraq Projects Focus on Getting Clean Water out of the Ground, to the People," *Stars and Stripes*, August 13, 2005, http://www.stripes.com.

2. Aseel Kami, "Veolia Baghdad Water Deal Worth $5 Bln—mayor," AFX News, July 16, 2009, http://www.finanznachrichten.de.

3. "Water and Sewage Sectors in Iraq: Sector Report—February 2013," Dunia Frontier Consultants, Washington, D.C., 2013; *Water in Iraq Factsheet*, U.N. Iraq Joint Analysis and Policy Unit, March 2013, http://www.jauiraq.org.

4. Quoted in David Wood, "Iraq Reconstruction Cost U.S. $60 Billion, Left behind Corruption and Waste," Huffington Post, March 6, 2013, http://www.huffingtonpost.com.

5. Quoted in John T. Bennett, "Panetta: Paying for Iraq War on Credit Was a 'Mistake,'" *U.S. News & World Report*, June 13, 2013, http://www.usnews.com.

6. Mark Thompson, "Inside the Secret War Council," *Time*, August 19, 2002.

7. This information is from the Bechtel website in the report "Setting the Record Straight: Bechtel's Response to Allegations about Its Work in Iraq," accessed December 12, 2012, http://www.bechtel.com. See also Daniel Henninger, "George Shultz, Father of the Bush Doctrine," *Hoover Digest*, July 30, 2006.

8. Neil Baumgardner, "Oscar Approves Army Acquisition Structure Re-organization," *Defense Daily*, November 1, 2001. Fluor CEO Alan Boeckmann was a member of the National Republican Congressional Committee, devoted to increasing the number of Republicans in the U.S. House of Representatives. Fluor's vice president was a member of George W. Bush for President, the fundraising arm for the president's campaign. See Aude Lagorce, "Fluor Upped at J. P. Morgan, U.S. Army Contract Cited," *Wall Street Journal*, June 29, 2007.

9. Elizabeth Becker and Richard A. Oppel Jr., "A Nation at War: Reconstruction; U.S. Gives Bechtel a Major Contract in Rebuilding Iraq," *New York Times*, April 18, 2003.

10. Ariel Cohen and Gerald P. O'Driscoll Jr., "The Road to Economic Prosperity for a Post-Saddam Iraq," Heritage Foundation, Backgrounder No. 1633, March 5, 2003, http://www.heritage.org.

11. Office of the Special Inspector General for Iraq Reconstruction, "Review of Major U.S. Government Infrastructure Projects in Iraq: Nassiriya and Ifraz Water Treatment Plants," SIGIR-EV-20-002, October 28, 2010, 7.

12. Michael Knights, "Infrastructure Targeting and Postwar Iraq," Washington Institute, PolicyWatch No. 725, March 14, 2003, http://www.washington institute.org.

13. "Technical Annex for a Proposed IDA Credit in the Amount of SDR 27.0 Million (US$40 Million Equivalent) to the Republic of Iraq for a Dokan and Derbandikhan Emergency Hydropower Project," World Bank, Report No. T7682-IQ, November 30, 2006, 33, http://www.worldbank.org. Quote in Barton Gellman, "Allied Air War Struck Broadly in Iraq," *Washington Post*, June 23, 1991.

14. Gellman, "Allied Air War Struck Broadly in Iraq."

15. Edward C. Mann, Gary Endersby, and Thomas R. Searle, *Thinking Effects: Effects-Based Methodology for Joint Operations*, CADRE Paper No. 15, Maxwell Air Force Base (Alabama: Air University Press, October 2002), 21–22.

16. "Iraq Water Treatment Vulnerabilities," memorandum from Defense Intelligence Agency to CENTCOM, Filename: 511rept.91, DTG: 221900Z, January 1991.

17. Quoted in Thomas J. Nagy, "The Secret behind the Sanctions: How the U.S. Intentionally Destroyed Iraq's Water Supply," *Progressive*, September 2001. Nagy also quotes a Defense Intelligence Agency document, "Status of Disease at Refugee Camps," dated May 1991: "'Cholera and measles have emerged at refugee camps. Further infectious diseases will spread due to inadequate water treatment and poor sanitation.' The reason for this outbreak is clearly stated again. 'The main causes of infectious diseases, particularly diarrhea, dysentery, and upper respiratory problems, are poor sanitation and unclean water. These diseases primarily afflict the old and young children.'"

18. See Barbara Crossette, "Iraq Sanctions Kill Children, U.N. Reports," *New York Times*, December 1, 1995. See also Joy Gordon, "U.S. Responsible for Human Toll of Iraq Sanctions," *Cap Times*, December 22, 2010, http://host.madison.com/ct.

19. Typhoid increased eightfold between 1991 and 1996. Felicity Arbuthnot, "Allies Deliberately Poisoned Iraq Public Water Supply In Gulf War," *Sunday Herald*, September 17, 2000. See also Center for Economic and Social Rights, *Special Report: Water under Siege in Iraq* (New York: Center for Economic and Social Rights, April 2003); Office of the Special Inspector General, "Review of Major U.S. Government Infrastructure Projects," 10.

20. Quoted in Center for Economic and Social Rights, *Special Report*, 6.

21. Quoted in ibid., 7.

22. From Loïc Fauchon, opening remarks at the 2012 World Water Forum, Marseilles, France.

23. David Batty, "Iraqi City Suffers Water Shortage," *Guardian*, March 24, 2003.

24. Bechtel–USAID contract, April 17, 2003, 12–13.

25. Dana Hedgpeth, "Bechtel's Projects Lacking In Iraq," *Washington Post*, July 26, 2007.

26. Quoted in Public Citizen Water for All Campaign, with Dahr Jaimal, *Bechtel's Dry Run: Iraqis Suffer Water Crisis* (Washington, D.C.: Public Citizen, 2004), 4.

27. From a report posted on the Bechtel website, "Bechtel, USAID, and the Iraq Infrastructure Reconstruction Program," accessed March 1, 2013, http://www.bechtel.com.

28. Fluor has a history of safety problems, from supplying formaldehyde-laden trailers to victims of Hurricane Katrina to causing an explosion at the Hanford nuclear facility in Washington in 1997. In total, Fluor has had thirty-four cases of "contract fraud and environmental, ethics, and labor violations" since 1995. It has been fined hundreds of millions of dollars but continues to receive billion-dollar contracts from the U.S. government. According to the nonprofit Transparency International, the construction industry is the most corrupt industry in the world. Philip Mattera, *Profiles of Twelve Companies That Have Received Large Contracts for Cleanup and Reconstruction Work Related to Hurricanes Katrina and Rita* (Washington, D.C.: Corporation Research Project, March 2006). See also "Federal Contractor Misconduct Database," Project on Government Oversight, accessed March 10, 2013, http://www.contractormisconduct.org.

29. Norris Jones, "Al Wathba Water Treatment Plant Gets Upgrade," Gulf Region Central District, U.S. Army Corps of Engineers, Defend America: U.S. Department of Defense News about the War on Terrorism, August 9, 2006, http://www.defendamerica.mil. See also Matthew Schofield, "Baghdad's Water

Still Undrinkable Six Years after Invasion," McClatchy Newspapers, March 18, 2009, http://www.mcclatchydc.com.

30. Quoted in "Iraq: Water Shortage Leads People to Drink from Rivers," IRIN, February 18, 2007, http://www.irinnews.org.

31. Matthew Schofield, "Baghdad in a Time of Cholera," The Real News, March 23, 2009, http://therealnews.com/t2.

32. Azeez Mahmood, "Fears of Cholera Epidemic in Kurdistan," Ground Report, May 5, 2008, http://www.groundreport.com.

33. Schofield, "Baghdad's Water Still Undrinkable."

34. See World Bank, "Iraq Country Water Resource Assistance Strategy," Report No. 36297-IQ, June 30, 2006.

35. Office of the Special Inspector General, "Review of Major U.S. Government Infrastructure Projects," 23.

36. Suez Environnement, "Degrémont Has Signed a Contract for the Design Procurement and Training Assistance in the Construction of a Drinking Water Treatment Plant in Al-Rusafa, Baghdad," press release, December 12, 2008.

37. "Baghdad Hopes Project Will Resolve Water Shortage," Radio Free Europe/Radio Liberty, February 12, 2010, http://www.rferl.org.

38. Khalid K. Al-Bayatti, Kadhum H. Al-Arajy, and Seba Hussain Al-Nuaemy, "Bacteriological and Physicochemical Studies on Tigris River Near the Water Purification Stations within Baghdad Province," *Journal of Environmental and Public Health* 2012 (2012).

39. "PM's Speech at Opening of Ifraz Water Project," Kurdistan Regional Government, March 22, 2007, http://www.krg.org.

40. Aiyob Mawloodi, "Ifraz Water Project Short on Funds," *Kurdish Globe,* February 25, 2012, http://www.kurdishglobe.net.

41. Special Inspector General for Iraq Reconstruction, *Learning from Iraq: A Final Report from the Special Inspector General for Iraq Reconstruction* (Washington, D.C.: U.S. Government Printing Office, March 2013), 74.

42. Christian Caryl, "The Democracy Boondoggle in Iraq," *Foreign Policy,* March 5, 2013.

43. "Ifraz Water Project to Supply Erbil until 2035," *Kurdish Globe,* December 27, 2009.

44. Ibid.

45. Ibid.

46. James Glanz, "For Iraq's Great Marshes, a Hesitant Comeback," *New York Times,* March 8, 2005.

47. Ralph S. Solecki, "The Bekhme Dam Project in Kurdistan Iraq: A Threat to the Archaeology of the Upper Zagros River Valley," *International Journal of Kurdish Studies* 19, no. 1–2 (2005).

48. See Neil King Jr., "Firms World-Wide Seek Billions to Cover their Gulf War Losses," *Wall Street Journal*, August 18, 1997. Ralph Solecki wrote, "Up to the time of its completion, the project cost $1.5 billion. . . . Consulting work was done by the San Francisco-based Bechtel International." Solecki, "Bekhme Dam Project in Kurdistan Iraq," 3.

49. Quoted in Joseph Kay, "Bechtel Awarded Iraq Contract: War Profits and the U.S. 'Military-Industrial Complex,'" World Socialist Web Site, April 29, 2003, http://www.wsws.org/en.

50. Solecki, "Bekhme Dam Project in Kurdistan Iraq."

51. For a detailed eyewitness account of the attack, see John Simpson, "Beyond the Hazards of Duty," Global Journalist, July 1, 2003, http://www.global journalist.org.

52. The project was funded by the Japan Bank for International Cooperation. See "Irbil and Tokyo Negotiate Water Treatment Plant Funding," *MEED*, November 24, 2006, http://www.meed.com.

53. David Hall and Emanuele Lobina, *Pipe Dreams: The Failure of the Private Sector to Invest in Water Services in Developing Countries* (London: Public Services International Research Unit, World Development Movement, 2006), 53.

54. See Qandil, *Sida Technical Proposal, Erbil City Water Network* (Erbil: Qandil, April 13, 2008), 6–7, 12, http://www.qandil.org.

55. At the Ifraz plant itself, the inspector general's office said personnel "identified several areas of concern regarding what they considered poor construction by the contractor," including falling concrete and clogged intake valves. Office of the Special Inspector General, "Review of Major U.S. Government Infrastructure Projects," 35–39.

56. "Survey Report: Erbil, Iraq," Associates for International Research, January 2012, http://www.air-inc.com.

57. Office of the Special Inspector General, "Review of Major U.S. Government Infrastructure Projects," 20, 22–24.

58. James Glanz, "Security vs. Rebuilding: Kurdish Town Loses Out," *New York Times*, April 16, 2005.

59. Shane Harris and Matthew M. Aid, "Exclusive: CIA Files Prove American Helped Saddam as He Gassed Iran," *Foreign Policy*, August 26, 2013, http://www.foreignpolicy.com.

60. Quoted in Jim Garamone, "Bush Says Massacre at Halabja Shows Evil of Hussein's Rule," American Forces Press Service, March 15, 2003.

61. Secretary Colin L. Powell, "Remarks for Al-Hurrah Television on the 16th Anniversary of the Halabja Massacre," March 16, 2004, http://2001-2009.state.gov.

62. Glanz, "Security vs. Rebuilding."

63. Henry Weinstein and William C. Rempel, "Iraq Arms: Big Help from

U.S.: Technology was Sold with Approval—and Encouragement—from the Commerce Department but Often over Defense Officials' Objections," *Los Angeles Times*, February 13, 1991.

64. Sam Dagher, "Uprooted for Decades, Iraqi Kurds Long for Home," *New York Times*, September 3, 2009.

65. "Iraqi Kurds Sue French Companies for Halabja Chemical Attack," RFI, June 11, 2013, http://www.english.rfi.fr.

66. On March 17, Japan International Cooperation Agency (JICA) president Sadako Ogata signed two agreements with the government of Iraq to provide loans to support reconstruction in Iraq. One of the projects was supposed to be the "Water Supply Improvement Project" in Kurdistan, which would ensure "a safe, stable water supply" to certain cities in the region. Cities targeted for this project were Halabja, Sulaimaniya, Erbil, and Dohuk. See "JICA Signed Japanese ODA Loan Agreement with Iraq," Japan International Cooperation Agency Report, ReliefWeb, March 17, 2009, http://reliefweb.int.

67. Special Inspector General for Iraq Reconstruction, *Learning from Iraq*, xii, 74.

68. Melik Kaylan, "Hard Times in Iraq," *Forbes*, August 19, 2010, http://www.forbes.com.

69. Quoted in Michael Schwartz, *War without End: The Iraq War in Context* (Chicago: Haymarket Books, 2008), 34.

70. World Bank, "Emergency Project Paper for a Proposed IDA Credit of SDR 66.5 Million (US$109.5 Million) Equivalent to the Republic of Iraq," Report No. 43153-IQ, May 19, 2008, 4, 9.

71. World Bank, "Implementation Status and Results, Iraq, IQ-Emergency Water Supply Project (P094650)," Report No. ISR9037, March 3, 2013.

72. Quoted in Muhammad Sharif Chaudry, *Fundamentals of Islamic Economic System* (Lahore: Burhan Education and Welfare Trust, 2009).

73. In 2010, UNESCO started the Initiative for Community Rehabilitation to help local communities restore and rebuild damaged *karez* systems. At the United Nations there is a resurgence of interest in traditional water systems, as evidenced in Harriet Bigas, Zafar Adeel, and Brigitte Schuster, eds., *Seeing Traditional Technologies in a New Light: Using Traditional Approaches for Water Management in Drylands* (Paris: UNESCO, 2009), which discusses *karez* and *qanat* systems. See also "Water Shortage Fueling Displacement of People in Northern Iraq, UNESCO Study Finds," ReliefWeb, October 13, 2009, http://reliefweb.int.

74. Bigas et al., *Seeing Traditional Technologies in a New Light*.

75. John F. Kolars and William A. Mitchell, *The Euphrates River and the Southeast Anatolia Development Project* (Carbondale: Southern Illinois University Press, 1991), 32–33.

76. Quoted in Itzchak E. Kornfeld, "Trouble in Mesopotamia: Can America

Deter a Water War between Iraq, Syria, and Turkey?," *Environmental Law Reporter* 34, no. 10634 (July 2004): 10635.

77. Saleem al-Wazzan, "Salt Levels in Shatt Al-Arab Threaten Environmental Disaster," Niqash: Briefings from inside and across Iraq, September 2, 2009, http://www.niquash.org. See also "Iraq: Drought Hits Rice, Wheat Staples," IRIN, August 31, 2009, http://www.irinnews.org.

78. From a talk at the World Water Forum, Marseille, France, 2012.

79. World Bank, *Water Resources Sector Strategy: Strategic Directions for World Bank Engagement* (Washington, D.C.: World Bank, 2003), 76–79.

Conclusion

1. Loïc Fauchon, "Out of Our Depth," in *The G8 2009: From La Maddalena to L'Aquila,* ed. John Kirton and Madeline Koch (Toronto: Newsdesk Media Group and the G20 Research Group, 2009), 126–28.

2. See Domenico Lombardi, "Strengthening the International Monetary Fund," in *The G20 Mexico Summit 2012: The Quest for Growth and Stability,* ed. John Kirton and Madeline Koch (Toronto: Newsdesk Media Group and the G20 Research Group, 2012), 96–97.

3. Johannes F. Linn, "The Future of the World Bank: Considering the Options," in Kirton and Koch, *G20 Mexico Summit 2012,* 100–101.

4. David Hall and Emanuele Lobina, *Pipe Dreams: The Failure of the Private Sector to Invest in Water Services in Developing Countries* (London: Public Services International Research Unit, World Development Movement, 2006), 50.

5. Ibid., 51.

6. World Bank, *An Evaluation of World Bank Support, 1997–2007: Water and Development,* vol. 1 (Washington, D.C.: World Bank, 2010), 3, 34–35, 64–65.

7. James Salzman, "Thirst: A Short History of Drinking Water," *Yale Journal of Law and the Humanities* 18, no. 3 (2006): 116.

8. World Bank, *Water Resources Sector Strategy: Strategic Directions for World Bank Engagement* (Washington, D.C.: World Bank, 2003), 15.

9. World Bank, *Evaluation of World Bank Support,* 35.

10. Quoted in Greg Palast, "The Globalizer Who Came in from the Cold," Greg Palast: Journalism and Film, October 10, 2001, http://www.gregpalast.com.

11. David Hall and Meera Karunananthan, "Our Right to Water: Case Studies on Austerity and Privatization in Europe," Blue Planet Project, March 2012, http://www.foodandwaterwatch.org.

12. "Italy Sets out Tariff Reform Methodology," *Global Water Intelligence* 14, no. 1 (2013).

13. "Paris Defends Re-municipalization Record," *Global Water Intelligence* 12, no. 5 (2011).

14. See International Monetary Fund, *France: Selected Issues,* IMF Country Report No. 13/3 (Washington, D.C.: IMF, January 2013), 73–74.

15. "'All Just a Misunderstanding'? Water Privatisation and Democratic Participation in the EU," Governance across Borders, June 26, 2013, http://gov ernancexborders.com.

16. Quoted in Mike Esterl, "Great Expectations for Private Water Fail to Pan Out," *Wall Street Journal,* June 26, 2006.

17. See Food & Water Watch, *The Future of American Water: The Story of RWE and the Politics of Privatization* (Washington, D.C.: Food & Water Watch, 2008), 14, http://www.foodandwatch.org.

18. Salzman, "Thirst," 115.

19. Quoted in ibid., 95.

20. A classic example of this anticolonial argument can be found in Frantz Fanon's *The Wretched of the Earth* (1961; repr., New York: Grove Press, 2005).

21. Human Rights Council, Fifteenth Session, Resolution 15/9, September 30, 2010.

22. U.N. General Assembly, Resolution A/RES/64/292, July 2010.

23. John F. Sammis, "Explanation of Vote by John F. Sammis, U.S. Deputy Representative to the Economic and Social Council, on Resolution A/64/L.63/ Rev.1, the Human Right to Water," U.S. Mission to the United Nations, New York, June 28, 2010, http://usun.state.gov.

24. Quoted in "In Historic Vote, UN Declares Water a Fundamental Human Right," Democracy Now, July 29, 2010, http://www.democracynow.org.

25. Ann Piccard, "The United States' Failure to Ratify the International Covenant on Economic, Social and Cultural Rights: Must the Poor Be Always with Us?," *The Scholar: St. Mary's Law Review on Minority Issues* 13, no. 2 (2010): 231.

26. "Why Won't America Ratify the UN Convention on Children's Rights?," *Economist,* October 6, 2013, http://www.economist.com.

27. "Human Rights," U.S. Department of State, accessed July 15, 2012, http://www.state.gov.

28. Farhana Sultana and Alex Loftus, "The Right to Water: Prospects and Possibilities," in *The Right to Water: Politics, Governance and Social Struggles,* ed. Farhana Sultana and Alex Loftus (London: Routledge, 2012), 2.

29. Quoted in ibid., 7.

30. See Maude Barlow, "Foreword," in Sultana and Loftus, *Right to Water.*

31. From a statement at the Sixty-fifth General Assembly Plenary, 117th Meeting (AM), General Assembly GA/11126. See "General Assembly Wraps up Two Meetings—On Achieving Human Right to Water and Sanitation; Revitalizing Conference on Disarmament," United Nations, Department of Information, News and Media Division, New York, July 29, 2011, http://unispal.un.org.

32. See Marleen van Rijswick and Andrea Keessen, "Legal Protection of the Right to Water in the European Union," in Sultana and Loftus, *Right to Water.* For further reading on Israel and Palestine, see Center for Economic and Social Rights, *Thirsting for Justice: Israeli Violations of the Human Right to Water in the Occupied Palestinian Territories,* report to the U.N. Committee on Economic, Social and Cultural Rights (Brooklyn, N.Y.: Center for Economic and Social Rights, May 2003).

33. For an overview of the West Bank's water system, see Ilaria Giglioli, "Rights, Citizenship and Territory: Water Politics in the West Bank" in Sultana and Loftus, *Right to Water.*

34. Quoted in Jessica Budds and Gordon McGranahan, "Are the Debates on Water Privatization Missing the Point? Experiences from Africa, Asia and Latin America," *Environment and Urbanization* 15, no. 2 (2003): 100.

35. Arjun Appadurai, *Fear of Small Numbers: An Essay on the Geography of Anger* (Durham, N.C.: Duke University Press, 2006), 104.

36. Quoted in "Greece and Suicide: A Hard Subject for a Sermon," *Economist,* Erasmus blog, October 21, 2013, http://www.economist.com.

37. Quoted in Ben McPartland, "France: Fired for Refusing to Cut Off Poor Families' Water," Save Greek Water, April 23, 2013, http://www.savegreekwater.org.

38. See Barlow, "Foreword."

39. Quoted in John Beahler, "City and Stream," *Illumination* (Fall/Winter 2010): 33.

40. Melanie Newman, "Analysis: Who Is Buying Our Donated Blood?," Bureau of Investigative Journalism, July 27, 2011, http://www.thebureauinvestigates.com.

41. Quoted in Maude Barlow and Tony Clarke, *Blue Gold: The Fight to Stop the Corporate Theft of the World's Water* (New York: New Press, 2004), 88.

42. Quoted in "World Bank Loans Linked to Child Mortality," Bretton Woods Project, February 7, 2012, http://www.brettonwoodsproject.org.

43. David Stuckler and Sanjay Basu, "How Austerity Kills," *New York Times,* May 12, 2013.

44. "Is Killing 4,000 Babies a Day Good Customer Service?," *Global Water Intelligence,* April 5, 2012, http://www.globalwaterintel.com. See also Laurence Ball, Daniel Leigh, and Prakash Loungani, "Painful Medicine," *Finance and Development* 48, no. 3 (2011), http://www.imf.org.

45. See "World Bank Refuses to Stop Funding African Land Grabs," *African Globe,* October 8, 2012, http://www.africanglobe.net.

46. Loïc Fauchon, "Finance, Governance, Knowledge: Pillars to Protect the World's Water," in Kirton and Koch, *G20 Mexico Summit 2012,* 156–57.

47. Susan Spronk, "Water and Sanitation Utilities in the Global South: Re-

centering the Debate on 'Efficiency,'" *Review of Radical Political Economics* 4, no. 2 (2010): 159.

48. Budds and McGranahan, "Are the Debates on Water Privatization," 88.

49. Hall and Lobina, *Pipe Dreams*, 5.

50. Erik Swyngedouw, "Dispossessing H²O: The Contested Terrain of Water Privatization," in *Neoliberal Environments: False Promises and Unnatural Consequences*, ed. Nik Heynen, James McCarthy, Scott Prudham, and Paul Robbins (New York: Routledge, 2007), 53.

51. Ibid., 52.

52. Transcribed from "Extra Features: Expanded Interviews," in *Flow: For Love of Water*, directed by Irena Salina (New York: Oscilloscope, 2008), DVD.

53. See World Bank, "Iraq Country Water Resource Assistance Strategy," Report No. 36297-IQ, June 30, 2006.

54. Stephen Healy, "Alternative Economies," in *The International Encyclopedia of Human Geography*, ed. Rob Kitchin and Nigel Thrift (Oxford: Elsevier, 2009).

55. Colin C. Williams, *A Commodified World? Mapping the Limits of Capitalism* (London: Zed Books, 2005), 5.

56. Jane Pollard, Cheryl McEwan, and Alex Hughes, eds., *Postcolonial Economies* (London: Zed Books, 2011).

57. "Water's Lessons from the Food and Beverage Industry," *Global Water Intelligence*, March 22, 2012, http://www.globalwaterintel.com.

58. Larry Elliott, Phillip Inman, and Helena Smith, "IMF Admits: We Failed to Realise the Damage Austerity Would Do to Greece," *Guardian*, June 5, 2013.

59. Don Lee, "Europe Austerity Strategy Is Hurting Growth, IMF Says," *Los Angeles Times*, April 19, 2013.

60. Quoted in Alexander Eichler, "Peter Doyle, Departing IMF, 'Ashamed to Have Had Any Association' with Organization," Huffington Post, July 20, 2012, http://www.huffingtonpost.com.

61. For instance, Robin Broad from the American University and John Cavanagh from the Institute for Policy Studies warned that the Bank's figures are "highly unreliable . . . and typically over-optimistic." See "World Bank Views on Poverty 'Econocentric,'" Bretton Woods Project, April 5, 2012, http://www.brettonwoodsproject.org.

62. Stuckler and Basu, "How Austerity Kills."

63. In Pittsburgh, half of the city is supplied by the municipal water system and half by the private company American Water. There, it is easy to compare the two systems. American Water customers pay 30 percent more for water yet receive more "boil water" notices than the other half of the city. When the German company RWE acquired American Water, it discovered that the company "had not met regulatory stipulations in various US states. In part, this was due

to insufficient investment by American Water in the previous 10 years prior to RWE acquiring its holding." Claiming it would take "over 200 years" to replace all the bad pipes it had inherited, and faced with mounting political resistance, RWE cut its losses and got out of the water business. See Lora Mae Aquinde, Andrew Bray, Sanya Gurnani, and Robert Kaminski, "The Feasibility of Privatizing Pittsburgh's Public Authorities to Forestall Bankruptcy" (independent study project, Carnegie Mellon University, spring 2009), 31, http://www.andrew.cmu .edu. See also leaked RWE Supervisory Board minutes dated September 16, 2005, http://documents.foodandwaterwatch.org.

64. Quoted in Alan Snitow, Deborah Kaufman, and Michael Fox, *Thirst: Fighting the Corporate Theft of Our Water* (San Francisco: John Wiley, 2007), 185.

RECOMMENDED READING

Bakker, Karen. *Privatizing Water: Governance Failure and the World's Urban Water Crisis.* Ithaca, N.Y.: Cornell University Press, 2010.

Barlow, Maude. *Blue Future: Protecting Water for People and Planet Forever.* New York: New Press, 2014.

Budds, Jessica, and Gordon McGranahan. "Are the Debates on Water Privatization Missing the Point? Experiences from Africa, Asia and Latin America." *Environment and Urbanization* 15, no. 2 (2002): 87–113.

Chellaney, Brahma. *Water, Peace, and War: Confronting the Global Water Crisis.* New York: Rowman & Littlefield, 2013.

Fishman, Charles. *The Big Thirst: The Secret Life and Turbulent Future of Water.* New York: Free Press, 2012.

Goldman, Michael. *Imperial Nature: The World Bank and Struggles for Social Justice in the Age of Globalization.* New Haven, Conn.: Yale University Press, 2005.

Guha, Ramachandra. *The Unquiet Woods: Ecological Change and Peasant Resistance in the Himalya.* Berkeley: University of California Press, 2000.

Hall, David, and Emanuele Lobina. *Pipe Dreams: The Failure of the Private Sector to Invest in Water Services in Developing Countries.* London: Public Services International Research Unit, World Development Movement, 2006.

Khagram, Sanjeev. *Dams and Development: Transnational Struggles for Water and Power.* Ithaca, N.Y.: Cornell University Press, 2004.

Lohan, Tara, ed. *Water Consciousness: How We All Have to Change to Protect Our Most Critical Resource.* San Francisco: AlterNet Books, 2008.

McDonald, David A., and Greg Ruiters. *Alternatives to Privatization in the Global South.* New York: Routledge, 2011.

Pearce, Fred. *When the Rivers Run Dry: Water—the Defining Crisis of the Twenty-First Century.* Boston: Beacon Press, 2006.

Robinson, Joanna L. *Contested Water: The Struggle against Water Privatization in the United States and Canada.* Cambridge: MIT Press, 2013.

Salzman, James. "Thirst: A Short History of Drinking Water." *Yale Journal of Law and the Humanities* 18, no. 3 (2006): 94–121.

Shiva, Vandana. *Water Wars: Privatization, Pollution, and Profit.* Cambridge, Mass.: South End Press, 2002.

Sultana, Farhana, and Alex Loftus. *The Right to Water: Politics, Governance and Social Struggles.* London: Routledge, 2012.

Suzuki, David, and Holly Dressel. "A River Runs through It: Fresh Water." In *More Good News: Real Solutions to the Global Eco-Crisis.* Vancouver: Greystone Books, 2010.

Swyngedouw, Erik. "Dispossessing H_2O: The Contested Terrain of Water Privatization." In *Neoliberal Environments: False Promises and Unnatural Consequences,* edited by Nik Heynen, James McCarthy, Scott Prudham, and Paul Robbins. New York: Routledge, 2007.

———. *Social Power and the Urbanization of Water: Flows of Power.* Oxford: Oxford University Press, 2004.

INDEX

Karen Piper is the author of *Cartographic Fictions* and *Left in the Dust*, which the *Los Angeles Times* called an "eco-thriller" that every "tap-turning American" should read. She received *Sierra's* Nature Writing Award and is a regular contributor to *Places* magazine. She teaches postcolonial studies in the Department of English and is an adjunct professor in the Department of Geography at the University of Missouri–Columbia.